Ideas in Action

A Guide to Critical Thinking and Writing

Rolf Norgaard

University of Colorado at Boulder

HarperCollins*College*Publishers

To Andrea—
friend, lover, wife, muse

Senior Acquisitions Editor: Jane Kinney
Project Coordination and Text Design: Proof Positive/Farrowlyne Associates, Inc.
Cover Design: Kay Petronio
Production Manager: Kewal Sharma
Compositor: Weimer Graphics, Inc.
Printer and Binder: R.R. Donnelley & Sons Company
Cover Printer: The Lehigh Press, Inc.

For permission to use copyrighted material, grateful acknowledgment is made to the copyright holders on pp. 303–304, which are hereby made part of this copyright page.

Ideas in Action: A Guide to Critical Thinking and Writing, First Edition

Copyright © 1994 by Rolf Norgaard

Library of Congress Cataloging-in-Publication Data

Norgaard, Rolf.
    Ideas in action : a guide to critical thinking and writing / Rolf
Norgaard. — 1st ed.
      p. cm.
    Includes bibliographical references and index.
    ISBN 0-673-46404-0. — ISBN 0-673-46705-8
    1. English language—Rhetoric.   2. Critical thinking.   I. Title.
PE 1408.N79   1994
808'.042—dc20   93-5809
                                          CIP

96   9 8 7 6 5 4 3

Contents

Part I   Discerning Ideas

Part II   Shaping Ideas

Part III Testing Ideas

Part IV Acting on Ideas

About This Book

Ideas in Action serves as an unobtrusive, flexible guide to the work that occurs when you analyze or argue; it addresses the ongoing challenge of shaping ideas. College writing invites you to respond to the ideas of others as you explore and defend your own. *Ideas in Action* can help you meet this challenge. Its goal: to give voice to the intelligence at work behind your prose.

If this is your first college composition course, the book will acquaint you with a reliable method for academic writing and reasoning. If you are taking an advanced composition course or an advanced seminar in your major, it can help you mature as a writer and thinker by reminding you why fundamentals are indeed fundamental. In either case, *Ideas in Action* can help you hone the persuasive edge that virtually all college writing requires.

In the Classroom

Many composition courses now use student writing, not a textbook or handbook, as the primary text in the classroom. This book does more than invite you to write; it serves the writing you're already being asked to do. Because *Ideas in Action* deals directly with the challenges that you face when shaping ideas on the page, it can help you at every stage of the writing process. It supports teaching and learning—a text that attends to your own creative work.

Some composition courses deal extensively with readings, often by means of an anthology. Such courses need a text that supplements the assigned reading and writing without breaking bank accounts or adding another 700-page book to an already packed syllabus. Relatively short, flexible, and, I hope, fun, *Ideas in Action* works in a reading-oriented course because it asks writers to approach their own work as discerning readers.

Ideas in Action also speaks to those of you who write in courses across the curriculum. Now common, these writing-intensive courses in various disciplines expect you to analyze and argue, yet they usually don't provide extensive writing instruction. The book meets an important need beyond the composition classroom by providing both the student and the instructor in such courses with a common language for understanding the essentials of academic writing and reasoning. It also encourages you to adapt those essentials to the context-specific demands of your own discipline.

This book, then, is meant for students who have something important to say in their writing and for classrooms in which ideas are taken seriously. It assumes that you already have an area of interest or expertise, or at the very least can derive a topic from a world of possibilities. It lends you help where the going gets tough: writing a cogent analysis or argument that reflects well on your knowledge and intelligence.

Organization

Because writing is not linear but recursive, I've written the book so that it offers many points of entry and many paths to follow. Wherever you begin, you'll want to return to chapters you've already read or jump ahead to specific sections as you address the immediate creative challenges in your own writing. This text can only come alive as your own writing lends it context, purpose, and utility.

You may choose to begin where I did. Part I helps you understand that ideas can take shape only as you draw relationships among them. The first chapter encourages you to read critically, to ask questions about ideas and their relationships. The second chapter shows you how to address in your writing the questions that readers will surely ask as they read. Here you become acquainted with the dynamic relationships among issues, assertions, and reasons. Those relationships allow you to shape ideas into coherent prose.

Part II helps you understand the distinction between observation and inference, and encourages you to make and defend inferences by analyzing and arguing. Because inferences are your springboard to analysis and argument, this section offers strategies for launching a paper. It helps you respond to questions at issue with reasoned assertions and credible support.

Part III provides strategies for testing your ideas. Here you learn how to troubleshoot and refine a provisional thesis and address questions that might arise as you explore ideas in a full paper. You learn that listening to readers, even arguing with yourself, can be an effective strategy for revising your work. Here, too, you'll connect the shape of ideas to the craft of style.

The book ends where much of your work begins: with specific, apparently unconnected assignments in a variety of courses. Part IV demonstrates how critical thinking and writing strategies apply to the various tasks you're asked to perform—from the essay exam to the research paper, from the lab report to the business memo, and on to the oral presentation. The book helps you return to your classes with a basic yet versatile method in hand. Each new paper need no longer present an inscrutable challenge.

Special Features

Several key features reflect this book's goals.

- Writing is treated as moving from whole to parts. You'll find discrete skills discussed in the context of your general intentions. It encourages you to address first the issues, assertions, and reasons that drive the thinking and writing you do in college.

- The book shows how reading, discussion, and critical thinking can inform the entire writing process. It turns writing into inquiry, your own text into a social act.

- By focusing on analysis and argument, the book addresses the essential challenge of academic writing: the testing and retesting of hypotheses. It views analysis and argument not as discrete modes but as the foundation for writing and reasoning in college.

- From the start, the book emphasizes the role that readers' questions play in shaping prose. By taking the relationship between reading and writing as its point of departure, the text helps you become your own best critic and a worthy critic of your classmates' writing. I hope this approach will encourage you to evaluate my advice and adapt it to your own contexts and purposes.

- The book makes extensive use of student writing to illustrate key points. By following drafts as they were revised from one workshop to the next, you will place your own writing in the context of peer editing and collaborative learning. Through these examples, you participate in a writing workshop with other college students. You will be able to learn from their mistakes and share in their successes.

- By focusing on relationships that lend shape to ideas, rather than on any one formula or format, the book helps you to recognize a common core of critical-thinking strategies that extend across the curriculum. These strategies allow you to adapt principles to your own needs. *Ideas in Action* can help you to think and write well in all of your courses.

A Final Word

I trust that no one will miss the end-of-chapter exercises and assignments common in composition books. *Ideas in Action* assumes that you are already writing; it catches you in the act and gives you practical guidance on the work at hand. Moreover, it accords student writing the respect it deserves. Your own papers provide ample opportunity to discuss and apply strategies that can help you think critically and write well. Workshops and seminars become electric experiences when participants share their best thinking and writing. This book invites you to do just that.

Acknowledgments

Many people have contributed to *Ideas in Action*, each renewing in a distinctive way my appreciation of what it means to write in a community of readers.

First and last, I owe an enormous debt to my students. Their papers—and their comments on my manuscript—have taught me about writing even as I was teaching them. Many have generously contributed their work to this project. Born in the classroom, not the private study, this book is as much theirs as mine. My thanks to you all.

This book was conceived when Constance Rajala of HarperCollins, visiting the University of Colorado at Boulder, sat in on my writing workshop. She first saw *Ideas in Action* not as a manuscript proposal but as classroom practice, where students and I work together to explore, refine, and test ideas. After class, as we shared a cup of coffee at the University Memorial Center, she overcame my skepticism that anything so interactive and dynamic could be rendered on the static and mute page.

Generous with both ideas and time, my colleagues in the University Writing Program have done more than support this undertaking: they coaxed and cajoled it to completion. Paul Levitt would invariably ask why he hadn't seen me at my computer or in Norlin Library, somehow giving me the courage to rise early the next morning. Elissa Guralnick inspired the initial conception of Chapter Three and, by example, helped me set high expectations for the entire project. In her own benign way, Hardy Long Frank encouraged me to wrestle an early version of Chapter Two into manageable shape. I owe special thanks to J. E. Rivers, whose attentive reading of the entire manuscript helped me release its meaning and its energy. By testing my advice in their own classrooms, far more instructors than I can name reminded me what we do when we teach—and why.

This book was born in and conceived for the classroom, but the University of Colorado at Boulder served as midwife. Answering Dean Middleton's call for improved undergraduate education, I devoted my energies to a publication that would enhance classroom teaching. Deans Seebass, Clough, and Dunn of the Engineering College gave me the opportunity to develop an innovative critical-thinking and writing program for engineering students, and with it the interdisciplinary context that shaped this book. Consulting on writing with faculty from fields as varied as physics, English, business, computer science, and linguistics helped me find a common set of critical-thinking and writing strategies that transcend disciplinary boundaries.

My community of readers, and the history of my indebtedness, extend to colleagues in rhetoric and composition across the country. Their published work—articles, books, and classroom texts—has both informed and enriched my own. But informal, even chance encounters have influenced me just as much. Whether from a distance or through lively conversation, a diverse group of colleagues has shaped my thinking, often in subtle ways: Chris Anson, Ann Berthoff, Patricia Bizzell, Richard Coe, Frederick Crews, Jeanne Fahnestock, John Gage, Richard Lanham, David Russell, Marie Secor, John Trimble, Kathleen Welch, and Joseph Williams, to name just a few.

I was assisted in my efforts by a veritable braintrust of reviewers: Karen Rodis, Dartmouth College; Katherine Adams, Loyola University; Margaret Himley, Syracuse University; Jack Prostko, Stanford University; Robert Schwegler, University of Rhode Island; John Schilb, University of Maryland—College Park; Richard Marius, Harvard University; Richard Lloyd-Jones, University of Iowa; Richard Larson, C.U.N.Y. Lehman; Judith Lee, State University of New Jersey at Rutgers; William Covino, University of Illinois—Chicago; James Stokes, University of Wisconsin—Stevens Point; Shirley W. Logan, University of Maryland—College Park; Carol Olsen, Valparaiso University; and Jo Allyson Parker, St. Joseph's University.

Their perceptive comments and suggestions made for a stronger book. Whatever blemishes remain indicate where I may not have heeded their better judgment.

At HarperCollins, Jane Kinney did more than inherit a project; she saw to its successful completion with astute advice and encouragement. Marisa L'Heureux, Miranda Schwartz, and Alison Brill brought to the book both their interest and their expertise. Lisa Dillman of Proof Positive/Farrowlyne Associates, Inc. offered her keen editorial eye.

Thus, the history of my debts becomes the tale of my good fortune. Nowhere more so than at home. Andrea was at once my most perceptive reader and my unfailing muse. Stefan gestated right along with this book, and began working on his words even as I wrote these.

Introduction

Years of writing instruction have enabled you to still the proofreader's red pencil. Sentence for sentence your writing's usually competent, clean, correct. You can manage descriptive reports, where facts follow upon facts, and narratives that chronicle events. But a compilation of information, by itself, often proves insufficient in college. You must do more than demonstrate your familiarity with course materials. The challenge you now face is to interpret texts, to find meaning in facts and events. Academic writing asks you to make and defend inferences based on what you read or observe.

To meet this challenge, you must bring complex, often ambiguous information to bear on a question at issue—one that calls for a reasoned response. To meet the concerns of your audience, you'll need to explore and clarify relationships among your ideas. In a word, you must *shape* your ideas—and sustain them as you justify your point.

A political science assignment, for example, may ask you to show the relevance of Machiavelli's *The Prince* to today's power politics. To respond, you'll need to do more than copy the shape of Machiavelli's ideas. You must shape your own ideas by analyzing his advice on how rulers can gain and maintain power, compare that advice to one or more significant moments in contemporary politics, and thereby formulate and defend your own view about Machiavelli's relevance. A successful paper would persuade readers that you understand Machiavelli perceptively, that you treat current politics in an informed and accurate manner, and that you relate theory and practice insightfully. You can do so only by drawing and evaluating relationships among ideas. The shape you lend to ideas allows you to explore, define, and defend your own insights. It also helps readers follow—or perhaps challenge—your thinking.

The Shape of Ideas

When I mention the word *shape*, you may conjure up dreary images of organization, format, and required patterns. You may even think of meaning and form as separate, sequential: first you have an assortment of ideas, then you try to find a form for them. Or perhaps a particular form has been imposed on you by a teacher or a textbook, a static structure to which you are told you must adapt your ideas. In either case, form and meaning are hardly on speaking terms.

They ought to be. Writing asks that you form *relationships* among ideas. Without relationships, ideas don't come together. Only as we recognize the functional relationships among ideas—that is, their shape or form—can we create meaning when we read or write. Those relationships, created by writers and perceived by readers, set ideas in action. Thus, to mean something, ideas must have shape. In fact, *idea* is the Greek word for "form."

In isolation, a single idea communicates very little. It's the relationships we create among ideas that lend them force, interest, and insight. Only by forging these relationships can we identify and respond to the issues that bring writer and audience together. We read, in turn, because relationships among ideas allow us to see matters in a new or unexpected way. Authors engage our attention not by flooding us with facts but by pursuing those relationships.

The consequences of separating form from meaning are as common as they are unwelcome. On the one hand we can have rambling prose where sparks of insight fade quickly. They remain undeveloped, unrelated to each other, and thus unappreciated, perhaps even unrecognized. When ideas don't come together, the writing falls apart. On the other hand, it is possible to have plenty of organization without much thinking. Standard organizational patterns can invite vacuous ideas that are then pressed, like luncheon meat, into one of several conventional shapes. When separated from the process of finding meaning, form quickly becomes a lifeless shell that discourages creative, incisive thinking.

To rescue your ideas from either fate, we'll consider how the dynamic shape you lend to your ideas creates meaning. Your thoughts won't convince anybody until you give them shape by drawing tight, vigorous relationships among them. Those relationships can serve as a dynamic tool for thinking—for finding and shaping meaning. Writing thus spurs critical thinking and active learning.

Five Misconceptions

If you have trouble shaping ideas as you write, it may not be for lack of effort. Your problems may stem from misconceptions that influence how you go about shaping your ideas. These conceptions may not be entirely false, but they are incomplete, and thus misleading. In challenging them and explaining why they are unproductive for writing analysis and argument in college, we can lay out the principles that guide this book. These principles will introduce you to the what, how, when, who, and why of shaping ideas in writing.

Misconception 1: When Writing, We Are Forming Content _____

Let's start with *what*. You may take for granted that what you shape when you write is your content. You label information and put it in order. You organize the things you have to say. Should you have trouble shaping your paper, the problem seems to lie in the complex information you wish to convey.

Let's rethink this premise. When you write, you are really *forming your intention*, not just content or information. An overall sense of purpose holds your writing together. You lend shape to your intention by articulating the point you wish to advance, by indicating why you are making it, and by explaining why it should elicit the belief of others.

And yet, content and information tend to occupy most of your attention. If you're like most writers in college, you have books piled high next to your computer and a stack of note cards filled with your own observations. Lack of information is not your primary problem; statistics, quotes, and firsthand observations buzz in your head. What concerns you is how to shape the information into a paper. Having made one statement, where are you to go from there? What should you put in or leave out?

Your professors may have warned you that they do not want a simple description of facts, or one more rehearsal of second-hand information. Instead they want you to analyze or argue, to assert something that is your own opinion and defend it with evidence and reasoning. Yet what else do you have but information and observation? That's precisely what your professors don't want.

By focusing exclusively on what to say, you are setting for yourself a descriptive task that is hopelessly encyclopedic. As information and data have no limits, you can soon find yourself overwhelmed with things to say but with few clues on how to go about saying them and little purpose to the saying itself. That's why experienced writers shape what they have to say by looking first to their *intentions*. They shape their writing by organizing words to accomplish specific ends. Unless you know to whom you are writing, and why, information will make little or no impression on you or your readers.

As you discover and refine your intention, you will learn how to shape what you have to say. When you must articulate and justify your intention, you actually discover that you have more to say than you thought you did. Moreover, you become an avid seeker of information and are better able to evaluate the new information you find. Only when you form your intention can you ask interesting questions or even know what constitutes useful or relevant information.

Misconception 2: We Shape a Paper by Arranging Parts _____

How, exactly, do you shape your writing? You may think of the process as the naming and arranging of parts, organization pure and simple. The task becomes one of dividing the information into parts and getting those parts in the right order. This approach places priority on formal arrangement, on the "skeleton" of your writing. Unless you find the right place for every element, the writing is out of joint.

Once again we need to rethink an assumption. A writer lends form to an essay not by arranging parts but by *establishing meaningful relationships* among ideas. Unless you know how parts relate to a common purpose, your intention, you may have little idea how to arrange them.

Not that you lack parts. You're already juggling more bits of information than you can manage. You may even resort to bold-faced headings in your draft to suggest some sort of order. But how are you to arrange these parts? And what point do they actually support? You sense that a random order won't do, but where would you find a meaningful order? A good paper, you recall, has a beginning, a middle, and an end. Perhaps those are your parts. Your work on the paper, after all, has a beginning, a middle, and an end, but your professor warned you not to retell the story of your research. Unable to offer plot summary, you may despair: beginning, middle, and end of *what*? Words can't just start, continue, and stop.

Parts have meaning only if you start with the whole—with the intention that establishes meaningful relationships among the parts. Each separate element in writing—a sentence, a paragraph, a larger section of your paper—is related to other parts only insofar as it reflects and fulfills your intention. Arrangement, then, means very little by itself. Experienced writers use arrangement as a means to accomplish an intended purpose.

It's not surprising that you might become preoccupied with arranging parts. After all, *format*—the outer arrangement and organization of writing—readily meets your eye when you read essays and articles. Some formats—lab reports, for example—are a matter of convention; you are expected to use them when writing in a particular discipline or on a particular subject. Preoccupied with format, you may not notice the underlying and essential *form* of the ideas. Form springs from the author's intention and establishes relationships among ideas that give writing shape and coherence. If you are expected to use a particular format, by all means do so; but look beyond mere organization to the relationships the format is meant to highlight. In writing that is carefully crafted, format serves a purpose—to help you grasp the interrelation among ideas.

By perceiving and constantly reexamining the logical relationships that follow from your intention, you can set ideas into dynamic relationships. We'll use those relationships to help you form your ideas. Only when you look for and understand relationships can the parts of your writing reflect your purpose.

Misconception 3: We Shape Our Writing Only After We Get Ideas

When do you lend shape to your paper? You might think of the task as a particular moment in the writing process, one sandwiched between other separate moments. Form seems to come after you get your ideas and gather your information but before you try to improve your tone, untangle an awkward sentence, or search for just the right word.

If you start from this premise, you may miss crucial opportunities to discover and shape ideas. The writing process is anything but linear. Stages such as thinking, writing, and revising do not occur in lock-step order. In fact, it may be misleading to think of separate stages at all. Writing is not a steady march forward, but a process of looping back to reconsider where you have been even as you work your way forward. *You are shaping ideas throughout the writing process*—from the earliest moments of discovering your intention to the final stylistic touches that you put on your work.

You may have problems shaping your paper because you have narrowed and isolated the task. You start your work by making close observations in the field or lab, or by looking closely at primary texts. You also pore through articles and books, and jot down ideas and observations on note cards. You measure progress by the number of cards. Shape? That comes days from now. Yet by disregarding relationships among ideas early on, you will find it hard to relate various observations or even shuffle your deck of cards. You will find it even harder to shape a hypothesis that you can test or formulate a research question that will help you sift through your growing pile of information.

With the deadline for the paper rapidly approaching, you figure you have to start writing out a full draft. Only then, with your sleeves rolled up, do you start what you think of as the forming of your paper—the shaping and arranging of content. The thick pile of cards looks a bit forbidding, but you see no point in culling them. After all, you've already done the research and it would be a shame to waste it. You figure there's little else to do but grit your teeth and churn out the paper. Hard work goes into the writing, but the work consists of gluing things together. Your paper becomes a collection of prefabricated parts—ideas, facts, cited references—that do not bear the stamp of your own design or reflect the shape of your thinking. Shaping the paper becomes dreary, assembly-line labor.

It's a mistake to consign the shaping of ideas to one isolated moment in the writing process. Any time you relate insights to each other or draw inferences from experience or observation, you are shaping ideas. When you try to formulate an assertion or pose a question, you are shaping relationships that will guide your paper's development. What's more, revision is no less a moment of creative formation than your first hesitant gropings for a thesis. Even what you might think of as style involves the shape and shaping of ideas. Any time you decide to begin a new paragraph, highlight a transition, or recast a sentence, you are rethinking relationships among ideas. Revision is nothing if not seeing relationships anew.

The shaping of ideas is not one stage; it is a way to make sense of the entire writing process. By exploring relationships among your ideas, you can know your own mind, and thus discover what you mean to say. Those very relationships, moreover, can help you communicate that meaning to others.

Misconception 4: The Author Alone Shapes the Writing _____

Isn't writing an author's private burden? After all, the author is the one slaving over the computer keyboard to get the paper written by tomorrow's class. And it's the author who will receive the grade.

If you find yourself struggling to shape your writing, the premise that this is the author's business and nobody else's may actually contribute to your difficulties. As author, you may be doing the actual writing, but your paper itself involves a *dynamic exchange between writer and reader*. Experienced writers take this exchange as their point of reference. They look to their rhetorical situation. In writing that matters, you begin with an issue or problem, something to say about it, and someone to whom it must be said. Your sense of audience helps shape your writing. Audience determines how you state the issue, how you present yourself and your point, and how you go about eliciting belief and goodwill.

Probably you do write with a particular reader in mind—the professor who assigns and grades your paper. Yet you may be unsure how to respond to this reader. Wanting to impress an expert audience of one, you may use the paper as an opportunity to tell all. Yet in so doing, you may fail to meet the interests and demands of even that one person. Real issues, perceptive assertions, cogent reasoning—these, not an avalanche of statistics and citations, are uppermost in your professor's mind. By writing merely for your professor, you miss an opportunity to write for many readers—among them, your professor. Don't write as a student addressing a teacher, but as a writer engaging many intelligent readers who sincerely want to know about your subject.

Frustrations with writing can stem in part from the isolation that follows from misconstruing, if not forgetting, your audience. You may fall into the habit of shaping prose to get it written, not to have it read. You may adopt the notion that what you are writing is yours alone to shape. Your prose may be driven by your own preoccupations, not genuine questions that are at issue between you and your audience. Although you may submit your paper to one professor, college writing asks that you also engage a wider audience—a community of thoughtful readers who share in the process of inquiry.

Perhaps you have seen a person practice karate or tai chi alone. The moves are called *kata* in Japanese, literally "forms." Only when a friend of mine explained them to me did I realize that they are based on the dynamic interplay of two people. Each move is designed to thwart or forestall a move that another person might make. When we see *kata* practiced in isolation, they may appear mechanical, a matter of going through the motions. Yet those forms are born of a dynamic relationship.

Like the forms of karate and tai chi, the process of shaping ideas, for all its apparent isolation, must take dynamic exchange as its point of departure. The shape you lend to your writing should answer the intellectual moves and emotional responses of your readers. Their potential questions, biases, hesitations, and outright objections can provide you with strategies for choosing your own moves, shaping your own words. By anticipating the concerns of your audience, you can make the dynamic exchange between writer and reader an ongoing part of your writing process. In fact, actual collaboration can make the exchange far more concrete and productive. Learning to read the papers of fellow students in a workshop setting can help you think more clearly and revise more effectively. That is why many writing courses are taught as workshops, where students read and discuss each other's work.

The shape of your writing guides the way in which your readers understand (or misunderstand) your intentions. Form thus involves acts of interpretation. If you ask *how readers might construe* what you write, you gain important clues about *how you might construct* your prose. The expectations held by your readers and the questions they pose can help you shape your ideas if you anticipate their response. After all, your writing takes on meaning only insofar as readers can discern meaning. When you anticipate and respond to the reader's interpretive task, you can actually lighten your own burden.

Shaping ideas is an activity shared by writers and readers. If writers express meaning by forming prose, readers look for meaning by recognizing form. Form is dynamic; it is one of the important means by which writers and readers interact. By reading critically and monitoring how you interpret a text, you can recognize and improve the shape of your own writing. Thus, if you wish to share your writing with others, you must first acknowledge the reader's share in shaping meaning.

Misconception 5: We Shape Ideas to Make Our Writing Readable _____

The fifth premise concerns *why* we set ideas in relationships. Shaping your paper seems a matter of making it more readable. Ease of communication appears to be form's chief virtue and function.

I'd like to suggest a better reason to work at refining your paper's shape. You should shape ideas not only to make your paper readable but, more importantly, to make it *worth reading*. Writers shape and reshape their prose in a continual effort to discover what they have to say and to make the saying of it enjoyable, memorable, and persuasive. Readers, in turn, slog through as much bad prose as they do because they are continually searching for the intellectual and emotional pleasure that comes from writing crafted with care. If you can give them that pleasure from the first word of your paper to the last, you will win them over.

Why bother reshaping a paper when the shape of your first draft might do? Because in reshaping you may find a crucial point that would otherwise remain buried. It could be a point that alters the thrust of your entire paper. Why might you—or your professor—prefer to read a paper whose shape has undergone careful scrutiny and revision? Because as a reader you are challenged and delighted by insights that are not obvious, by insights that can emerge only when the focus of a paper has been clarified over several drafts. In shaping your paper, you refine your intention and take responsibility for the conclusions you have drawn. It's challenging work because it makes writing an act of self-discovery. The ideas you express on the page should reflect an ongoing act of inquiry and invite readers to join in. By focusing on the shape and shaping of your writing, this book can help you discover what you think—and why.

Critical Thinking and Writing in College

These five misconceptions about shaping ideas can influence how and what you write. They also influence how your writing will be read. We communicate not in a vacuum but in the company of other readers and writers who themselves hold assumptions. The shape of our ideas thus has a powerful social dimension. When we write, we are engaging and responding to each other as members of a community. The shape we lend to our writing allows writers and readers to interact because it arouses and fulfills desires; it raises expectations that are either met or left unsatisfied.

The papers you write in college are produced and received in such a "discourse community"—or more precisely, several overlapping discourse communities. Expectations and assumptions hold these communities together. The immediate community may be the class itself, with its professor and students. The assignment for the paper and the discussions that take place in the classroom provide context for both writer and reader, student and professor.

You also participate in one or more disciplinary communities. As you use and acknowledge the work of others, you participate in a process of shared inquiry. Depending on the disciplines you are studying, you may encounter conventions that guide how members of each community shape meaning. Different types of writing—a scientific lab report, a business case study, or a critical analysis of a poem—reflect how members of the community inquire into ideas, how they establish the validity of their points, and what style they find most effective and efficient for communicating with each other. These genres function as a kind of collective memory, a way of recalling and preserving the expectations shared by readers and writers in specific communities.

College itself is one of the communities in which you participate. It holds certain expectations of its writers and readers, whatever their discipline. College invites you into a world of inquiry where ideas and their credibility matter. You and others come together to discuss issues, advance conclusions about them, and evaluate reasons for those conclusions. You arrive at, test, and refine hypotheses. You ask critical questions about your ideas and about whether the relationships you draw among them are coherent and reasonable. When professors assign papers, they want to see your own ideas in action. To do so, they look to the shape that you give to your ideas—and your papers. In college, the shape you lend to your writing matters so much because it reflects the shape of your thought.

Because academic writing emphasizes ideas set in relationship, it asks you above all to make those relationships clear and defend them before skeptical readers. Thus, college stresses *analysis* and *argument* over other types of writing with which you may be more familiar, such as narration and description. Many of you excel when writing a narrative in which you organize information chronologically or a description in which you marshall material through loose, topical association. But when asked to pursue a rigorous analysis or cast an explicit argument, you may struggle. For all your native intelligence and disciplinary training, you face a new and different task. Sheer information and random impression no longer suffice; you are now called upon to relate observation to inference, to place information in the service of a point. Virtually all college writing asks you to make a point, but analysis and argument foreground reasoned inquiry in a rigorous way. You find yourself challenged when asked to write the very prose on which your academic and future professional success depends.

Why do analysis and argument place special demands even on mature writers? These forms, common in academic contexts, require you to shape your writing by discovering meaning. The dynamic relationships you draw among ideas are what give analysis and argument shape.

Analysis requires that you observe closely, note patterns or develop interesting categories, and draw inferences from what you see. It need not imply the dreary task of picking something apart, nor should it smack of a pedantic obsession with irrelevant detail. Analysis asks you to take apart in order to reconstruct and, in so doing, to impart a meaning or significance that was not immediately apparent. Analysis thus involves a synthetic act of mind. And therein lies its utility, its power, and—yes—its fun. Analysis asks you to use observation and inference to pull things together and arrive at an interpretive conclusion. It asks you, by looking closely, to make fresh sense of the whole.

Like analysis, argument asks you to arrive at and defend conclusions that are not obvious or about which reasonable and intelligent people might disagree. Like analysis, argument is a synthetic act. You may break down your argument into specific reasons that support your view and meet your readers' objections, but those reasons should all point to your conclusion. Analysis and argument differ to the extent that argument addresses an audience that is not disposed to your viewpoint. To win over such an audience, you need not use threats, fallacious reasoning, or insincere appeals. Argument involves the civilized and civilizing search for good reasons. It encourages all of us to take responsibility for what we say and do; it asks us to earn our conclusions. In the process, it may even help us live more responsibly.

As you write in college, you will find some instances of analysis and argument to be very explicit. Conclusions will be clearly stated, and reasons marshalled in an orderly array. Other instances of analysis and argument will be far more subtle. To recount a Civil War battle, you may find that you have to analyze evidence and conflicting perspectives. And the telling of it may involve you implicitly in arguing for or against a particular interpretation of events.

Analysis and argument are thus closely related ways of thinking. They are basic human activities, yet college asks you to pursue them with special rigor. Both analysis and argument require you to express an interpretation or formulate an assertion that lies beyond immediate observation, accepted fact, or chronological sequence. In doing so, you will find that the distinctions between analysis and argument are not absolute but gradual. Analysis can verge on argument just as argument usually requires sustained analysis. The differences between analysis and argument on the one hand and outright description and narration on the other may prove far more telling. Indeed, the differences may help explain the challenge of shaping analysis and argument.

We love stories. When we sit at the dinner table (if indeed the custom is still practiced), we retell the day's events or describe its situations. When television replaces intimate conversation, we find that reporters and talk-show hosts ask us to understand our world by casting our concerns in terms of stories (narration) or by accumulating and dispensing information (description). Rarely do we analyze and argue in a rigorous or explicit way, where we put forward our own conclusions and test our reasons for having them. Because of this, analysis and argument may be unfamiliar to you, or you may not be well practiced in crafting them.

You may feel challenged by analysis and argument for another reason. Unlike narration and description, the form of analysis and argument depends almost entirely on the shape of your ideas. Granted, when you tell a story or describe something, you also need to shape your prose. You can do so by following the natural contours of the thing you are describing or by recounting the chronology of the events that contribute to your story. In description and narration, form sometimes comes ready-made. Not so with analysis and argument. They ask you to make inferences that extend beyond observation and event. They require you to formulate assertions based on those inferences and then defend those assertions. In analysis and argument, the only shape that exists is the one that you create to serve your own particular purpose. Analysis and argument are difficult because they force you to think clearly about the conclusions you reach, your motives for reaching them, and the reasons that allow you to reach them.

Analysis and argument thus depend on original and rigorous thought. This explains not only their importance and prevalence in college writing but also their power. If you can shape writing that expresses your thinking, you empower yourself. And in writing such prose, you can empower others with your thought.

The following pages can help you sort through the questions to ask when shaping your writing in college. You've already made a good start. By reconsidering the assumptions behind your work, you've found that exploring and shaping ideas asks you to

- discover and refine your intentions so that the information you accumulate can serve a purpose;

- perceive and develop relationships among ideas so that you can demonstrate how you have earned your conclusions;

- make the shape of your ideas an ongoing concern so that writing becomes, from first to last, a process of critical thinking;

- relate writing to the interpretive act of reading so that the shape you bestow to your ideas anticipates the expectations and reactions of your readers; and

- revise and refine your paper so that by getting it into shape you are discovering and communicating the shape of your own thoughts.

This book will help you shape ideas consciously, coherently, and creatively—ideas that represent your thinking at its best.

Part I

Discerning
Ideas

Reading the
Shape of Ideas

1

Whether you are writing or reading, you are finding your way in a world of issues, concerns, and ideas. If you become lost when you write, or for that matter when you read, you often can get back on track by asking the right questions. This strategy means reading texts—even your own text—in a critical, self-conscious way.

As writers, we find and communicate meaning by actively shaping ideas. As readers, we also have a hand in constructing meaning, for a text makes sense only if we recognize relationships among those ideas. Reading, then, is also a matter of shaping meaning. When you read critically, you're looking for more than information or facts. You are looking for—and shaping—ideas.

As you read, you are interacting with an author, much as that author is interacting with readers. Both reading and writing are dynamic transactions. By reading critically, you attend to that transaction more closely than you otherwise might. You ask probing questions and assess how writers respond. In turn, critical reading can help you write with the interests of readers in mind. By thinking like a reader, writers can shape ideas that will win, hold, and persuade an audience.

Reading Critically by Asking Questions

Reading becomes critical not when you find fault with a text but when—true to the Greek meaning of *kritēs*—you seek to become a "discerner" or "judge" of meaning. To read critically, you must take responsibility for your act of interpretation.

This sort of reading asks far more from you than you may realize. You can't just sit back and let words wash over you, nor can you read simply for information, facts, or the author's main idea. Critical reading is labor-intensive because you must ask questions. You must discover and evaluate ideas in relationship to each other.

The question of relationships goes to the heart of what happens when we read. Readers find meaning only by finding meaningful patterns. Those patterns highlight some elements while subordinating others. Without this sort of patterned differentiation, reading would result in nothing more than a cognitive blur.

To find patterns in a text you must set yourself in relationship to it. Far from being a private, one-sided, or passive affair, reading, like writing, entails social interaction. It sets in motion a tug and pull between reader and text, audience and author. This interaction requires that readers negotiate two competing demands. On the one hand, critical reading requires humility. To interpret responsibly, you must honor the text. You must respect and take seriously the words on the page. Yet critical reading also asks that you assume authority. You have an obligation to challenge ideas, to evaluate and respond to a text by weighing its claims against available evidence. Only when you read both humbly and authoritatively—both with and against the grain of a text—can you discover and test its ideas.

To read critically, you must ask the right questions. Three questions should guide your encounter with a text.

- What is the question at issue?
- What is the author's point?
- Do the author's reasons elicit belief?

These questions will help you shape the ideas you read. And, in turn, they will help you shape your own thinking and writing. Widely applicable, these questions have a long history reaching back to ancient Greek orators and rhetoricians. They remain helpful today, for they are the questions that readers naturally ask when engaging a text. They are also the very questions that effective writers seek to answer.

These questions are always in play. The expectations you bring to a new text represent your memory of prior encounters with other texts—encounters that have been guided by these very questions. Your expectations also reflect the needs and desires of the discourse community to which you belong. If those expectations are not met, the meaning of what you read can suffer. Your task as a critical reader is to weigh how or even whether these questions have been answered.

The questions become particularly apparent when writing goes astray, when readers look for and fail to find coherent answers. In this chapter we will look at some examples of student writing that failed to answer one or more of these questions. Through them, we can identify three reasons why ideas lose their shape. The reasons may surprise you. Lack of a predictable organization is not the chief source of errancy. The reasons go deeper and have to do with how we agree on the kind of shared conversation we might have, how we identify or express intention, and how we accord credibility to the statements we read.

By examining these three questions in writing that goes astray, you will become familiar with techniques for finding your way through the complex, sophisticated prose you read in college. Later in this chapter we will apply these questions to published texts. Then, in Chapter Two, we'll discuss strategies for helping you address the questions as you write. After all, the questions we as readers raise are the same ones we as writers should be sure to answer.

What Is the Question at Issue?

To merit a reader's serious attention, writing needs a reason to be written and read. College writing almost invariably turns on a *question at issue* for both writer and reader. Writers use that question to focus their response; readers use it to orient themselves to the concerns that the writer will address.

Let's pose this question ourselves as we read the first example, written by a student named Jerry. He has been asked to write a two-page essay—one that advances and supports a view about a matter of some concern or interest. I've numbered the sentences for easy reference.

(1) The sun is coming up over Boulder, Colorado, and the school children prepare for breakfast. (2) The choices are eggs and bacon, French toast, Pop Tarts, any of a dozen hot and cold cereals, TV news, and cartoons. (3) Here life is full of choices, choices, choices.

(4) The American business community has supplied us with more than enough choices. (5) However, it looks like the commercial expansion of our industry has brought with it some severely detrimental side effects. (6) We can no longer afford to overemphasize economic growth in light of the data on our social ills, such as air pollution, traffic congestion, widespread drug abuse, child-care scandals, or watershed contamination.

(7) Moreover, American commerce—our manufacturers and distributors—have long been developing foreign markets. (8) Our cultural values demand that American business penetrate foreign markets.

(9) However, domestic industrial waste is one of several growing problems which require a review of not only our domestic industrial expansion, but more importantly for my purpose, a mature review of our commercial intentions internationally.

When you read Jerry's prose, you look for some way to orient yourself. As you move from breakfast choices (sentences 1–3) to the dark side of economic growth (4–6), from American cultural values (7–8) to industrial waste and domestic expansion and foreign intentions (9), you find yourself, literally and figuratively, all over the map. Each paragraph does have a transition, a local connection. However, in the absence of an overall purpose, the connections remain only local. Jerry makes a number of interesting points but, taken as a whole, his writing amounts to free association.

You have difficulty orienting yourself to Jerry's writing because he has not articulated a *question at issue*, a point of disagreement that concerns both him and his readers. Something should prompt the writing—and rarely will it be the mere urge for self-expression. Jerry's immediate, if somewhat artificial reason for writing may be that his professor has required a paper. Yet most assignments implicitly ask writers to establish for themselves a genuine concern or problem. Writers do so by identifying the question at issue. When established and clearly stated, the question at issue can focus a writer's energies and help readers interpret a text.

By failing to engage a question at issue, Jerry's writing wanders. He hasn't said anything wrong, but he remains unclear about the kind of conversation he is having with his readers. He may not even have thought about who his readers are and what concerns or expectations they may have. Outlining the paper or collecting more information won't lessen Jerry's struggle to shape his writing. Critical thinking is the only thing that will help him draw relationships among his various ideas. For only by thinking critically about his material and his audience can he decide what is at issue. Only then can he focus his writing sharply. He will have a reason to write, a question to answer, a problem to solve.

Questions at issue force themselves on writers and readers alike because time and space are constrained. Our impatience with Jerry's essay stems from the expectation among college readers that an essay will get to its point quickly. Delay only annoys. When writers disregard the conditions under which an audience reads, they compromise the very process by which readers make sense of the writing.

Jerry provides us with our first lesson in critical reading: writer and reader communicate not in a vacuum, but in a context. To find direction, both as we write and as we read, we have to understand the *rhetorical situation*. Specifically, we need to know

- what question at issue prompts the writing,
- what roles author and audience inhabit and what expectations they share, and
- how constraints such as time and space orient what we do with words.

Unless readers have a sense of the rhetorical situation, they won't be able to orient themselves. Critical reading thus starts where communication itself starts:

with writers and readers, and an issue that, while bringing them together, nevertheless remains a point of discussion, even disagreement.

Because rhetorical situations help shape the texts we read and write, authors try to capture the distinctive exigence behind their texts in what we might call an *occasion*. Occasions offer clues about the rhetorical situation in which writer and reader find themselves. In so doing, the occasion establishes the relevance of the prose. It speaks to a question that every reader naturally asks: Why should I read this? When you write an analysis or argument, you should imagine your readers looking over your shoulder and asking that question. When you answer it early in your essay, you have an occasion. A good occasion convinces readers that they should pay attention to what you write.

What Is the Author's Point?

Writers pose questions to answer them, and to have us believe in the response. Readers, in turn, find an author's answer worthwhile only if it provides a credible response to a question at issue for them. Lest readers have any doubt about an essay's intention, writers generally answer the question at issue with one key statement—the *thesis statement*—that lends a concise point to their response.

A second example of prose gone astray, written by Karen, challenges us to find her intention, and thus teaches us further lessons about shaping ideas as we read.

> (1) Every year bulldozers cut down 200,000 square miles of Brazilian rain forests for farmland, timber, and grazing land. (2) This loss of forest cover is the major factor contributing to myriad environmental problems, including soil erosion, species extinctions, loss of soil productivity, and the destruction of the ozone. (3) Although one could see this as a conflict between Brazil's economy and its environment, Brazil could slow needless deforestation and ironically save billions of dollars through the removal of misdirected national policies that encourage the clearing of rain forests. (4) Policies regulating raw wood exportation, current logging concessions, and land development all encourage the clearing of rain forests.

We probably have as much trouble following Karen's writing as we did Jerry's. The reasons, however, differ. If Jerry was uncertain about the kind of conversation he was having and the issue that prompted him to write, Karen seems confused about the point she wishes to make. Despite her earnestness, Karen doesn't get far because conflicting intentions take her in several different directions. Let's take a closer look.

Karen opens by describing the extent of deforestation. She then gives a list of secondary environmental effects ranging from soil erosion to ozone depletion. Although Karen seems to be setting herself the task of describing each of these problems, sentence 3 sets off in a different direction. The first word of this sentence—*Although*—points to a logical contrast between the economy and the environment. The contrast, however, is never developed. The reader is tempted to interrupt by asking, "How *do* you see the conflict; what *is* the relationship between economy and environment?" Because the remainder of the sentence doesn't address these questions, confusion mounts. The main clause straddles analysis and argument with the ambiguous word *could*. Does Karen wish to argue that Brazil should eliminate policies destructive to rain forests, or does she wish to analyze the potential effects of eliminating those policies?

We never find out, as the fourth sentence sends us in still another direction. Although it seems to promise that Karen will analyze why certain policies encourage the clearing of rain forests, it also intimates that she will describe three areas of activity to which those policies apply. Despite her mention of raw wood exportation, logging concessions, and land development, we still don't know what Karen wants to say about these activities or the policies that govern them.

For all its apparent density, Karen's prose wanders as much as Jerry's. The errancy stems chiefly from her uncertain intention. Moreover, Karen's shifting intentions obscure the specific issue that prompts her discussion. They also fail to show how she will go about supporting any one particular assertion. Karen may have a topic, but she needs to say something *about* her topic, something that bears the imprint of her own thinking. Her task is all the more difficult because she may have only secondhand acquaintance with deforestation. Even if she can report the conclusions of others, she may not be able to advance a perceptive point of her own.

This second example prompts a question that should guide your critical reading and, in turn, your own writing: What point does the essay advance? That is, what statement would its author have you believe? Many authors reply by clearly announcing a core assertion, a *thesis*. But even if only implied, this assertion remains the idea that makes everything else in the essay necessary.

Writers and readers alike accord such importance to the thesis because it influences the entire essay. To understand its influence, view *thesis* as a *relational*, not static, term. A thesis looks in two directions.

• It looks back toward the occasion by giving an answer to the question that prompts the essay.

• It also looks forward to the support and development that the writer must provide if we are to accept that answer.

As a tool for critical reading and thinking, the thesis can help you identify the author's point and test lines of reasoning. It expresses the author's opinion on a question at issue. It can also serve as a hypothesis by which writer and readers can explore and refine ideas. For a thesis to be anything more than a hypothesis, reasons must make it credible.

Do the Author's Reasons Elicit Belief?

Writers make assertions about questions at issue because they want to elicit our belief. To win that belief responsibly, writers call on *reasons* to justify their assertions. In the absence of reasons, analysis and argument lose their shape. A final example of vagabond prose will help us uncover this third source of errancy. We'll hear now from Daniel.

(1) While the United States is willing and able to spend money, the federal government is heavily burdened with the largest national deficit to date. (2) Even though the debt is still increasing, it does not receive adequate attention from Congress because congressmen are more concerned about being reelected than reducing the deficit. (3) Congressmen, therefore, purposely underestimate fiscal spending and purposely overestimate the growth of the economy. (4) In addition, they spend too much money on social programs.

(5) A major problem that Congress must correct is underestimating spending and overestimating revenue. (6) Congressmen purposely make these estimating errors to gain more supporters. (7) By underestimating fiscal spending and overestimating the economy's growth, Congress allows itself to spend more money, and individual congressmen gain more supporters for reelection.

(8) Another way congressmen win votes is by spending money on social programs. (9) Although these programs should be supported, too much federal money is spent on them. (10) A lot of people receiving these government funds do not really need them and are just using our legislatures. (11) Congress is being used because they feel that by giving more money to more people, they will be able to win people's votes. (12) This is of course true, but government does not have money to spend foolishly.

(13) The federal deficit is not a problem that will immediately go away, but hopefully individual congressmen will show some responsibility. (14) This could be done by worrying more about the debt than being reelected.

On a cursory reading, Daniel's writing may not seem to go astray. We can point to the second sentence of the essay as stating his intention. What's more, the essay seems to have discernable shape. The third and fourth sentences of the introductory paragraph set up the middle two paragraphs. What, then, is vagabond about an essay that plots its organization so carefully?

Daniel's writing wanders quite simply because the thinking doesn't follow. Despite its surface organization, the essay breaks the rules it sets for itself; it departs from the conditions and consequences of its own assertions. When making claims, Daniel doesn't take responsibility for supporting them, or even for questioning whether the assertions he makes can be substantiated. Readers probe an essay's credibility when they study the link between an assertion and the reasons offered in its support. Critical reading thus culminates in the issue of belief: Are we to believe what we read?

With Daniel's prose, we remain skeptical. For all of his surface formatting and tidy paragraphs, Daniel wanders because he misses the inherent connection between intention and fulfillment, assertion and support. His credibility and our belief suffer as a result. Let's take a more careful look.

Daniel's problems start in the first paragraph, where he tries to express his main point. When he asserts in the second sentence that the debt does not receive "adequate attention," he implies that he has some way of measuring adequacy. How much attention is "adequate"? We never find out. Likewise, when Daniel claims that congressmen are more concerned about being reelected than reducing the deficit, we assume that he has some way of determining "concern." He certainly couldn't turn to congressmen themselves, for they would never admit openly that they place reelection over national interest.

We see from the second sentence that Daniel has not one but two points that he wishes to focus on: adequate attention and reelection concerns. Each of those points forces the reader to circle back and question whether it can be supported.

Experienced authors shape their writing by following through on what they say, by playing out the conditions and consequences implicit in their own statements. When Daniel tries to find reasons for his assertion, he wanders. We ask how the third sentence follows from the second, how estimates of fiscal spending and economic growth can follow from claims of inadequate attention and misplaced concerns about reelection. Because the points don't follow, we have trouble discerning the shape of Daniel's argument. The fourth sentence once again confirms and frustrates our need for follow-through. How is it that we now turn to social programs? Why not defense programs? How does spending on social programs make congressmen's attention to the deficit any more or less adequate?

As Daniel tries to expand sentences 3 and 4 into a sustained discussion that will support his main point, his own statements sabotage his efforts. The second paragraph hinges on the claim that congressmen "purposely" under- or overestimate. Yet how can one prove intention in this case? Unable to do so, Daniel can only resort to restating time and again his original assertion. The third paragraph suffers the same fate. Unable to justify how much is "too much" spending, Daniel falls back on sweeping indictments of social programs. By failing to follow through on his statements, Daniel never gets far, despite the appearance that his paragraphs march in disciplined sequence.

Our third example of vagabond prose makes clear that surface organization is itself an inadequate means to shape ideas that will elicit belief. Here, form has become mere format; all we have is a skeleton that attests not to the coherence of the paper but only to the absence of lively, careful thought. The surface organization is phoney, the control faked—and both writer and reader know it. Daniel's problem can be traced to flouting the conditions and consequences of his own words. Whereas Jerry was uncertain about the kind of conversation he was having or the issue prompting it, and Karen was unsure of her intention, Daniel has failed to explore his own statements, to follow where they seem to lead. He merely repeats assertions without backing them up, and thus loses the credibility he is trying to earn.

Here are several ways to consider credibility as you scrutinize what you read and write.

- You can ask, as we did with Daniel's paper, what the thesis requires in the way of analysis or proof.
- You can evaluate the reasons an author advances in support of a point, and further, the ideas that lie beyond those reasons.
- You can also notice where the reasoning stops and where emotional or other sorts of appeals come to the fore.
- You can uncover hidden assumptions that allow an author to place reasons in support of an assertion.
- And finally, you can determine to what extent an author has taken questions or opposing views into account when developing an assertion.

By questioning whether the author's reasons elicit belief, you can test the adequacy and logical coherence of the thesis and its support. This can also help you examine the shape of the author's thinking and even anticipate the overall shape of the text. You are then better able to test whether the shape of ideas serves or undermines shared inquiry.

In finding our way through Jerry's, Karen's, and Daniel's prose, we have noted questions that readers would ask of virtually any essay or written document that makes an assertion.

- What is the question at issue?
- What is the author's point?
- Do the author's reasons elicit belief?

These questions can help you consider the shape of reason in what you read and write. They are powerful questions because they concern the motivations, intentions, and means that generate and shape content. They are the questions that call ideas into action.

Varieties of Prose Strategy

Nonfiction prose seems to offer a nearly infinite variety of forms. So many, in fact, that you may not recognize what is common among them. Consider instead that prose offers various ways of responding to just a few underlying questions.

Because critical reading poses those questions, it can help you examine the many strategies by which writers respond to them. Virtually any well-crafted text will address in some manner questions about the issue at hand, the point advanced, and the reasons meant to elicit belief in that point. The manner in which authors treat these questions can and should vary widely, for therein lies the creative challenge of writing nonfiction prose—and the pleasure we derive from reading it. As readers and writers, we can appreciate and make sense of widely differing texts because we can discern these underlying questions at work. We can use and enjoy many prose strategies because we share a common method for finding meaning in them.

An Invitation to Critical Inquiry

Much of the prose you read takes a straightforward approach to answer these questions. Consider, for example, editorials in your daily newspaper. Here's one from *The New York Times* of October 5, 1990, written by Anthony Lewis. He scrutinizes American policy in the decade leading up to Iraq's invasion of Kuwait in August 1990. As you read, look beyond the author's political persuasions to the manner in which he engages underlying questions.

Paying for Reagan
Anthony Lewis

(1) There has been much soul-searching since Aug. 2 about failures of American policy that helped to encourage Saddam Hussein's aggression. But not enough attention has been paid to the man whose folly led the way: Ronald Reagan.

(2) In three significant ways, President Reagan gave the Iraqi leader reason to believe that he did not have to worry about American opposition. Mr. Reagan played down human rights concerns, winking at horrendous cruelties by Saddam Hussein. He destroyed U.S. energy policy, making us more vulnerable to oil threats. And he treated international law with contempt.

(3) Few recent inhumanities in the world have been as shocking as Iraq's use of poison gas to kill thousands of its own Kurdish citizens in 1988. And it was unconcealed. Reporters went to the devastated villages. The world saw the bodies on television.

(4) And what did the United States do? Secretary of State George Shultz, to his credit, condemned Iraq for the use of chemical weapons. But the larger message sent by the Reagan Administration to Saddam Hussein was that it did not care.

(5) The Administration lobbied against, and blocked, Congressional efforts to impose sanctions on Iraq in 1988 because of the use of poison gas. It continued to extend $500 million a year in credit guarantees to Iraq to buy U.S. food products.

(6) At a special international conference on chemical weapons, held in Paris in January 1989, the United States strongly opposed efforts to name Iraq as a violator. Because the Administration gave a low priority to human rights, and because it wanted to sell goods to Iraq, it groveled.

(7) Before the gassing of the Kurds, Saddam Hussein had used chemical weapons in the war with Iran. The Reagan Administration made no forceful objection to that either.

(8) "In retrospect, it would have been much better at the time of their use of poison gas . . . if we'd put our foot down." Richard L. Armitage, an Assistant Secretary of Defense in the Reagan Administration, said that after the invasion of Kuwait.

(9) "The mistake we made," he added, "was not pushing very hard and loud for international action." The Reagan Administration, in short, missed a chance to deter Saddam Hussein.

(10) Shortly after Mr. Reagan was elected President, he said energy conservation meant being too hot in the summer and too cold in the winter. His policy was in keeping with that ignorant sneer.

(11) Funds for research on energy conservation were cut toward the vanishing point. Energy efficiency standards for cars and appliances were cut back, opposed, delayed. And the Reagan Administration just about ended the search for solar and other renewable energy sources.

(12) By the conservation measures started in the Carter Administration, the United States had reduced its dependence on imported oil to 28 percent of its total supply. Now about half the oil we use is imported.

(13) Ronald Reagan's contemptuous attitude toward international law hardly needs to be described. He reversed the historic American position, going back to Theodore Roosevelt's time, of respect for international law and international legal institutions.

(14) In disregard of treaties and other obligations, the Reagan Administration made war on Nicaragua. When Nicaragua sued in the World Court, the Reagan Administration rejected the Court's judgment and withdrew from its jurisdiction.

(15) Again, Saddam Hussein heard the message he wanted: The United States does not care about international law; it will look the other way if I break the rules.

(16) President Bush carried on the failed Reagan policies. When Congress imposed sanctions on Iraq but allowed a Presidential waiver, he waived them—and his people were on Capitol Hill opposing effective sanctions just a few days before the invasion of Kuwait. He did nothing for energy conservation. His invasion of Panama was another expression of contemptuous disregard for international law.

(17) We can hope that Mr. Bush has learned from the experience of these last two months: learned at least that it does not serve American interests to disregard a tyrant's cruelties or to trample on international law.

(18) But Mr. Reagan never learned. I thought of him when the superb public television series on the Civil War last week described how President Buchanan's vacuity helped to bring on the war. Americans paid for that war for 100 years. We shall be paying as long for Ronald Reagan's folly.

Aware that busy readers would immediately look for the question at issue, Anthony Lewis supplies it straightaway. The opening paragraph establishes common ground between writer and reader by acknowledging the nation's soul-searching even as Lewis directs attention to his immediate concern: the overlooked role of a past president in encouraging Saddam Hussein's aggression.

With the third sentence, Anthony Lewis's thesis is clear: Reagan gave Saddam Hussein reason to believe that he had nothing to fear from the United States. The remainder of the second paragraph offers, in turn, a brief sketch of the reasons that Lewis will offer to support his assertion. Lewis shapes his editorial by developing those reasons.

Such a straightforward response does more than orient an audience or ensure readability. It invites *critical inquiry*. If Anthony Lewis's assertion is to become credible, he must elicit and earn belief by offering reasons that stand up to tough questions.

Consider Lewis's second reason: "[Reagan] destroyed U.S. energy policy, making us more vulnerable to oil threats." Does it, in fact, support his thesis? To find out, we must turn to the body of the editorial, specifically paragraphs 10–12. Having announced his reasons, Lewis is now compelled to support them and tie all of them directly to his thesis. Yet Lewis's discussion elicits more questions than belief. Even if we presume, for the moment, that a weakened energy policy has made us "more vulnerable to oil threats," wouldn't that vulnerability prompt, not hinder, our opposition to Iraq's annexation of oil-rich Kuwait? Ideas may unravel when you scrutinize the relationships among them. You are reading critically when you examine the shape of reason in any text and arrive at your own conclusions.

A Respect for Reasoned Opinion

A belief in shared inquiry persuaded Thomas Jefferson to address readers' questions directly in a cornerstone of our democracy—The Declaration of Independence. Indeed, those questions shape its very beginning.

> When in the course of human events, it becomes necessary for one people to dissolve the political bands which have connected them with another, and to assume among the powers of the earth, the separate and equal station to which the Laws of Nature and of Nature's God entitle them, a decent respect to the opinions of mankind requires that they should declare the causes which impel them to the separation.

In one sentence, Jefferson handles all three questions. If the long subordinate clause that opens the sentence establishes the occasion, Jefferson's intention becomes clear as the sentence drives to its conclusion: the intention is separation. Yet if our founding fathers were to gain solidarity among their supporters, move the undecided to join their cause, and justify the colonies' actions to other nations, they could not content themselves with merely announcing America's independence. They had to "declare the causes," and thereby offer a credible defense of their action that would win both belief and support. In this sense, the document is as much a declaration of reasons as a declaration of independence. It is, in fact, an argument.

College should foster Jefferson's respect for reasoned opinion. As you read and write in a community of inquiring minds, you discover issues that deserve consideration, seek out and refine answers to those issues, and test your conclusions by justifying them with reasons that will earn the belief of others. As you move from discipline to discipline, course to course, the prose you read and write varies. Yet you will notice throughout a preoccupation with questions that concern the shape of ideas. Good writing answers those questions.

Layers of Reasoning

Books, essays, and scholarly articles that analyze or argue have a special obligation to treat readers' questions in a forthright manner. All the more so when the case being built relies on *layers of reasoning*. Consider, for example, Andrew Hacker's article "The Myths of Racial Division." Here is his introduction, along with his analysis of one of several black-and-white myths that he debunks.

The Myths of Racial Division
By Andrew Hacker

(1) The urge to emphasize racial division in America is hard to resist. Few nations have etched so deep a black-and-white separation as our own. Even South Africa allows for Coloureds, while Latin countries have mulattos and mestizos, as well as Creoles and quadroons. But here even children of mixed marriages end up regarded as black. And while citizens may cherish their European origins, being white retains primacy in most of their minds. At times, race seems to surpass even gender as our major schism.

(2) It shouldn't. We now have information about how much impact race has in areas such as school achievement, hiring, family life, and crime—and it should spur us to rethink the actual impact of race and ethnic separatism. If anything, there is evidence that race is becoming a *less* salient factor for growing groups of Americans. Here follows a brief debunking of a variety of black-and-white myths, which, upon inspection, turn out to be grayer realities.

(3) *The black family is disintegrating, while the white family remains intact.* Since Daniel Patrick Moynihan's 1965 report found black families trapped in a "tangle of pathology," conditions seem to have gotten worse. Two-thirds of black babies are now born outside of wedlock, and more than half of black homes are headed by women. A majority of black youngsters live only with their mother; and in most of these households she has never been married.

(4) Almost everyone agrees that the increases in nonmarital births and female-headed households are causes for dismay. But why should race be the crucial variable? Readily available reports show that low income and

education outweigh race in causing family instability. Absent fathers abound in depressed counties where the residents are almost wholly white. In rural Maine, for example, out-of-wedlock rates exceed those for blacks in several states.

(5) As it happens, extramarital births and households headed by women are subject to social trends, which touch all races and classes in similar ways. The Census figures for female-headed families for the last four decades show that both black and white families have disintegrated at virtually identical rates. In 1950, 17.2 percent of black families were headed by single women, against 5.3 percent of white families (a black-white multiple of 3.2). In 1990, the figures are 56.2 percent and 17.3 percent respectively (a black-white multiple of 3.2). Plainly, what we have been seeing are not so much race-based differences as concurrent adaptations to common cultural conditions. True, the black figure has always been three times larger, and here is where "racial" reasons have an influence of their own. But those forces were at work well before 1950, prior to talk about "pathology." Of course, the current 56.2 percent rate for black households is depressingly high. But then the 1990 figure for whites is almost identical to the one for blacks lamented in Moynihan's report.

(6) The point here is not whether family structure is important, but whether its dynamic over the last thirty years has been different along racial lines. It hasn't been. Given the ubiquity of absent fathers—black and white—little will be gained by lecturing one race on its duties. To call on black Americans to show greater discipline would seem to suggest that only they have deviated from national norms. Black families will become more stable when all households evolve a stronger structure.

(7) Where out-of-wedlock births are concerned, there is actual racial convergence. What we hear most is that 66 percent of black births are to girls and women who are not married. However, close study of the figures reveals that the black-white multiple is less than half of what it was forty years ago. So while black out-of-wedlock births are at an all-time high, the white ratio has been ascending at a far faster rate. Even in typical mid-American cities such as Davenport, Iowa, and Dayton, Ohio, the current white figures are 27.8 percent and 31.4 percent. In 1950, 16.8 percent of black births were out of wedlock, while 1.7 percent of white births were (a black-white multiple of 9.9). In 1970, the proportions were 37.6 percent and 5.7 percent respectively (a multiple of 6.6). Today, the figures are 66 percent and 16 percent (a multiple of 4.1). The chief reason for the decrease in the multiple is the availability of abortion. Although black women constitute only 13 percent of women of childbearing age, they account for more than 30 percent of the pregnancies terminated each year.

Andrew Hacker uses the first paragraph to establish his occasion: the perception that race is our nation's major schism. The article challenges that perception, as he makes clear with his thesis in the second paragraph: race is "a less salient factor" than many of us would presume. What reasons does Hacker advance to convince us of his point? A wealth of information now allows us to question a variety of black-and-white myths. Those myths—and the evidence he uses to debunk them—shape his discussion.

Readers' questions help Hacker develop his case and, in turn, help the reader evaluate that case. Let's consider how he debunks the first of several myths—namely that "the black family is disintegrating, while the white family remains intact." That very statement provides the immediate question at issue for this section of the article. Hacker develops this occasion throughout the third paragraph with information that would seem to lend credence to that statement. He responds to this occasion in paragraph 4, where he states that low income and education outweigh race as factors that influence family stability. How does Hacker make this assertion credible? He organizes his discussion around two specific bodies of evidence: households headed by women (paragraphs 5 and 6) and extramarital births (paragraph 7). Moreover, he starts each of those discussions with an assertion that he then justifies. Thus, at various levels, Hacker shapes his article by drawing relationships among issues, assertions, and reasons.

As you read in college, you may find it difficult at times to grasp the shape of ideas. Some reasoning is indirect or poorly organized; some may be fallacious. In a complicated analysis or argument like Hacker's, you'll find layers of reasoning, where a set of reasons will support one conclusion, and that conclusion will itself be one of several reasons that justify the author's main assertion. Lest you become overwhelmed by complex prose, always evaluate the question at issue, the assertion that answers it, and the reasons for that assertion.

Close, Not Superficial Analysis

The following short yet relatively complex passage shows just how carefully you must read. Here we find Martin Luther King, Jr., addressing local clergy in a brief excerpt from his "Letter from Birmingham Jail."

(1) You deplore the demonstrations taking place in Birmingham. (2) But your statement, I am sorry to say, fails to express a similar concern for the conditions that brought about the demonstrations. (3) I am sure that none of you would want to rest content with the superficial kind of social analysis that deals merely with effects and does not grapple with underlying causes. (4) It is unfortunate that demonstrations are taking place in

> Birmingham, but it is even more unfortunate that the city's white power structure left the Negro community with no alternative.

The question at issue is not expressed directly. A closer reading sends us back to sentence 2, where we are meant to ask what *did* bring about the demonstrations. King's answer is likewise not easy to spot, for we have to recognize the irony in his otherwise polite rhetoric. The second half of sentence 4 reveals the point of King's argument: the city's white power structure left the Negro community with no alternative. How so? What reason does King provide? Sentence 3 doesn't seem to hold a clue if we read it quickly—and straight. Yet King's critique is all the more damning because the biting irony in this sentence points out just how indirect and insufficient the white community's response has been. The black community had no alternative precisely *because* the white power structure rested content with superficial analysis, with surface effects not underlying causes.

Why is this passage so difficult to read? We have to look beyond the simple fact of the demonstrations, beyond immediate information, to what King was doing with words. Moreover, we have to look beyond the polite, deferential rhetoric to his argument's hidden ironic edge. King's purpose in this passage, and in the letter itself, is to provoke close, not superficial, analysis. He is asking his audience to do the very kind of hard thinking that critical reading requires of you.

Inquiry in the Meditative Essay

Even exploratory prose such as the meditative or reflective essay can best be appreciated in light of readers' questions. Despite the apparent formlessness of such essays, they nevertheless respond, if only obliquely, to those questions. Yet the strategies by which the questions are addressed may be highly distinctive and aim for special effects. Roger Rosenblatt's brief essay "The Man in the Water" offers an example.

The Man in the Water
Roger Rosenblatt

(1) As disasters go, this one was terrible, but not unique, certainly not among the worst on the roster of U.S. air crashes. There was the unusual element of the bridge, of course, and the fact that the plane clipped it at a moment of high traffic, one routine thus intersecting another and disrupting both. Then, too, there was the location of the event. Washington, the city of form and regulations, turned chaotic, deregulated, by a blast of real

winter and a single slap of metal on metal. The jets from Washington National Airport that normally swoop around the presidential monuments like famished gulls are, for the moment, emblemized by the one that fell; so there is that detail. And there was the aesthetic clash as well—blue-and-green Air Florida, the name a flying garden, sunk down among gray chunks in the black river. All that was worth noticing, to be sure. Still, there was nothing very special in any of it, except death, which, while always special, does not necessarily bring millions to tears or to attention. Why, then, the shock here?

(2) Perhaps because the nation saw in this disaster something more than a mechanical failure. Perhaps because people saw in it no failure at all, but rather something successful about their makeup. Here, after all, were two forms of nature in collision: the elements and human character. Last Wednesday, the elements, indifferent as ever, brought down Flight 90. And on that same afternoon, human nature—groping and flailing in mysteries of its own—rose to the occasion.

(3) Of the four acknowledged heroes of the event, three are able to account for their behavior. Donald Usher and Eugene Windsor, a park police helicopter team, risked their lives every time they dipped the skids into the water to pick up survivors. On television, side by side in bright blue jump-suits, they described their courage as all in the line of duty. Lenny Skutnik, a 28-year-old employee of the Congressional Budget Office, said: "It's something I never thought I would do"—referring to his jumping into the water to drag an injured woman to shore. Skutnik added that "somebody had to go in the water," delivering every hero's line that is no less admirable for its repetitions. In fact, nobody had to go into the water. That somebody actually did so is part of the reason this particular tragedy sticks in the mind.

(4) But the person most responsible for the emotional impact of the disaster is the one known at first simply as "the man in the water." (Balding, probably in his 50s, an extravagant mustache.) He was seen clinging with five other survivors to the tail section of the airplane. This man was described by Usher and Windsor as appearing alert and in control. Every time they lowered a lifeline and flotation ring to him, he passed it on to another of the passengers. "In a mass casualty, you'll find people like him," said Windsor. "But I've never seen one with that commitment." When the helicopter came back for him, the man had gone under. His selflessness was one reason the story held national attention; his anonymity another. The fact that he went unidentified invested him with a universal character. For a while he was Everyman, and thus proof (as if one needed it) that no man is ordinary.

(5) Still, he could never have imagined such a capacity in himself. Only minutes before his character was tested, he was sitting in the ordinary plane among the ordinary passengers, dutifully listening to the stewardess telling him to fasten his seat belt and saying something about the "no smoking sign." So our man relaxed with the others, some of whom would owe their lives to him. Perhaps he started to read, or to doze, or to regret some harsh remark made in the office that morning. Then suddenly he knew that the trip would not be ordinary. Like every other person on that flight, he was desperate to live, which makes his final act so stunning.

(6) For at some moment in the water he must have realized that he would not live if he continued to hand over the rope and ring to others. He *had* to know it, no matter how gradual the effect of the cold. In his judgment he had no choice. When the helicopter took off with what was to be the last survivor, he watched everything in the world move away from him, and he deliberately let it happen.

(7) Yet there was something else about our man that kept our thoughts on him, and which keeps our thoughts on him still. He was *there*, in the essential, classic circumstance. Man in nature. The man in the water. For its part, nature cared nothing about the five passengers. Our man, on the other hand, cared totally. So the timeless battle commenced in the Potomac. For as long as that man could last, they went at each other, nature and man; the one making no distinctions of good and evil, acting on no principles, offering no lifelines; the other acting wholly on distinctions, principles and, one supposes, on faith.

(8) Since it was he who lost the fight, we ought to come again to the conclusion that people are powerless in the world. In reality, we believe the reverse, and it takes the act of the man in the water to remind us of our true feelings in this matter. It is not to say that everyone would have acted as he did, or as Usher, Windsor and Skutnik. Yet whatever moved these men to challenge death on behalf of their fellows is not peculiar to them. Everyone feels the possibility in himself. That is the abiding wonder of the story. That is why we would not let go of it. If the man in the water gave a lifeline to the people gasping for survival, he was likewise giving a lifeline to those who observed him.

(9) The odd thing is that we do not even really believe that the man in the water lost his fight. "Everything in Nature contains all the powers of Nature," said Emerson. Exactly. So the man in the water had his own natural powers. He could not make ice storms, or freeze the water until it froze the blood. But he could hand life over to a stranger, and that is a power of

nature too. The man in the water pitted himself against an implacable, impersonal enemy; he fought it with charity; and he held it to a standoff. He was the best we can do.

Although Rosenblatt may not engage questions directly, they nevertheless orient both the essay's carefully crafted shape and our own reading. The first two paragraphs state the occasion in a variety of ways to question and seek out the grounds of the discussion. The occasion extends into the next two paragraphs, where the exploits of Usher, Windsor, and Skutnik, described in paragraph 3, provide counterpoint to the simple narrative of heroism in paragraph 4. In the process, we learn about the Air Florida crash and the ensuing rescue attempts. Yet background information is not offered for its own sake. It serves the author's deeper concern and our own growing interest: What accounts for this disaster's emotional impact?

At the end of the second paragraph, the author would have us believe that in the crash of Flight 90 "human nature . . . rose to the occasion." Yet what seems to be Rosenblatt's main point becomes itself an opportunity to explore the term *human nature*, juxtaposing as it does human character and natural element. Reflective essays often withhold conclusions or use several tentative answers that play off or comment on each other. They also may not offer organized reasons so much as follow turns in logic, association, and inference whose plan and purpose may only become apparent at the essay's close. Such is the case with Rosenblatt's essay, for only in the last paragraph do we find that "the man in the water had his own natural powers."

What reasons did Roger Rosenblatt use to elicit our belief? They may not march in orderly array, yet they persuade us. We find them in paragraphs 5 and 6, where, when ordinary activity becomes crisis, we discover the natural power of knowledge and deliberate choice in our lives. We find reasons as well in paragraphs 7 and 8, where the battle in the Potomac reveals the power one man gives to others—and to us. We may only discover the reasons that elicit our belief when we search the prose to find them. Yet unlike vagabond prose, this essay does contain reasons—good ones. Meditative essays invite inquiry when they represent carefully honed intentions and calculated effects, not impromptu ramblings.

Whatever form your college reading and writing takes, you owe it to yourself to discover and evaluate what other authors mean and what you have to say in response. Because prose strategies are endlessly varied, your best course lies in asking the right questions. A means to critical reading and thoughtful writing, the three questions we've discussed help you make rational decisions about which opinions to accept and which to reject.

Writers as Readers

Questions help you probe the texts you read. But they can also help you write. By reading critically, you can write more intelligently as you respond to those texts. You also become more adept at using textual sources to advance your own case. Finally, critical reading gives you a valuable perspective on your own writing, enabling you to revise drafts so that they will meet the demands of skeptical readers. By thinking like a reader, writers hone their skills—and their ideas.

College draws a particularly close connection between reading and writing because you must often respond to and evaluate texts. Academic writing is largely text based. And texts are everywhere. Some are fiction—the poems, novels, and plays that you read in literature courses. Other texts describe, explain, analyze, or argue in the language of nonfiction prose. Still others may not even seem like texts to you—the immigration registers on Ellis Island or financial statements issued by the leading employer in your town. Indeed, texts extend beyond the written word to include movies, artwork, and advertisements. Some theorists even speak of cultural texts, such as funerals and sorority rushes. However different they may seem, texts ask you to observe and infer, to look closely at patterns of ideas and experience as you draw conclusions about what they mean.

To write about these texts, you must not only discover and interpret their patterns but also establish patterns in your own thinking. The questions that readers pose about a text—questions about issues, assertions, and reasons—now become the very ones to which you must respond. As you address them, these questions can help you discover and shape your own ideas.

As a writer, you will also address current issues as they arise in public debate. All your life, you will respond to others. To respond well, you must fully understand the positions that others hold. A superficial grasp of someone else's ideas may undermine your own reply or even anger the very people you wish to persuade. To respond as an informed citizen, you must "read" the nature of debate, much as you would a text. And as you advance your own case, you often will need to evaluate and use textual sources and the testimony of experts. For your writing to be informed by the best minds, you must be able to read the shape of their ideas. Once again, critical reading bears on your work as a writer.

Finally, critical reading prompts you to ask useful questions about your own prose. As you generate drafts and revise them, you will play both reader and writer, each perspective complementing and reinforcing the other. Revision starts with your ability to evaluate your own text critically, with the eye and ear of your most skeptical reader. To re-envision your writing, you must look past your own preoccupations to questions that your readers will invariably pose. Only by addressing their concerns can you offer writing meant to be read. Writers are at their best when they can evaluate and revise their own words.

To help you write with readers in mind, we need to understand in greater detail how the questions they pose work and interrelate, and how you can respond to them in your own writing. Doing so will focus our attention on concerns essential to college writing:

- engaging an issue directly in the spirit of shared inquiry,
- lending conceptual focus and rigor to your point, and
- substantiating the assertions that you make.

These priorities are best met by prose strategies that strive for clarity, not special effects. Moreover, a straightforward approach helps you meet the constraints of time and space that govern communication in college. A direct approach also provides a suitable basis for exploring applications across the curriculum. Finally, addressing readers' questions directly requires far more skill and creativity than you might expect. Even the most accomplished writers share this challenge: using the writing process to shape and refine ideas that will elicit a reader's belief.

Your chief resource remains your own willingness and capacity to monitor how you form meaning. This critical, self-conscious approach helps you understand the implications of what you read and write and the questions you are asking when doing both.

Writing to Form Ideas

2

The questions that readers pose are the very ones to which writers ought to reply. Readers orient themselves by asking

- What is the question at issue?
- What is the author's point?
- Do the author's reasons elicit belief?

They expect in return a reasonable degree of guidance from the author. Academic writing should not ask readers to become sleuths, nor should it encourage authors to become secret agents. An author's perceptive insights deserve to be readily grasped. As a reader, you can do your part by posing questions that contribute to a perceptive, critical reading.

Writers, in turn, must wrestle with readers' questions directly on the page. Since readers of *your* writing will be posing these very questions, help them by providing clear answers. Readers' questions should prompt you to formulate

- an *occasion* that focuses an issue or concern likely to engage your reader's interest;
- a *thesis* that, in expressing your point, invites shared inquiry; and
- *reasons* that support your point and thus help you develop your paper by projecting its essential organization.

By answering questions you take advantage of a reader's innate curiosity and skepticism and use them to lend your writing shape and power. Not only will you make your writing more readable, you'll improve the thinking behind it.

These three elements of form are far from separate categories, mere slots to fill in. They provide an integrated set of critical-thinking tools, and thus bear closely on each other. Indeed, the *relationships* you create among them allow you to explore and shape ideas as you analyze or argue. They can refine your thinking even as they contribute directly to the writing that must get done.

How do these elements of form—occasion, thesis, and reasons—actually work? And how do their relationships with each other create a web of meaning that is more than the sum of separate parts? In this chapter we will explore the dynamic relationships among these elements. We'll start where most papers start, with authors helping readers understand what they are doing with words. Authors often provide this help in the introductions to their papers. Knowing full well that readers need and desire some orientation at the outset, authors of essays use their introductions to indicate for their readers and themselves the key relationships they are drawing. Introductions, in turn, allow us to examine closely each of the three elements—the thesis and its two companions, occasion and reasons. As discrete elements, they hold little intrinsic interest. They become useful to you and to your readers only when you link them together. By knowing what is at stake with each element and by establishing relationships among them, you can anticipate readers' questions and integrate even hostile, probing objections into a process of shared inquiry.

Speaking of Form: Five Voices

Experienced authors will be the first to tell you that introductions are difficult to craft. Why? Introductions often have you writing about writing. They require that you consider relationships among ideas even as you speak about your subject. Moreover, as you set words on the page, you may not be entirely clear about your own intentions. For all their difficulty, introductions help you establish the occasion, articulate the thesis, and project the reasons that organize the text to follow. In so doing, they offer a laboratory for exploring the very relationships that lend meaning to prose.

You may draft an introduction as you start to write, but you will surely return to it often during the writing process. You'll want to reconsider and revise it as you clarify your purpose in writing the full paper. For readers it is much the same. As you take a document in hand, you may start with its introduction, yet you can never simply dispense with it as you read on. Throughout your reading you are considering how or whether its promises have been fulfilled, its claims supported. The introduction need not become a fixation, but for writers and readers alike it orients and informs. It may be a point of departure, but it also is a place to which you return as you find your bearings and evaluate your journey.

As you hear from the following five writers, consider how their introductions orient you to the shape of their ideas. We'll use these introductions to identify key principles that can help you form ideas. Although they are by no means perfect, they do succeed in launching a tightly reasoned analysis or argument. (At the end of this chapter, you'll find the full papers that demonstrate how the writers developed their ideas.) By looking for and applying the principles at work in their introductions, you can emulate their achievement.

An aerobics instructor for seven years, Cindy came to college to study kinesiology, the science of human movement. Using the aerobics class as her "text," she analyzes the effect of hand-held weights, or heavy hands.

(1) "Burn those calories! (2) Get that heart rate up!" screams the instructor. (3) The music pulsates, the pace quickens. (4) With the motto "more is mightier," you clutch your weights and swing them in cadence with the fast tempo. (5) Like other health club regulars, you may assume that these hand-held weights enhance an aerobic workout. (6) Yet aerobics performed with heavy hands actually compromises fitness. (7) By using weights you can overestimate exertion, cause anaerobic fatigue before significant cardiovascular benefit occurs, and jeopardize your body's muscular and skeletal structures.

Another writer, Paula, worked for three summers as a ranger with the United States Forest Service. The experience helped her look behind the headlines during the spectacular 1988 fire in Yellowstone National Park.

(1) The United States Forest Service (U.S.F.S.) uses a type of fire management called "let it burn" that allows lightning-induced wildfires to burn freely in wilderness, without human interference. (2) When the U.S.F.S. allowed the 1988 summer fire in Yellowstone National Park to burn unchecked for weeks, the media were harshly critical. (3) Journalists repeatedly blasted the U.S.F.S. fire management program and insisted that they propose a new one. (4) Although the media, and consequently the public, think that the U.S.F.S. should use a fire suppression method, I believe that the U.S.F.S. should continue to observe a policy of "let it burn." (5) Fire suppression, which does not allow *any* fire to burn freely, results in a crown fire that can be ten times more destructive than the ground fire produced in "let it burn." (6) While fire suppression inhibits the growth of prime tree species, "let it burn" helps maintain a healthy and diverse forest.

A native of Montana, Kurt has always had an interest in the Old West—and in Custer's Last Stand. Drawing on published eyewitness accounts and current research, he makes a case about the fate of Custer's men that contradicts the popular, larger-than-life version of the battle.

(1) Edgar S. Paxson's famous painting of the remnants of the cavalry dying in hand-to-hand combat with the Indians represents a popular but

false version of Custer's Last Stand. (2) Evidence strongly suggests that Custer's men committed suicide when the end was imminent. (3) Eyewitness accounts by Indians in the battle and recent discoveries of spent cavalry shells around the graves substantiate the theory that many of the soldiers killed themselves or executed mutual death pacts. (4) Soldiers preferred a quick death to what they believed would be a slow and painful end in Indian hands.

By playing off the text of Paxson's painting, Kurt finds and develops his own point.

Another writer, Del, looks closely at the text of Mark Twain's *The Adventures of Huckleberry Finn* to question a common interpretation of the novel. A native southerner, Del calls on his own classroom experience to frame his reading of the text.

(1) Reading *The Adventures of Huckleberry Finn* in a predominantly black school presents a serious obstacle: student and parental objections to the book as racist. (2) A common defense of the novel holds that the close relationship between Huck and Jim prompts Huck's moral development—a development that takes him beyond racial attitudes. (3) But I would argue, however reluctantly, that black students and parents are right. (4) Jim and Huck's relationship reveals not Huck's reputed moral development but rather his continuing racism. (5) Few readers would question that, early in the novel, Huck's response after Jim bests him in an argument reflects racist attitudes. (6) But the central episode in the fog that many readers point to as establishing close friendship and signalling moral development also turns on a racial slur. (7) Even Huck's response near the end of the novel to Jim's refusal to leave the wounded Tom Sawyer is made bittersweet by Huck's continuing racism.

Patricia takes as her text T. S. Eliot's *Murder in the Cathedral*, a play about the martyrdom of Thomas à Becket. She shapes her argument by looking closely at the function of the chorus in the play. Published in *The Explicator*, a journal devoted to close reading, Patricia's essay reminds us that academic writing need not choke on chalk dust. She engages us because she raises an intriguing question, asserts a provocative insight, and marshals close observations of the text to justify her reading—and reward us for ours.

(1) When Carole M. Beckett observes that "the dramatic function of the women of the Chorus [in *Murder in the Cathedral*] is to comment upon the events which they witness," she, like others, skirts the perplexing critical

question of why the chorus is composed solely of women. (2) What, in the design of the play, would necessitate an all-female chorus?

(3) The second priest in the play sees little use for the chorus of women:

> You are foolish, immodest and babbling women....
> You go on croaking like frogs in the treetops:
> But frogs at least can be cooked and eaten.

(pp. 20–21)

(4) These women, however, do perform a vital function: they expand our understanding of martyrdom through a metaphor of birth. (5) The female chorus reminds us that both women and martyrs give birth to new life. (6) For a woman, it is the life of her child; for a martyr, it is the life of his belief. (7) In the play, the women's chorus shows us how before giving birth, a martyr, like an expectant mother, must wait and suffer.

These introductions provide access to the author's ideas even as they set the shape of the analysis or argument to follow. They place the essay in context by indicating why the author is speaking and what interests bring reader and writer together. In this sense, introductions offer texts about context. Yet they also provide a commentary on the full essay to follow. They help highlight the author's core assertion and suggest how it will be developed. Thus, introductions both situate and predict. They point to the situation out of which a text emerges even as they help writer and reader orient the words to follow.

Although the writing styles and topics of these five authors vary, their introductions allow them—and you the reader—to establish the shape of their ideas. You can do the same in your own writing by observing a few fundamental principles. We'll start by considering the thesis; it's the point around which the occasion and reasons turn.

Establishing Your Point: The Thesis

As a veteran of writing classes, you are no stranger to the term *thesis*. But for all its familiarity, the term may conjure hazy notions. You know that a thesis is your main point, that it's better to mention it early rather than late, that a strong one is better than a weak one. That's not much to go on. Here's more.

Your Thesis Should Assert an Arguable Opinion

When you *assert* something, you do more than refer to a general topic. To make an assertion that can serve as a thesis, you must say something *about* the topic;

you must establish or predicate a relationship between two or more concepts. To do this, you will use verbs to link words and phrases. Look at the following transformations from topic to thesis. To draw attention to the shape of ideas in these thesis statements, I've boldfaced the key verbs and italicized the concepts they draw into relationship. Those relationships, not broad topics or individual concepts, allow you to shape ideas.

Topic	**Thesis**
The use of heavy hands in an aerobics class	*Aerobics performed with heavy hands* actually **compromises** *fitness*.
U.S. Forest Service policies for managing fires	*The U.S.F.S.* **should continue to observe** *a policy of "let it burn."*
The death of Custer's men	*Custer's men* **committed suicide** *when the end was imminent.*
Racial attitudes in *The Adventures of Huckleberry Finn*	*Jim and Huck's relationship* **reveals** not Huck's reputed moral development but rather his *continuing racism*.
The function of the chorus in T.S. Eliot's *Murder in the Cathedral*	*Women [in the chorus]* **expand our understanding of martyrdom** *through a metaphor of birth.*

Not all assertions, however, are useful as thesis statements should you wish to analyze or persuade. Only an *arguable opinion* will serve you well, one that isn't trivial or self-evident. It should express a view on a subject of some concern, articulate an important but unnoticed insight, or advance a claim that readers are inclined to debate. An arguable opinion is one that can be disputed. It indicates your willingness to analyze or debate a question at issue. It also requires you to provide good reasons for your view.

The mark of a good thesis, then, is its *potential refutability*. Readers cannot evaluate a thesis intelligently unless they can also consider alternative views. Likewise, a writer cannot defend a thesis well without exploring objections to it. The only way to discover what you really think is to evaluate views and evidence that oppose or qualify your current position. To defend a thesis, you must in some sense attack it yourself. A perceptive thesis worthy of your reader's attention requires you to take an intellectual risk—reasonable risk, to be sure, but a risk nonetheless. Writing in college asks you to share in a process of inquiry by placing your ideas in open, reasoned debate.

Two Pitfalls

As you search for an arguable opinion, you will want to avoid two common pitfalls: asserting facts and asserting personal taste. Although such assertions do more than state a topic, they do not lead to workable thesis statements for an analytic or argumentative paper. They don't take intellectual risks or lead to shared inquiry. Understanding why can save you the frustration of heading down a blind alley.

The following assertions offer no more than statements of fact.

- Heavy hands are now used in many aerobics classes.
- The 1988 Yellowstone blaze sparked a debate about fire-management policies.

Useful as a fact may be in supporting your thesis, it cannot itself serve as a thesis. Why? Because you can't analyze or argue the facts themselves. General truths or self-evident observations don't lend themselves to development. If you were to phrase such factual or self-evident statements as questions, each would elicit a clear-cut yes or no answer. Facts are facts. They don't prompt analysis or argument, nor do they call for support.

Likewise, personal statements of taste such as the following hinder the shared inquiry that analysis and argument should foster.

- The presence of an all-women chorus makes *Murder in the Cathedral* a good play.
- Custer's men were foolish cowards to commit suicide.

Although your own tastes, values, and personal opinions lie behind virtually every analysis or argument, you cannot rest your case on an assertion whose grounds of support must be wholly personal. Support for a thesis should not amount to the mere tastes or prejudices of the individual making the assertion. Although you may find that the presence of an all-women chorus makes for a good play, this personal yardstick for dramatic excellence may do little to convince others. So too with the assertion about foolish cowardice on the part of Custer's men, for the statement hinges on a purely personal view of those men and their presumed suicides. Declarations of personal taste betray an unwillingness to open up assertions to shared scrutiny and judgment. Instead of fostering a debate about the merits of an idea, the purely personal thesis insists upon them. It shouts that one's own private view of reality is the correct one and that it is therefore unarguable. Such a thesis leads not to shared inquiry but to closed minds.

Testing and Defending Your Hypothesis

You may swallow hard at the thought of formulating a thesis. But if you keep your conclusion provisional, treating it as a scientist would a hypothesis for an experiment, you can shape your analysis or argument without pages of vagabond prose. By wrestling with the formulation of your thesis, you can scout out potential difficulties, examine the path your paper may take, identify areas where you may need more information, and even discover what you really believe.

When asserting an arguable opinion in your finished essay, announce your point early. Instead of drifting toward an opinion, analyze or argue in its defense. Your paper will likely have a final paragraph or concluding section. But don't wait until then to show your cards or figure out for yourself what your point is. In a first draft you may drift toward a point as you sift through evidence. Readers will have little patience with you, however, should you drift in your final version. A paper that fails to establish its point at the outset risks being misread—or not read to its end.

Responding to an Issue

An arguable opinion is far more than an isolated assertion. It acquires its force because it looks in two directions: to the issue that prompts it and to the reasoned support that such an opinion requires.

To be workable as a thesis, an assertion cannot be just any arguable opinion. It must be an opinion that responds to an issue before a particular audience. Although the assertion "fire-management policies deserve attention" may work as a thesis in some situations, it will clearly miss the mark before an audience already debating those policies. This example underscores that a thesis is always situated, never context-free. If a thesis is an arguable opinion, then what makes it arguable is determined by both issue and audience. You will find yourself without an arguable opinion if your assertion lacks an appropriate occasion or an appropriate audience. Never a self-contained statement suitable for all seasons, your thesis must grow out of your own rhetorical situation.

Some issues are inherent in the situation to which you must respond. The occasion is set for you. If you are writing an editorial on a ballot question, your occasion readily presents itself in the question of how one should vote. If you are writing an in-class essay exam, the occasion likewise presents itself in the form of the essay questions themselves. To respond appropriately, you must fashion a thesis that meets the exigencies that prompt the writing or anticipates the exigencies that govern its reading. Even when you have the freedom to specify an otherwise open occasion, your thesis will work well only if it responds to the issue you articulate.

Supporting Your Point

The arguable opinion you present as your thesis does more than state your view on an issue; it places on you the obligation to support your assertion.

If you think of your thesis merely as your main point, you risk losing its dynamic character. A thesis is not a static, isolated point; it is a vector—a line of reasoning that will thrust or propel you in a certain direction. In shaping your thesis, your job is to anticipate whether the journey in support of that thesis will be feasible, productive, and worthwhile. To assert, for example, that Custer's men committed suicide, you must anticipate and stand ready to provide the sort of evidence normally required of suicide investigations: reports from those who last saw the victim, physical evidence, and indications of psychological motivation.

An analytic or argumentative thesis requires that you think rigorously about the development of your assertion. A thesis is your *contract* with the reader. When crafting it, be sure that you can fulfill its terms; when developing it, be sure you have justified its claim. As you jot down your list of things to talk about, ideas to cover, or examples to mention, you may find yourself with items that relate to your thesis only because they concern the same general topic. Your thesis requires, however, far more than loose topical association with its support. Your thesis obligates you to find reasons for that thesis, not just points to cover or subtopics to mention. Reasons are the means by which you justify the claims of your thesis and fulfill its contract. In finding reasons for your thesis, you have to analyze or argue *why* your thesis holds true, rather than describe *what* your thesis is about. Your task is to find and justify a perspective on your subject.

When pressed to justify your assertion, you may be tempted to back off with the reply, "But it's just my opinion." An assertion may be your opinion, but if it responds to a shared concern or question at issue, it is an opinion in which your readers have some stake or interest. A thesis asks you to earn your opinion. The hesitations, doubts, and probing counterarguments of your readers play a role in how you develop your paper. In supporting your thesis, you are not well served by insisting on it in a shrill voice. An arguable thesis holds open the possibility of a rival hypothesis, a counterthesis. Support for your thesis actually entails that you recognize your view may be open to dispute.

Scouting Your Thesis

If you wish to test and improve your thesis, you'll need to scout its potential opportunities and hazards by clarifying its relationships to occasion and reasoned support. Your most important tool will be your ability to think ahead, to recognize consequences before you actually face them. When scouting your thesis, ask yourself the following three interrelated questions.

- Does the thesis assert an arguable opinion?
- Does the thesis respond to a concern or question at issue?
- Does the thesis lend itself to reasoned support?

Relationships among these questions allow the thesis to acquire its pervading influence. As you draft and revise your full paper, those relationships help you decide what does and doesn't belong in your discussion. By viewing your thesis in relational terms, you will find that it is more than the central idea of a unified composition; it is the very means of unifying it.

Engaging the Issue: The Occasion

Openings, you've been told, should elicit the reader's interest. They should "grab," "hook," "engage," "entice," or otherwise "excite" the reader about the paper. Although correct, the advice is incomplete. Winning attention for your prose is in itself not too difficult. The challenge lies in directing and focusing the attention.

Perhaps you've had your interest grabbed by a bulletin board notice boldly headlined

S   E   X

only to be disappointed at the fine print beneath: "Now that I've gotten your attention, the Delta Tau Delta fraternity is holding a car wash." The striking quotation, amusing anecdote, or powerful example may indeed prompt curiosity. But unless you direct the attention you have created, your occasion can become a source of confusion, even irritation. Instead of setting up your analysis or argument, it can derail your efforts.

If you seek to interest your readers merely by entertaining them, you are forced to rely on your own verbal artistry and virtually nothing else. Pulitzer Prize winners can pull this off. But for most writers, trying to wow your reader with fancy footwork can leave you flat-footed or even flat on your face. You needn't reach for special effects—weighty philosophical statements, clever anecdotes, or stylistic pyrotechnics. Your occasion is not an isolated set piece, an opening hurdle you must clear before you get down to the business at hand. Your occasion actually *establishes* the business at hand. It voices the concern that motivates your entire essay.

Speaking to the Issue _____

Experienced writers engage their readers by directly engaging an issue that they share. You can only find something to say by discovering yourself in a rhetorical situation—one in which something needs to be said and someone needs to hear it. If you call on a shared concern to engage your reader, the engagement becomes both mutual and genuine. Moreover, by speaking to an issue, you can spark not only interest but also your own reasoned response.

Why engage an issue at the outset? An issue is your point of contact with your audience. It's the question whose answer you and your readers have yet to agree on—either because you openly disagree, or because you have yet to settle on a suitable response. Your audience looks for this question at issue when they ask, "Why should I read this?" Writers ask themselves a version of this same question ("Why am I writing?") and try to answer it early.

You have another good reason to engage a question at issue. Only an issue can make information relevant. Without an issue, you and your readers are awash in information, knee-deep in data. If you open by providing them with information that doesn't serve to focus an issue, you give them little motivation to read on. If writers themselves haven't discerned what is pertinent or what question deserves an answer, readers have little reason to become engaged. An issue or concern frames a writer's purpose and thus gives an audience a reason to read.

What makes for an issue? Front-page controversy, opposing views, the burning issues in your neighborhood or our nation. But you needn't reach for high drama or pro–con argument. Virtually any concern or interest can serve as an occasion if it will encourage readers to look with you at a new question or to look anew at what they thought was an old one. To generate interesting writing and interested reading, be sure that your occasion poses a question at issue for yourself and for others and can prompt a reasoned reply.

Why engage the issue *directly*? Readers need a reason to give you a hearing, and they will generally allow you a paragraph, at most a page, to prove you are worth it. College instructors may slog their way to the end, but they too will become either bored or engaged after a page. First impressions stick. But apart from the demands of readers, you as a writer have good reason to start quickly. By engaging an issue, you are immediately engaged in shaping your ideas and your writing.

Prompting Response _____

Your occasion should also prompt response—namely, your own point. Your occasion should set up your thesis; it should pose a question that you answer. A successful occasion does more than generate interest; it focuses interest on your thesis. Your occasion and your thesis must therefore be closely linked; they must speak to each other. To get your occasion and thesis in sync, choose an occasion that lies nearest to your thesis, or choose a thesis that responds most directly to your occasion. Your opening can thereby "occasion" your thesis. After all, the attention your occasion wins is helpful only if readers attend to your point.

Sometimes the occasion that prompts the writing is clear from the context that writer and reader share. The rhetorical situation is concrete, immediate. It makes plain what the circumstance is, who the players are, and what expectations govern their exchange. In these cases, your writing may require only a very abbreviated occasion, if any at all. Consider the case of a real estate analyst who has been asked to recommend for or against the purchase of an investment property. All the analyst need do is acknowledge the situation that occasions the writing.

> In reply to your request for a recommendation on the rental property at Ninth and North Streets, I find that the price, location, and earning potential of the property all speak in favor of your purchase.

When you write essay exams or respond to a given problem or concern, you need not invent a new occasion. Simply point to the one with which you have been presented and move directly to your own assertion.

If you are not presented with an occasion, you often can find one by examining assumptions or attitudes. The occasion that prompts Cindy to write about heavy hands follows from the assumption that they improve an aerobic workout. By questioning that assumption, she uncovers contradictions between the effects of heavy hands and the objectives of an aerobic workout—contradictions that lead her to assert that heavy hands actually compromise fitness.

Del and Patricia use similar strategies. Both note contradictions between what a certain text actually does and what readers, critics, or even characters in the text think it does. Del notes that many readers respond to objections that *The Adventures of Huckleberry Finn* is racist by viewing the growing friendship between Huck and Jim as evidence of Huck's development away from racism. He then questions this reading by looking at key moments in the novel often thought to demonstrate that development. The contradictions he uncovers prompt him to assert that Huck does in fact remain a racist. For Patricia, writing about *Murder in the Cathedral,* the contradiction lies in the attitude of the second priest, who sees little use for the chorus of women even though T. S. Eliot specifies that the chorus be composed of women. That contradiction is echoed in the attitude of critics, who likewise see little or no meaning in the fact that the chorus is female despite the playwright's explicit casting. Both attitudes prompt Patricia—and her readers—to take a closer look. In much the same way, your occasion should encourage readers to take a closer look at a written text or the text of their own experience.

Your occasion can also prompt a thesis in another way—by explicitly engaging an opposing view. In Paula's paper on fire-management policies, counterargument serves as the occasion for her own argument. She uses the media's criticism as a springboard to develop her defense of the "let it burn" policy. The occasion as a whole drives to the thesis, with background information provided as necessary to set up the opposing view. The thesis, in turn, answers the concerns of journalists and citizens. Although the reasons that Cindy provides for her thesis justify the "let it burn" policy, they never lose sight of the opposing view that she raised in the occasion.

Even when immediate circumstance, prevailing attitudes, or pro–con arguments suggest an occasion, take the initiative to frame your occasion in an imaginative way. When Kurt began his paper on Custer, he found it difficult to engage and direct the interest of his readers. And then he remembered a painting— "Edgar S. Paxson's famous painting of the remnants of the cavalry dying in hand-to-hand combat with the Indians. . . ." Kurt could have said simply, "Contrary to accepted opinion that Custer's men died in battle, evidence strongly suggests that they committed suicide when the end was imminent." But how much less colorful and evocative that occasion would have been. Paxson's painting embodies the accepted opinion, the heroic myth of Custer's Last Stand, that Kurt hopes to explode. Its close and imaginative connection with the thesis is the mark of a good occasion.

That connection is vital. Without a close link to your thesis, your occasion will either *funnel* or *misfire*.

The Funnel

Funnelled openings typically start broad as authors inch their way into the paper—often hoping to come up with a point as they go.

> The instinct to design and build has always been part of the human experience. Since the earliest of times, human beings have been known as makers. Bridges in particular have fascinated us because they challenge our ingenuity to span distant points. Bridges in all cultures not only serve transportation and commerce but also represent a culture's values and mark its technological prowess. The bridges of New York City have long been acknowledged to be both engineering feats and cultural monuments. The disrepair of these bridges and the general decay of the Big Apple's

infrastructure represent perhaps the most pressing challenge of the next century. Traditional testing methods do not permit engineers to spot hidden problems before they become visible, and untreatable. However, noninvasive techniques for the detection of structural failure now provide civil engineers with a new weapon in the fight to preserve the city's bridges.

An occasion becomes a funnel when you delay addressing a specific issue. Here, the author only comes to it in the final two sentences. Three symptoms mark the opening funnel.

- *Plot summary* that retells what readers already know
- *Background information* that does little to focus or flesh out the question at issue
- *Broad, abstract generalizations* that fail to set up your immediate concern

By putting off the question that your essay addresses, opening funnels can easily put off your readers.

Many writers do use the opening of an essay to acknowledge the context that informs their work and to present or recall useful information, prior discussions, and relevant research. You can do so most effectively, however, if you use your occasion to lend focus to the question at issue. If you find yourself merely "talking about" your topic—retelling plot, giving information that doesn't point to an issue, or making broad generalizations—chances are you have not yet found your occasion. You are also overlooking a tool that can help you refine your thinking and writing. Funneling may help you to find ideas while writing an early draft. But once you know where you are headed, there's no point in having your reader retrace your errant steps. By addressing an issue at the outset, you can take advantage of the focus that a crafted occasion can provide.

The Misfire

Even if an occasion doesn't funnel, it can still misfire. Recall the poster headlined "SEX" that bore little or no relation to the car wash it advertised. If your occasion doesn't match the thesis, the reader will be either surprised by the unexpected thesis or frustrated by unfilled expectations raised in the occasion. In either case, the reader perceives the opening of the paper as a false start. The mismatch might be traced to a lapse in logic, but it can also be due to a shift in tone or perspective. As a result, occasion and thesis are not in sync. The timing's off. Each suggests a course that is many degrees away from the other.

Here's an occasion where even the briefest story misdirects our attention.

(1) Steve was valedictorian, captain of the football and basketball team, class vice-president, and had a full scholarship to a major university. (2) The night before graduation, Steve and two of his friends decided to have a drinking contest chugging pints of vodka. (3) Steve won the contest, but he lost his life. (4) TI, the Teen Institute for the Prevention of Alcohol and Drug Abuse, is an organization successfully preventing deaths such as Steve's. (5) They are doing this through education and the provision of role models.

Unfortunately, the interest in Steve roused by the dramatic occasion (sentences 1–3) doesn't transfer to the Teen Institute. What's more, the thesis (sentence 4) and the reasons that project the paper's organization (sentence 5) don't follow from Steve's story at all; in fact, quite the contrary. If "education" and "role models" are what the Teen Institute provides, the story about Steve would have us believe that he lacks neither; in fact, he could pass as a role model himself. Because "successful" prevention can refer to anything that staves off death from drugs or alcohol, we learn little about the Teen Institute's programs and even less about how the institute relates to Steve's case. Given that the story focuses on an isolated if not unique binge, we wonder whether "successful" prevention is possible. We're left in a muddle; the occasion has sabotaged the very connections it ought to foster.

The story of Steve suggests that an introductory hook is engaging only if it offers a direct and coherent line to a strong thesis. The same could be said of the following striking quotation.

(1) "It will never be climbed," cried Zebulon Pike when he discovered the mountain which now is Pikes Peak. (2) In 1806, Zebulon Pike tried to climb the Peak but aborted his effort because he was not prepared for the snowy terrain. (3) The first to climb the mountain was Dr. Edward James in 1820. (4) Since then travel up Pikes Peak has increased. (5) The Pikes Peak Highway, the Cog Railway, and the Barr Trail have been established over the years.

Zebulon Pike's exclamation hooks us every bit as much as the story of Steve did. But once again the line to a thesis is slack. The opening cry suggests that the paper will be about Pike's discovery and the first successful ascent of the mountain. But the following sentences redirect our attention to terrain, climbing history, increased travel on Pikes Peak, and finally to different routes and modes of transportation. Each successive sentence forces us to redraw the line that might link occasion and thesis. Without a clear link, the paper fails to justify the striking quote with which it opened or capitalize on the interest that it generated.

No matter how catchy your occasion may be, if it doesn't establish the connection between an issue or concern and your thesis, it will put readers off rather than draw them in.

> (1) In a recent airplane crash, two pilots were heard talking about the sexual habits of a flight attendant right before takeoff. (2) This incident and others have raised the question, "How good are our pilots?" (3) Pilots are not up to their level of performance because they are pushed into flying early on account of the constant demand for airplane pilots. (4) Pilots today must overcome inexperience, fatigue, and poor concentration in the cockpit to enable them to do their part in keeping the skies safe.

If "sexual habits" is to capture our attention, it remains unclear what we should be attending to. Is the question at issue the airplane crash or tasteless banter in the cockpit? The second sentence promises to set us straight, yet the unclear reference to "this incident" keeps us wondering. The question "How good are our pilots?" only confuses matters further, as it might refer to sexual prowess and not necessarily to the airplane crash. How then are we to read "level of performance" and "constant demand"? What about "cockpit"? Uncertainties and double entendre only multiply as the paragraph continues.

My guess (and it's only a guess) is that the author wishes to address Federal Aviation Administration policies that regulate the training and flight schedules of airline pilots—policies that might prove dangerous in an era of pilot shortages. The point is that an occasion shouldn't have us guessing. Without a clear indication of the question at issue, the assertion advanced, or the audience involved (pilots, flight attendants, passengers, FAA administrators?), the occasion only obscures meaning and alienates readers. Some readers may find themselves chuckling over the angle taken by this writer, others put off by the sexual innuendo. But as this paper taxis down the runway, never quite taking off, we find ourselves, like the pilots in the occasion, distracted.

Ongoing Relevance

Your occasion orients your readers at the beginning of your paper, but its work isn't finished with your introduction. An occasion pervades your entire paper and establishes its relevance. Your occasion helps you and your readers gauge whether your discussion bears on the problem at hand. It creates for your writing a sense of urgency, importance, or interest. Even when you are not talking about the concern that set you off to write, your words should bear the stamp of your occasion. You should be able to say, at every point, "Yes, this is why I am writing," and your reader should be able to say, "This is why I am reading."

An occasion can even help you with your conclusion. Instead of merely summarizing your discussion, you can return to the occasion that first set it off with the satisfaction of having come full circle. Recall the essay's question at issue to bring out the implications and significance of your essay's reply. By making clear why you bother to write, you help ensure that readers will bother to hear you out.

Testing Your Occasion

To sharpen your occasion, ask yourself the very questions that are on your readers' minds.

• Does the occasion capture interest by engaging an issue, problem, or concern?

• Does the occasion focus that interest on the response that it is meant to prompt—your thesis?

Positive answers mean that your occasion is more than the beginning of your paper. It is a beginning that serves the ends of analysis and argument: reasoned inquiry.

Eliciting Belief: Good Reasons

A reason offers a justification that answers the question "Why should I believe this thesis?" Your thesis can become credible only when you establish connections that link an arguable opinion with other assertions that offer support, evidence, or justification. Connections among assertions permit writers to support, and readers to accept, the claims advanced.

Two sets of examples related to the topic of heavy hands can help you appreciate how important it is to draw relationships among assertions.

(1) Aerobics performed with hand-held weights compromise fitness. Using weights causes anaerobic fatigue before significant cardiovascular benefit occurs.

(2) Aerobics performed with hand-held weights compromise fitness. Participants ought to avoid aerobics classes that use heavy hands.

Whether the opening assertion in each set serves as a conclusion (as in the first example) or a reason (as in the second) depends on how you link the statements. You decide which links to draw and which to forgo based on the concern that occasions the discussion and the point that reflects your intention. You can draw attention to those connections by using such words as *because* and *therefore*. Yet even when they are missing, as in the above examples, you naturally tend to supply them yourself. The very metaphors we use to describe the process of thinking point to those connections: *line of reasoning* and *train of thought* speak not of parts but of relationships.

Orienting Readers to Your Reasons

Because assertions become reasons only when set into relationship with the thesis, experienced authors try to make those relationships as clear as possible. A useful way of doing so is to answer the question "Why?" straightaway by projecting the organization of your reasons. A *projected organization* makes explicit the connection between the arguable opinion that calls for support and the reasons that justify the arguable opinion.

The term *projected organization* may remind you of more familiar ones— *plan, blueprint* or *outline*. But a projected organization is more than a mere laundry list, or a preview of coming attractions: "First I will discuss this, and then I will discuss that." It orients readers to the shape of your prose and, more importantly, to the underlying logical relationships. It makes clear, at least potentially, the exact connection of each reason to the thesis and the connection of those reasons to each other. Without reasons, of course, an opinion is nothing more than a personal preference or whim that needn't convince anybody. But even with reasons your thesis will remain unconvincing if your readers fail to grasp their connections. Your projected organization forestalls any such confusion. From the very outset readers know what you're up to.

Answering "Why?"

Earlier in this chapter when we read the introductions crafted by our five authors, we found that they do more than assert an opinion; they offer reasoned support. Cindy cites three reasons why heavy hands compromise fitness. Likewise, Paula argues for the "let it burn" policy because it helps control future fires and maintains the health of the forest. Both Cindy and Paula provide a direct response to the question "Why?"

Yet directness need not imply a lack of imagination or style. Consider Kurt's projected organization for his paper on Custer. He supports his view by addressing three key aspects of suicide investigation—eyewitness accounts, physical evidence, and psychological motivation—without resorting to an explicit list. Moreover, by introducing these three reasons over two sentences, he avoids the monotonous rhythm that could follow from allotting one reason per sentence.

Del avoids a common problem in his paper on *The Adventures of Huckleberry Finn*—a lapse into narrative and description—because he chooses to discuss only those moments when readers tend to presume Huck's moral development. Although he projects an organization that touches on early, middle, and late sections of the novel, he does so not to summarize the novel but to focus on key scenes that support his point—namely, that Huck is still mired in racism.

When Patricia analyzes *Murder in the Cathedral*, she must likewise avoid narrative and description. How easy it would be to retell the martyr's story as it relates to the experiences of a pregnant mother, or for that matter to catalog all those birth metaphors. No, Patricia prefers to answer the question that drives analysis and argument—the question "Why?" Her explanation of the metaphor sets up the reasons why it expands our understanding: "In the play, the women's chorus shows us how before giving birth, a martyr, like an expectant mother, must wait and suffer." The very shape and energy of that sentence drive home two key terms—*wait* and *suffer*—that themselves have become pregnant with meaning. By exploring them, she shapes the paper to follow.

Explaining Your Reasons

Because the projected organization is only a springboard to the development of your paper, you need not spell out everything in detail. Instead, briefly indicate your reasons. How brief is brief? It's your judgment call. But judge according to the needs of your audience. If your projected organization is too short, you may seem vague or cryptic. If it's too long, you may well lose your readers in a blueprint so detailed and undifferentiated that you have nothing left to say—and they're glad.

Because you may not know how much information your reader needs, you may be unsure about the best length for your projected organization, or, for that matter, for your occasion. In general provide information that puts your occasion, thesis, and reasons into sharp relief and shows their general relationship. Once you do so, readers have a framework in which to place the wealth of information that is sure to follow. Remember, your introduction is not the only place to bring information to bear on your case. You can always provide more details as you go along. One place to do so is in a background paragraph that follows your introduction but precedes your actual analysis or argument. Better yet, fold in information as you need it when developing your reasons.

As you try to fulfill the contract implicit in your thesis, you may find that your paper develops in ways that you did not foresee, or even in ways that you may not like. I've often heard students confess, "But this is not the paper I want to write." I can only answer, "True, but this is the kind of paper your thesis requires." This frustration reflects the consequences of freedom—and it's a frustration all writers know. Having freely chosen to advance an assertion, you may find yourself surprised, even dismayed, at the consequences that follow from your decision. What you want to talk about may differ from the support your thesis requires. If so, either adjust your expectations or revise the thesis so that its conditions are ones you can and want to fulfill. But whatever you do, be sure to establish a clear and consistent connection between thesis and reasons. When you do so, you are not merely toying with elements of form; you are discovering what you actually think.

Missed Connections

To discover what you think, you must draw a connection between thesis and reasons. Miss it, and your assertions go without support. Miss it, and what evidence you do provide fails to add up to a point. Here are some common pitfalls that prevent you from making a clear connection between your thesis and your projected organization.

The abbreviated list   A short list of one-word items can identify what points your paper will address. But those brief tags may not help you or your reader grasp the logical connection between thesis and projected organization. Consider Cindy's paper on heavy hands. An abbreviated list, such as "exertion, fatigue, and muscular and skeletal structures," would have simply enumerated areas she wished to touch on without offering what she does in fact provide: a reasoned and reasonable link to her thesis.

Loose topical association   If you organize your paper by generating "things to say about the topic," you won't fulfill the conditions of proof that your thesis places on you. For example, had Paula merely discussed a series of subtopics about the Yellowstone fire, she would not have made her core assertion credible. To do so, she called on reasons. Even if you stay with the same general topic throughout your paper, your prose will ramble unless you consistently link evidence to assertion.

New, unrelated assertions   If your projected organization fails to establish its connection to the thesis, evidence becomes unmoored from your assertion. Points that should support your claim then become new assertions that vie for attention as the thesis of your paper. For example, had Patricia not maintained a clear connection between her reasons and her thesis, her discussion of Eliot's play might have gone off on any number of tangents.

Circular restatements   You can also fail to establish a connection when the reason you offer in support of a thesis merely repeats the same assertion. If you wish to argue, for example, that "junior-high math and science programs should encourage women to consider careers in technical fields," you merely repeat the claim if you support it with the assertion that "such encouragement would introduce women to career choices that they may not have contemplated." Instead of supporting a claim, you are spinning your wheels.

Questionable assumptions   Assumptions allow you to connect the thesis you present with the reasons you provide. That connection falls apart, however, when your audience does not share your assumption. If you justify the assertion that "students should support striking university clerical staff" with the reason that "student involvement shows solidarity with the strikes," you assume that students should do anything that demonstrates solidarity. Readers who refuse to accept this assumption will also refuse to accept your thesis. Be sure to justify any assumption that your readers are likely to reject. Analysis and argument rely on your reader's willingness to entertain connections among ideas.

Incidental reasons   When you offer reasons for the conclusion you have drawn, provide those that will most likely convince readers or answer their concerns. Incidental reasons will not make your claim credible. For example, to argue that a state should adopt a mandatory helmet law for motorcyclists, you need to do better than remark, as one student did, that new helmet designs don't impede hearing. This observation may respond to one of several hesitations that bikers have about wearing helmets, but it doesn't address the claim that wearing helmets should be mandatory.

One-sided reasons   The connection between thesis and projected organization can also unravel when the reason offered for a conclusion fails to take into account counterarguments that readers may have. Readers may object to a mandatory helmet law because it violates personal freedom. Unless you indicate your awareness of objections and express a willingness to meet them in the body of your discussion, your reasons will not fully answer the question "Why is the thesis credible?"

Each of these pitfalls can lead you to violate your contract with your reader—your promise to justify your thesis with reasoned support. In any early draft, such problems can prompt some useful brainstorming, or even a basic reassessment of your contract. But as you write a polished draft for your readers, you'll want to honor and justify that contract. Good reasons serve your thesis by meeting the implicit demands for support that accompany an arguable opinion.

Developing Your Reasons

In addition to linking reasons to your thesis, the projected organization also anticipates the discussion to follow. It launches the development of your paper. Why? The reasons you suggest are not yet reasons you have established conclusively. You have merely pointed to your reasons, much as a concert program announces music yet to be heard. Reasons don't become compelling until you flesh them out. The interest, curiosity, and expectations you generate in your projected organization call for gratification, for a full and complete treatment of the ideas you announce. A projected organization suggests how you will earn and justify your thesis, but the actual earning and justifying are something for your paper as a whole to accomplish. A projected organization that does not call for further treatment closes down your discussion instead of opening it up. It functions more as a summary or abstract of your paper than an invitation to explore the reasons that support your point.

You can't explore those reasons all at once. You have to move through your reasons and evidence in a linear fashion, with one point following another. The projected organization announces the key steps in that progression. Those steps may represent paragraphs in a short essay, sections of a longer paper, or even chapters in a book. Whatever their length, the steps serve as the key stages in developing a line of reasoning. Because the projected organization captures the essential logic of those stages, it serves as a tool to help you consider whether they make sense.

At a very basic level, the projected organization provides clues about the order of those steps. If you announce that you will speak about Tom, Dick, and Harry, readers will expect you to treat them in that order. Likewise, readers will expect the categories to remain consistent; they would only be confused if you actually organized your paper by different categories altogether—let's say, personality, appearance, and intelligence. Your projected organization can also help you examine the logical development behind what might otherwise be a random or impromptu order. Which reason logically comes first? Which reason permits you to introduce information that the reader will need to make sense of later points? A projected organization allows you to order proofs in a progressive pattern, to set simultaneous ideas into reasoned development. Because your projected organization lays out ideas in sequence, it can even serve as a brief guide to the signposts and transitions you might provide as you develop the full draft.

By helping you to articulate connections, the projected organization becomes not a one-time checklist of items to cover but a means to develop the reasoning that should drive your paper.

Checking for Reasons

Use the projected organization as a tool for discovering, evaluating, and refining the relationships that shape your thinking. To do so, ask yourself two questions.

• Does the projected organization answer the question "Why?" by providing reasons that support the thesis?

• Does the projected organization launch the discussion by suggesting its progressive development and logical coherence?

When tested and refined, your projected organization affords a bridge from simple assertion to reasoned discussion, from an opinion you'd like to advance to an essay that promotes shared inquiry. It promises readers an amplification that rewards them with evidence and new insight—one that should elicit their belief.

Five Papers in Full

Heavy Hands: Do They Work or Hurt?
Cindy White

"Burn those calories! Get that heart rate up!" screams the instructor. The music pulsates, the pace quickens. With the motto "more is mightier," you clutch your weights and swing them in cadence with the fast tempo. Like other health club regulars, you may assume that these hand-held weights enhance an aerobic workout. Yet aerobics performed with heavy hands actually compromises fitness. By using weights you can overestimate exertion, cause anaerobic fatigue before significant cardiovascular benefit occurs, and jeopardize your body's muscular and skeletal structures.

Aerobics classes seek an exercise intensity of between 70 and 85 percent of your maximal capabilities for twenty to sixty minutes. On demand, your body increases the blood flow and thus the oxygen supply to the working muscles. As the music tempo increases and movements quicken, your heart must increase its rate of contraction and the volume of blood it pumps out per beat or stroke. Together heart rate and stroke volume determine cardiac output, the amount of blood pumped through the heart per minute. When you exercise on a regular basis, your heart makes physiological adaptations to help alleviate the stress that exercise puts on the body. Specifically, your heart becomes stronger and grows larger, thus increasing the stroke volume and enabling your heart to pump more blood per contraction. By improving your heart's efficiency, aerobic exercise contributes to your cardiovascular fitness.

When you use heavy hands in an aerobics class, you limit cardiovascular adaptations because you tend to overestimate your exertion. Consequently, your exercise regime does not reach the recommended level of intensity. Unlike standard aerobics classes, those using weights overemphasize arm movements without significant leg action. As a result, your body must increase blood flow to the upper limbs if it is to supply working muscle with oxygen and nutrients. Use of your arm muscles tends to produce higher heart rates but lower stroke volumes because these smaller muscles can accommodate less blood than your leg muscles. This effect leads you to misinterpret just how hard your heart is working. Because exertion is estimated as a percentage of your maximal heart rate (for your age), if you increase your heart rate but not your stroke volume, you're bound to overestimate your exertion.

You may think that heavy hands improve cardiovascular fitness, but anaerobic fatigue usually sets in before you accomplish any real aerobic conditioning. Anaerobic activities rely on immediate stores of energy in your muscles (not on stores of fat) because those activities are initiated without the need for additional oxygen. Once you use up those immediate stores of energy, muscle fatigue sets in. Specifically, when you use heavy hands during an up-tempo, quick-movement aerobics class, your body utilizes white muscle fibers. These fast-twitch anaerobic fibers fatigue within just a couple of minutes, causing the "burn" felt during your workout. Because this energy depletion often forces you to rest your arms, hand-held weights reduce activity and decrease intensity, thereby leading to a smaller cardiovascular load and lower levels of exertion. Heavy hands invite anaerobic fatigue, and thus limit the cardiovascular benefits you derive.

With your muscles now exhausted, your heavy-hands aerobics class may well have you dance right into injury. Up-tempo and upbeat, an aerobics class involves accelerated arm swings and arm circles. Because hand-held weights place an extra burden on your shoulder, you have an injury that's just waiting to happen. Your shoulder joint is supported by both ligaments and muscles. When the muscles fatigue, ligaments are all that's left to support your heavier than usual hands. Picture a rubber band with a weight tied to one end. Now rotate the weight in a circle. The rubber band may stretch to ten times its original length. But unlike that rubber band, your shoulder's ligaments, once stretched, do not return to their original length. When you use heavy hands, "push it to the limit" becomes "pull the ligament to its limit." Muscle and tendon strains and shoulder dislocations may be your immediate rewards, reconstructive ligament surgery your eventual fate.

Instead of improving fitness, heavy hands actually lower exertion, prompt anaerobic fatigue, and invite physical injury. They're a fad—and an unfortunate one. Aerobics classes do promote muscular endurance, weight loss, lean body tissue, coordination, and positive cardiovascular adaptations. Weights, however, are not the way. Any instructor who claims otherwise is pulling your leg—or rather, your arm!

Let It Burn—Please!
Paula Schwalbe

The United States Forest Service (U.S.F.S.) uses a type of fire management called "let it burn" that allows lightning-induced wildfires to burn freely in wilderness, without human interference. When the U.S.F.S. allowed the 1988 summer fire in Yellowstone National Park to burn unchecked for weeks, the media was harshly critical. Journalists repeatedly blasted the U.S.F.S. fire management program and insisted that they propose a new one. Although the media, and consequently the public, think that the U.S.F.S. should use a fire suppression method, I believe that the U.S.F.S. should continue to observe a policy of "let it burn." Fire suppression, which does not allow *any* fire to burn freely, results in a crown fire that can be ten times more destructive than the ground fire produced in "let it burn." While fire suppression inhibits the growth of prime tree species, "let it burn" helps maintain a healthy and diverse forest.

When "let it burn" management is used, a wildfire burns off only the debris and undergrowth that have accumulated on the forest floor. These ground fires have relatively small flames because they are not fed by a large amount of fuel. Trees that live within a "fire system" develop protective adaptations such as thick bark, closed pine cones, or a resilient root system. Ground fires do not affect these trees; in fact, the trees retain their green foliage and appear untouched after the fire. This was not the case in the Yellowstone National Park fire. For decades, an old management policy had used fire suppression in order to preserve the park's scenic beauty for a flourishing tourism trade. The fire of 1988 was a classic example of a crown fire caused by the outdated suppression method. A crown fire fueled by an excessive amount of duff, litter, and shrubs on the forest floor literally "explodes" and takes everything in its path. Flames engulf the trees entirely and "jump" from one to the next, leaving a forest devoid of foliage. The media devoted much of their time to lamenting Yellowstone's blackened, sparse appearance. They should also applaud the fact that Yellowstone is finally back on its natural path to ecological succession.

Ecological succession, a process that changes bare soil into a forest or grassland, is dependent upon "let it burn" management. California's redwood forests and the Rocky Mountains' mixed pine-spruce-fir forests are examples of ecosystems that have undergone the continuous process of ecological succession. Ground fires change the dominant species in a forest at least three times over a hundred-year period by allowing new species to release their seeds and reproduce. For example, Colorado's ponderosa pine have thick, closed cones that can pop open and release seeds only when exposed to a fire's high temperature. Lodgepole pine is another tree indigenous to Colorado that grows after a ground fire has created the mineral-rich environment that it finds favorable. Fire suppression can destroy these trees' ability to compete and evolve into a healthy, widely speciated forest.

When fires burn partially decomposed matter, the ash is used as fertilizer by all trees. With fire suppression too many trees grow in an ash-free, nutrient-poor soil. Competition for water and minerals among different species increases, and trees readily succumb to disease and insect infestation. In 1970, for instance, much of the Sugarloaf, Colorado, area had developed into a dense pine tree stand (forest) after decades of fire suppression management. Pine beetle infestation occurred, and hundreds of acres of trees had to be cut down to prevent the disease from spreading.

In the last fifty years the United States Forest Service has learned by trial and error that fire suppression has too many negative effects on a forest. Accordingly they applied "let it burn" to wilderness areas. They must continue to use "let it burn" to prevent future fires from being as severe as Yellowstone proved to be. Reinstating fire suppression management passes the buck to future generations, leaving them with uncontrollable fires and diseased forests. The media should study their topic more carefully before they pass their "misunderstanding" on to the impressionable public. Let it burn!

Custer's Last Stand: The Truth
Kurt Alme

Edgar S. Paxson's famous painting of the remnants of the cavalry dying in hand-to-hand combat with the Indians represents a popular but false version of Custer's Last Stand. Evidence strongly suggests that Custer's men committed suicide when the end was imminent. Eyewitness accounts by Indians in the battle and recent discoveries of spent cavalry pistol shells around the graves substantiate the theory that many of the soldiers killed themselves or executed mutual death pacts. Soldiers preferred a quick death to what they believed would be a slow and painful end in Indian hands.

Over two thousand Indians survived Custer's Last Stand. In the following fifty years, whites made various attempts at interviewing some of these eyewitnesses. Although many of the interviewers were interested only in selling a story or protecting the military's reputation, reviewers agree that at least two authors, Walter Camp and Thomas Marquis, objectively sought the truth. Walter M. Camp wrote *Custer in '76: Walter Mason Camp's Notes on the Custer Fight* after he spend twenty-five years interviewing Indian and white participants in the campaign. According to Robert Utley of *American West*, Camp was "a meticulous and assiduous gatherer of original materials." Reporting his extensive interview with Turtle Rib, who at the time of the battle was an experienced Sioux warrior under Chief Lamedeer, Camp writes, "The Indians were up close and the soldiers were shooting with pistols. He saw some of the soldiers shoot each other."[1]

Even more convincing, because of its many relevant interviews, is Thomas Marquis's *Keep the Last Bullet for Yourself*, a work described by Joseph Medicine Crow, official historian of the Crow Tribe, as "a highly original contribution based on first hand and on the spot research."[2] Marquis writes that although vision during the battle was obscured by dust and smoke, small groups and individual Indians witnessed instances of suicide and apparent execution of death pacts among the soldiers. For example, to the Indians around Chief Lame White Man it appeared that the soldiers in one of Custer's detachments were "fighting among themselves. They were shooting each other as well as shooting themselves." Tall Bull, a Cheyenne warrior, saw a soldier shoot and kill three companions in rapid succession. These and other eyewitness accounts are linked to the version of the battle that Marquis states was commonly accepted by the Cheyenne. This account tells of a pitched battle that lasted for an hour or more, then suddenly concluded as the smoke and dust cleared and the Indians noticed that the soldiers were "wiped out." The Cheyenne account does not include a bloody hand-to-hand finish to the battle, only that the cavalry mysteriously "vanished from existence." No Indian saw a large

---

[1] Robert M. Utley, "Custeriana," review of *Custer in '76: Walter Mason Camp's Notes on the Custer Fight*, by Walter M. Camp, *American West*, November 1976, 46.

[2] Thomas B. Marquis, *Keep the Last Bullet for Yourself* (New York: Reference Publishers, 1976).

enough portion of the battle to conclude that a large number of soldiers committed suicide. However, these accounts do support the broadly applicable archaeological evidence found recently.

In 1984, archaeologists Richard Fox and Doug Scott of the U.S. Park Services Midwest Archaeological Center headed an archaeological dig of the Custer battlefield. They were not looking for specific evidence of suicide, but they found it—a striking number of bullets from the army-issued Colt handguns located near the soldiers' position. Had a soldier fired at an oncoming Indian and missed, the bullet would have continued traveling away from the battle ridge. Yet because only fourteen Indians died in the entire battle, the rest of the bullets that were found must have been aimed at other targets on the ridge. Fox and Scott interpreted this finding as meaning that in the end the Indians engaged the soldiers in hand-to-hand combat and killed the cavalry with their own sidearms.[3] There are two serious problems with this analysis. First, it is unlikely that in hand-to-hand combat an Indian would have chosen to wrestle a soldier for a weapon with which he had had very little experience when he could simply use his well-proven tomahawk. A more serious criticism comes from the fact that Indian eyewitnesses make no mention of hand-to-hand combat with the soldiers. Like the eyewitness accounts, the archaeological evidence supports the suicide theory. The pistols were used against the soldiers, by the soldiers.

The repulsive thought of a soldier's putting a bullet through his head is believable when we look at what fellow soldiers believed the alternative to be. In 1890, newspaper editor John F. Finerty summed up the general conception of the alternative when he wrote, "Our soldiers . . . in the Indian campaigns had ever before them the terrors of fiendish torture and mutilation in case of capture by the Indians."[4] Whether or not the Indians actually tortured their captives is not important. What is important is that the soldiers believed that they did. And the evidence of that belief is overwhelming. Marquis quotes twelve sources that describe the plans of soldiers to commit suicide rather than face torture by the Indians. The most relevant account comes from some of Major Reno's men who testified before a Congressional subcommittee that they "gave intense thought to suicide as an alternative to torture." Still, thinking and acting are not the same. Would a soldier actually kill himself or follow through on a death pact? Custer thought so. After an entire eighty-three-man cavalry unit died in the Fetterman fight against the Cheyenne, the general wrote, "Colonel Fetterman

---

[3] Jim Robbins, "A New Look at Custer's Last Stand: Diggings Throw Light on Battlefield Mystery," *American West*, July–August 1985, 50–57.

[4] John F. Finerty, *War-Path and Bivouac: Or, the Conquest of the Sioux* (Chicago: Donohue, Henneberry & Company, 1890).

and Captain Brown no doubt inflicted this death upon themselves. These officers had often asserted that they would never be taken alive by Indians."[5] If even battle-hardened officers could be so overcome by fear, certainly raw recruits, 30 percent of the Seventh Cavalry, were also capable of suicide.

Thus it would seem that a large percentage of Custer's soldiers committed suicide. But is that important? Why can't Americans nostalgically believe that the men of our military fought bravely until the end? Because it is not the truth. War is not a glorious fight by our altruistic soldiers against an evil and threatening enemy. War is a man-made institution with human participants subject to human weakness. In order to understand it so that it can be handled most effectively in the future, we need to understand its past. We need to face the truth.

Huck's Continuing Racism
Delmas E. Hare

Reading *The Adventures of Huckleberry Finn* in a predominantly black school presents a serious problem: student and parental objections to the book as racist. A common defense of the novel holds that the close relationship between Huck and Jim prompts Huck's moral development—a development that takes him beyond racist attitudes. But I would argue, however reluctantly, that black students and parents are right. Jim and Huck's relationship reveals not Huck's reputed moral development but rather his continuing racism. Few readers would question that, early in the novel, Huck's response after Jim bests him in an argument reflects prevailing racial attitudes. But the central episode in the fog that many readers point to as establishing close friendship and signalling moral development also turns on a racial slur. Even Huck's response near the end of the novel to Jim's refusal to leave the wounded Tom Sawyer is made bittersweet by Huck's continuing racism.

Huck's sympathy with the prevailing racial attitudes of the day is clear early in the novel. When he remarks that Jim had "an uncommon level head" and was "most always right," his qualification, "for a nigger," leaves little doubt that Huck believes that blacks have inferior intelligence. Two arguments between Huck and Jim in Chapter XIV bear this out. In the first, concerning King Solomon, Huck is not a clear winner and, in fact, may be the loser. Accordingly, Huck decides Jim is obsessed "by a notion" and

---

[5] George A. Custer, *My Life on the Plains: Or, Personal Experiences with Indians* (New York: Sheldon & Company, 1874).

drops the argument. Then, when he tries to convince Jim that it is natural for Frenchmen to speak French, Jim uses a very tidy syllogism that utterly defeats Huck's attempt to argue. Having just been bested in an argument, Huck states, "You can't learn a nigger to argue."

Huck's deepening relationship with Jim would change all that—or so some readers would have us believe. Indeed, they point to the episode in the fog as providing a turning point in that relationship. Would that it were so. Instead, the exchange between Jim and Huck following that episode reveals the continuing racism underlying their relationship. Twain prefaces the racial slur with one of the most touching scenes in the novel. When Jim realizes that he has been tricked by Huck, he responds:

> When I got all wore out wid work, en wid de callin' for you, en went to sleep, my heart wuz mos' broke bekase you wuz los', en I didn' k'yer no' mo' what become er me en de raf'. En when I wake up en fine you back ag'in, all safe en soun', de tears come, en I could 'a' got down on my knees en kiss yo' foot, I's so thankful.

Then, answering Huck's earlier question about the debris on the raft, Jim says, "Dat truck dah is *trash*; en trash is what people is dat puts dirt on de head er dey fren's en makes 'em ashamed" (emphasis mine). For anyone privy to the meaning of southern insults, there is none worse than to be called [white] trash. Often taken as an act of contrition, Huck's response to Jim's remark shows neither contrition nor compassion. He says that Jim's comment "made me feel so mean I could almost kissed his foot to get him to take it back." Jim's statement has a power similar to a curse; his calling Huck trash makes it true. Huck clearly sees the need to apologize, not for his cruel act, but in his own self-interest. He wants Jim to take back the insult. Yet as strong as his desire is to have the insult recalled, his racism makes it extremely difficult for him to act. He says, "It was fifteen minutes before I could work myself up to go and humble myself to a nigger." Even in a scene that reveals Jim's affection for him, Huck maintains a deep-seated racism.

That racism persists to the novel's end. When Tom gets shot as a direct result of his foolishness and game-playing, Jim refuses to abandon him, even though his refusal will likely mean a return to slavery. Huck reveals his racism by paying Jim a supposed compliment: "I knowed he was white inside." Far from being a compliment, Huck's statement is the ultimate denial of Jim's humanity. Jim is black, a black human being, and for Huck to reject his blackness is to reject Jim. He may be Huck's true friend—but only if he can think of Jim as being "white inside." Thus, even at the end of the novel and even in attempting to express his affection and admiration for his friend Jim, Huck remains a racist.

Many would have us believe that *The Adventures of Huckleberry Finn* is a story of a friendship that reflects a boy's moral development, one that moves him beyond racism. Careful reading of the text proves otherwise. In fact, Huck is a kind of racist common in the South and elsewhere to this day—the kind who, in cases of individual relationships, buries much of his overt racism. "I ain't no racist," Huck would say, "one of my best friends is a nigger."

T. S. Eliot's Murder in the Cathedral
Patricia Mosco Holloway

When Carole M. Beckett observes that "the dramatic function of the women of the Chorus (in *Murder in the Cathedral*)[1] is to comment upon the events which they witness," she, like others,[2] skirts the perplexing critical question of why the chorus is composed solely of women. What, in the design of the play, would necessitate an all female chorus?

The second priest in the play sees little use for the chorus of women:

> You are foolish, immodest and babbling women. . . .
> You go on croaking like frogs in the treetops:
> But frogs at least can be cooked and eaten.

(pp. 20–21)

These women, however, do perform a vital function: they expand our understanding of martyrdom through a metaphor of birth. The female chorus reminds us that both women and martyrs give birth to new life. For a woman, it is the life of her child; for a martyr, it is the life of his belief. In the play, the women's chorus shows us how before giving birth, a martyr, like an expectant mother, must wait and suffer.

To introduce his metaphor of birth, Eliot first shows us that both the women in the chorus and the martyr are waiting. The women open the play waiting "close by the cathedral" where they acknowledge they "are forced to bear witness" (p. 11). As it turns out, they will bear witness to the birth of a martyr. At this point in the play, even though they are not consciously aware of waiting, intuitively they are expectant; they wait and wait. In fact,

---

[1] T. S. Eliot, *Murder in the Cathedral* (New York: Harcourt, Brace and Company, 1935). All subsequent references to the play are from this text.

[2] Although numerous critics have discussed the function of the chorus, no one specifically addresses the question of why the chorus is composed solely of women. For a general discussion of the choric function in the play, see Carole M. Beckett, "The Role of the Chorus in *Murder in the Cathedral*," *Theoria*, 53 (1979), 71–76; E. Martin Brown, *The Making of T. S. Eliot's Plays* (London: Cambridge Univ. Press, 1969); David E. Jones, *The Plays of T. S. Eliot* (Toronto: Univ. of Toronto Press, 1960); William J. McGill, "Voices in the Cathedral: The Chorus in Eliot's *Murder in the Cathedral*," *Modern Drama*, 23 (1979), 292–96; Louis Tremaine, "Witnesses to the Event in *Ma'Sat Al-Hallaj* and *Murder in the Cathedral*," 67, *The Muslim World*, 33–46.

they repeat the word "wait" eleven times in just this first passage. This repetition, as well as words such as "bear" and "barren," suggests a metaphor of birth. Similarly, Thomas' diction also points to a birth metaphor when he notes soon after he enters the play:

> Heavier the interval than the consummation.
> All things prepare the event.
>
> (p. 23)

Like the expectant women, he too is waiting for the birth of the martyr. Ironically, that birth will come only with the "event" of his death.

The women in the chorus, however, do not refer literally to Thomas' death. Instead, they speak metaphorically about an imminent, ominous birth:

> the air is heavy and thick.
> Thick and heavy the sky. And the earth presses up
> against our feet. . . .
> The earth
> is heaving in parturition of issue of hell.
>
> (pp. 40–41)

The image of a round earth pressing up and the words "heavy" and "thick" suggest the physical appearance of women about to give birth. The word "parturition" itself literally depicts the act of childbirth. Later in the play, the women will repeat the image of a "heaving earth" as they again convey the metaphor of birth: "I have felt the heaving of earth at nightfall, restless, absurd" (p. 64).

Both the women and Thomas await the "absurd" birth described by the chorus, and as they wait, they suffer. The women agonize when they realize they await the death of Thomas. They fear the birth of which they speak because it will be a "parturition . . . of hell"—the hell of their suffering when they experience the physical loss of their beloved Thomas. Like the expectant women, Thomas, too, suffers as he awaits his delivery. He suffers not only mentally through the temptations to his pride and power, but also physically through the pain of his death—the death that will deliver him into his heavenly birth.

Eliot uses the symbol of blood to link the suffering of the martyr and the suffering of the women. Just before he sheds his own blood, Thomas notes:

> I am . . . ready to suffer with my blood
> This is the sign of the Church always
> The sign of blood.
>
> (pp. 72–73)

Blood is not only a sign for martyrdom, it is also a sign for motherhood. The shedding of Thomas' blood frightens the women, who would naturally associate it with the pain of childbearing, and their first reaction is to rid themselves of this sign of suffering:

> Clean the air! clean the sky! wash the wind! take stone
> from stone and wash them.

(p. 74)

They echo the birth metaphor a last time when, in the same speech, they refer to themselves as wandering "in a land of *barren* boughs."

If, as seems to be the case, Eliot wants to show the similarities between giving birth and the making of a martyr, then a chorus composed of women makes sense not only thematically, but also structurally. After all, it is women who know best how to wait, suffer, and give birth.

Part II

Shaping
Ideas

Inferring, Analyzing, Arguing

3

This chapter explains why and how you can shape ideas to analyze and argue. We'll start by exploring the relationship between your observations and the inferences, or conclusions, you draw from those observations. That relationship plays a role even in apparently straightforward tasks like describing a situation or narrating an event. Analysis, however, asks more of you. It requires you to make your inferences explicit and to evaluate the evidence and justify the reasoning that allowed you to arrive at them. Argument, too, asks you to evaluate and defend explicit inferences, but with an added twist. Your inferences are themselves at issue. Because they are a matter of debate, you must argue for your view even as you refute the views of others. Argument asks you to defend your inferences by shaping your ideas to accommodate your audience's needs, questions, and objections.

You can control and sustain the thinking required of you in analytic and argumentative writing by shaping your paper around an occasion, thesis, and reasons. The relationships you draw among those elements can support even very complex essays—essays whose reasoning is all the more persuasive because the prose is anything but formulaic.

Observation and Inference

When you see smoke, you might infer the presence of fire. Thunderheads on the horizon might likewise promise rain. We all reach conclusions by drawing inferences. Our inferences allow us to make sense of what we observe by enabling us to reason from evidence and premises and thereby arrive at conclusions about our world. The process is so common, so natural, that you may not always be aware of how you reach the many conclusions you arrive at each day.

When my copy of *Harper's* magazine arrives each month, I immediately turn to "Harper's Index," a regular feature that entices and plays with our everyday leaps from observation to inference. It simply lists quantifiable facts, as in these excerpts from the September 1991 issue.

• Average number of weeks it took the poultry industry to produce a full-grown chicken in 1940: 12

• Average number of weeks it takes today: 6

• Chances that a chicken sold in a supermarket is infected with salmonella: 1 in 3

From these facts we make inferences—some wise, some rash—about how the care and feeding of chickens relates to the safety of the poultry we eat. Those connections are nowhere to be found on the page, only in our own mental steps from observation to inference. Here's more from the same issue.

• Percentage of Americans who say their best friend is their father: 0

• Percentage of Fortune 1000 companies that offer paternity leave: 31

• Percentage of eligible American men who take paternity leave: 1

If the second item in the series suggests that corporate America is to blame for the lack of strong friendships with our fathers, the third item promptly sets the focus on men themselves. Why do so few men avail themselves of paternity leave when it is offered? And could it be that men's own expectations about their role in the workplace inhibit them from developing close, enduring bonds with their children? Leaps from observation to inference multiply, always qualifying each other, as we examine our own experience and gather more information.

College writing asks you to pay rigorous attention to the nature of your inferences, the reasoning behind them, and your motivations for arriving at them. Instead of having you ramble casually from one page to the next as you sift through observations, search out possible assertions, and cast aside others, the analytic or argumentative paper inverts the process. It asks you to articulate an arguable opinion and then offer a pointed defense. The challenge of academic writing lies, then, not only in arriving at an assertion, but also in sustaining and justifying the reasoning that brought you there.

To illustrate this process, let's consider a political cartoon—Bob Gorrell's comment about difficulties at NASA. As you cast your eye over the editorial page in your newspaper, you may allot to a cartoon no more than a few seconds. A chuckle, an assenting nod, or a flash of indignation may mark your response. Yet behind your immediate reaction lies a series of complex mental activities that allows you to infer something from what you observe on the page. The same essential activities occur as you read a poem or novel, examine a research article, or study a textbook. In this chapter, we'll use Gorrell's cartoon to illustrate why making and justifying inferences lie behind much of the analytic and argumentative writing you do in college.

© 1990 GORRELL—THE RICHMOND NEWS

Gorrell's cartoon seems to concern recurring technical problems that have plagued the Space Shuttle and the Hubble Space Telescope. (The latter was rendered partially blind by an improperly ground mirror.) But are these technical difficulties really the focus of the cartoon? Might it not be about NASA's reliance on public relations? Or does it concern the causes behind NASA's decline since its preeminent technical achievement, the *Apollo 11* moon landing? How, exactly, do you know what the cartoon means?

If you simply describe the cartoon as you see it on the page or narrate the events to which the cartoon refers, you still depend on inference—on the process of shaping observation into a meaningful assertion. By looking at description and narration, we can appreciate how important it is to make your inferences explicit and to evaluate their credibility. To do so, in turn, requires that you analyze or argue.

Description

The apparently simple task of description poses two problems: selection and arrangement. Because it seems pointless to describe every last detail, you have to choose what to include and what to leave out. Moreover, you have to order the virtually simultaneous impression that the cartoon makes on you into a description governed by the linear progression of the written word. Do you start describing the cartoon by mentioning the map of the world, or need you mention it at all? What about the control panels with their dials and knobs or the two television monitors? When you mention the figure with the raised hand, do you also mention the clipboard, the lab coat with its pocket of pencils and pens, the man's expression, his double chin and rotund figure, or the badge that bears the acronym NASA?

To decide, you must make inferences about the meaning of what you observe. And in doing so, your description is already moving in the direction of interpretation. Making this move is not wrong; in fact, this cartoon—and much of what you read in college—is asking you to interpret. But you must be aware of making this step from observation to inference and the reasons that prompt you to form particular conclusions.

To show just how much interpretive activity goes on when you read a cartoon (or any text, for that matter), let's start by formulating a bare-bones description. For the moment, set aside matters of inference and interpretation. By selecting certain details and leaving others out—that is, by shaping the description—the description will of necessity be predisposed to accommodate certain interpretations.

> Gorrell's cartoon, featured in *The Richmond News*, pictures a man standing in front of an array of scientific control panels. To one side is a television monitor bearing the label "Hubble." On the monitor we see only static. To the other side is a television monitor labeled "Shuttle," on whose screen we see a lemon. The man has a worried expression. He wears a lab coat that barely fits over his rotund figure, and clipped to it is a badge with the acronym NASA. Raising one hand in the air, he proclaims, "That's one small glitch for man, one giant headache for the boys in P.R. . . . !"

Not much left to the cartoon, you might say. And in one respect this is true. What's missing is the meaning, the very point of the cartoon. And yet, in another respect description offers the evidence you need for inferring something about the cartoon. In this sense, description records all that you have to go on. It's the heart of the cartoon, and perhaps all that the cartoon itself offers. If you're looking for meaning, it can only be found in the interaction between reader and text. That interaction involves making inferences. You arrive at an interpretive conclusion by reasoning from evidence.

My bare-bones description of the cartoon is peculiar in that I have tried to separate inference or interpretation from available evidence. Rarely does description work this way, except perhaps in the most rigorous scientific writing.

Many academic disciplines use description as a central part of their methodology for drawing and reporting inferences. Ethnographers, for example, rely on detailed, thick description to record what they observe; they then draw informed, reasoned inferences from their observations. Description invariably asks you to see something in your observations by prompting you to make a meaningful selection and arrangement of elements in your field of vision or the field of your experience.

But what meaning or interpretation does your description point to? Description alone cannot help you if you are unsure what point of view to hold, why you might hold it, or whether that point of view is even appropriate. Such are the concerns at stake with your response to Gorrell's cartoon, and for that matter with most of the texts you read and study in college. If you wish to answer these questions, you must place description in the service of analysis and argument.

Narration

Like virtually all political cartoons, Gorrell's responds to the events of the day. A story, to be sure, lies behind the cartoon. Yet narration, like description, carries with it inherent challenges. First you must decide on the level of detail that the story requires, a matter that affects its pacing. If the lines of static interference on the television monitor marked "Hubble" recall manufacturing errors in the telescope's mirror that impair its operation, to what extent do you tell the story? What of the mirror's design and manufacture, the discovery of the error, the ensuing embarrassment and public-relations headache, and plans for sending a repair mission into space?

A second and more fundamental challenge concerns the arrangement of the story: where to begin and where to end. Problems with the Hubble Space Telescope are only one aspect of the cartoon. What about nagging difficulties with the Space Shuttle? How are you to relate these two aspects of the story? The challenges multiply further when you realize that the statement made in the cartoon recalls Neil Armstrong's famous words as he first set foot on the moon: "That's one small step for a man, one giant leap for mankind." The story suggested by this cartoon thus goes back over twenty years, and includes NASA's past achievements as well as its now tarnished reputation and troubled public image. Yet in another respect, the cartoon speaks of one moment alone, one in which a NASA employee proclaims headaches for the boys in P.R.

To tell the complicated if not convoluted tale suggested by the cartoon, you must first know the point and purpose of your story, and the logical and emotional effect you intend. Once again, you are thrown back to questions about the cartoon's meaning and how its treatment of events leads you to recognize that meaning. In a narrative, you might tell any one of several stories that could convey the cartoon's perspective on events. But what, exactly, is the cartoon's perspective, its point of view? An explicit defense of your answer to that question lies beyond narrative alone, just as it lies beyond description. Writers in many academic disciplines now use narratives—whether oral or written—to document case material; they may even use narrative to present findings in an engaging manner. But when they do, they must confront, as you do, the question of the narrative's point. To respond to that question, you must likewise place narrative in the service of analysis and argument.

Much of the writing you do in college seeks to create meaning for the reader by making and defending inferences. A variety of traditional modes, among them description and narration, can be used to meet this challenge. But to do so, the writing must carry an edge—an analytic or argumentative edge. In this sense, analysis and argument inform and underlie much of academic writing. We'll consider analysis and argument not as separate modes but as the necessary means of justifying inferences in a process of shared inquiry.

Analysis: Making Inferences Explicit

Analytic writing extends beyond gathering and transmitting information; it seeks to impart meaning for your readers. Analysis asks you to advance the best possible interpretation that accounts for available evidence. Moreover, analysis accepts the burden of establishing and justifying the reasons for that interpretation. The task sounds straightforward enough, except that available evidence is invariably messy, contradictory, and downright confusing.

Analysis helps you master messy evidence by enabling you to sort and classify what would otherwise be a dizzying array of observations, information, and facts. The trick is knowing on what basis you ought to sort and classify. Clearly you need some purpose or point of view that prompts you to organize observations in one particular way. Without some initial inferences about your observations, any organization would be as good (or as misguided) as any other. Even in its earliest stages, analysis needs a point of view, an organizing idea, a tentative hypothesis. To generate an organizing idea, however, you need to have some mastery over the material, mastery that only analysis can provide. Analysis thus seems to present a dilemma so circular that it resists solution.

Far from being a flaw that you might wish away, this circularity accounts for the power of analytic thinking. When you analyze you are constantly shuttling back and forth between observation and inference, between messy details and an organizing idea, between evidence and interpretive assertion. And it's this very back-and-forth motion that allows you to observe more clearly and to see your way to ever more appropriate inferences. But the process of analysis works well only if you make your inferences explicit and subject them to scrutiny. The form you give to your analysis can make this task easier.

Analytic writing, then, both expresses and tests your analysis. It is conclusion and experiment rolled into one. Analysis that does not lead to a statement synthesizing the whole is always unfinished. In turn, an interpretive statement that does not fully justify itself according to the evidence is always incomplete. You might say that analysis is always under way, always traveling toward a more apt interpretation that pulls together ever more nuanced observations.

Where in all of this is Gorrell's cartoon? Throughout. The cartoon may be what you read, yet its meaning lies in how you read it. The same holds true of any "text," be it a short story, experimental data, or your own experience. You weave meaning as you shuttle back and forth between observation and inference. To determine what the text means, you cannot rely solely on your imagination, nor can you look for the most creative or outlandish interpretation. No, inference must always be governed by observation. You can't claim more than the evidence allows, nor can you ignore evidence that doesn't fit.

As to the meaning you create of Gorrell's cartoon, analysis requires that you observe the cartoon closely and then draw inferences based on what you see. In the process you work toward ever more appropriate assertions. A written analysis can provide a persuasive defense of your thinking if you

- clarify the *occasion* that prompts your discussion,

- articulate at the outset an explicit *thesis* that expresses your interpretation, and

- test that interpretation against evidence by offering *reasons* for your view, a brief summary of which can project the organization for a full paper.

Because these three elements of form stem from questions that readers ask, they can help you refine and justify your interpretation as you write. Each successive draft can thereby match your growing awareness of available evidence.

Let's see how these three elements can serve as critical-thinking tools by looking over the shoulder of a student who is starting to write a brief analysis of Gorrell's cartoon. You'll find these elements to be equally effective tools for a variety of college assignments. A junior majoring in aerospace engineering, Brian is intrigued by the cartoon, but he and other students in his class are still debating what it says. They help each other by posing and answering readers' questions to find possible interpretations that Brian might develop about the cartoon. By evaluating these interpretive assertions, he treats them as hypotheses subject to revision. In the process, he encounters several common problems that make analysis difficult. You may encounter some of them yourself as you interpret other texts. But as he works through these problems, his understanding of the cartoon becomes ever more sophisticated.

Moving Beyond the Self-Evident

Brian's first stab at a thesis accords with some aspects of the cartoon, and so it's a promising start.

> Gorrell's cartoon ridicules the technical difficulties that NASA's space programs have encountered.

Brian figures he can support his thesis with two reasons: the television monitor labeled "Hubble" refers to problems with the telescope's mirror, and the monitor labeled "Shuttle" implies that a host of technical difficulties reveal the shuttle to be something of a lemon.

But Brian's classmates jump in to ask about the cartoon's occasion. Don't the very technical difficulties that he has listed as reasons for his thesis also serve as Gorrell's occasion for drawing the cartoon? They notice, moreover, that what Brian thought were two separate reasons for his thesis are but two examples of one point—technical difficulties. In fact, now that he checks his answers to all three readers' questions—his occasion, thesis, and reasons—they all seem to say virtually the same thing. If Brian were to write a paper at this point, all he could do is repeat himself endlessly, always asserting the obvious: that two NASA programs have technical problems. That's self-evident and hardly the basis on which to develop an analysis.

As you interpret a novel for your English class or analyze a case study for your finance professor, you'll find, as Brian did, that we go to the trouble of articulating and defending inferences only when they move beyond the self-evident assertion. You can move beyond the self-evident by searching for an assertion that requires some justification—an assertion that answers a question to which there might be more than one reply.

Looking More Closely

Brian goes back to the cartoon for another look. Only by observing more closely can you discover a perspective that bears analysis. What about that reference to P.R.? And what about the comparison between "small glitch" and "giant headache"? Realizing that his first interpretation is but a start, Brian sets out to refine his point. Here is his second attempt.

> Gorrell asserts that NASA's headaches lie in public-relations difficulties, not technical glitches.

Brian has tied the public-relations reference to technical problems. He also has a better sense of the cartoon's occasion, technical glitches. It's those glitches that prompt Gorrell to say something more, to say something about NASA's public-relations headaches.

But what about the reasons around which Brian can organize his analysis? The words in the cartoon's bubble are a start. When Brian had a hard time coming up with anything else, his classmates pointed out that simply paraphrasing what was already stated didn't amount to much analysis. If he were to develop this thesis, he could do no better than say something circular and self-evident, such as, "The cartoon is about P.R. headaches because its bubble says that glitches have brought on P.R. headaches." Once again, Brian steps back from his own interpretation to see if he might not be accounting for some evidence. He has the nagging feeling that he's just stating the obvious, that there's more to the cartoon.

No matter what the course, college asks you to look more closely. One way to push your analysis of a novel or a business case study toward a more insightful interpretation is to ask yourself whether it accounts for all your observations. When you look—or read—more closely, you'll find new evidence that may complicate or enrich your interpretation. Analytic writing encourages you, like Brian, to take another look.

To Brian's surprise, the class points out that he has said virtually nothing about the main figure in the cartoon—the very man who makes the key statement. That figure seems to be a NASA scientist, for he is wearing an official badge and is standing in a control room. In fact, he has all the accoutrements of the stereotypical scientist: lab coat, an array of pens and pencils in a breast pocket, and a clipboard at the ready. At first Brian couldn't seem to get much mileage from this insight. He then realized, however, that the scientist is interesting because he stands in implicit contrast to figures not physically rendered in the cartoon, the "boys in P.R."

Public relations. Brian is familiar with the term and its standard definition—"the business of inducing the public to have understanding and goodwill toward a person, firm, or institution." But the abbreviation to "P.R." and the reference to "boys" lead Brian to believe that a less virtuous connotation is implied: slick Madison Avenue image making.

Now the implicit comparison between the scientist and the boys in P.R. becomes telling indeed. The scientist presents anything but the favorable image that the boys in P.R. would have us see. He is rotund, balding, and out of shape; the lab coat is bursting at the buttons. Facial features carry a double message: the mouth and eyes suggest consternation, yet the double chin and large jowls communicate an air of fat-cat self-contentment. To Brian's ever sharper eye, the figure in the cartoon hardly bespeaks technical competence or scientific achievement. In fact, given what we see on the television monitors, he comes off as inept. We certainly don't catch sight of a lean and rigorous scientific mind.

Justifying Your Inferences

With new observations to account for, Brian makes a third go at expressing the cartoon's essential point.

> Gorrell asserts that NASA's headaches stem from overpromising technical achievement to create a positive, confident public image.

It's slow progress, but Brian's thesis keeps getting more powerful, more interesting, more responsive to the wealth of detail in the cartoon. The new thesis has also helped Brian sharpen the occasion for his paper. Instead of merely asserting the self-evident, he now can use what is self-evident as an occasion that sets up his thesis: "*If technical problems have created public-relations headaches for NASA*, Gorrell's cartoon asserts that those headaches stem from overpromising technical achievement to create a positive, confident public image."

What about the reasons that would allow Brian to defend his thesis? He has amassed an impressive body of observations, but at the moment they have the appearance of haphazard insight. To organize observations into powerful reasons, Brian needs analytic categories. One such category might be the implicit comparison between the frumpy scientist and the slick image that the boys in P.R. would have us see. Brian could use this comparison to justify the distinction in the thesis between technical achievement and public image. He could then call on another analytic category—images of technical failure—to show that P.R. hype about technical achievements backfires when programs perform poorly or fail. Brian plans to use these categories to develop the reasoning that would justify his thesis.

It all sounds reasonable and well-organized until Brian's classmates question whether these categories really support his thesis. Where, for example, does he make a case for "overpromising"? And where in the cartoon is the "positive, confident public image" that he says NASA has created? By looking closely at the relationship between his thesis and the reasons that project the organization of his paper, Brian realizes that he had better rethink his inferences by observing the cartoon more closely. He must do more than make inferences; he must justify them.

Brian's latest thesis was not successful because he tried to infer something that wasn't in the evidence. If he started out by not reading closely enough, Brian may now be reading a bit too much into the cartoon. As you interpret literary texts, historical records, or financial statements, you must balance these two tendencies. How? By earning the conclusions you reach as you offer your readers a well-reasoned case for them. If you overstep that evidence by advancing an assertion that doesn't hold up, skeptical readers will put little stock in what you say.

Re-vision: Looking Anew at Evidence

But Brian is far from discouraged. When in hot pursuit of the P.R. angle, he noticed two further aspects of the scientist's statement. As Brian thinks about them, they grow in importance. Given that a scientist is voicing the cartoon's key statement, the comparison between "small glitch" and "giant headache" is hardly what one would expect. In fact, that comparison reverses expectations about what a scientist would typically say about technical failures for which he might be responsible. Quite simply, the statement trivializes problems with the Shuttle and the Hubble Space Telescope. It also seems to catch the scientist shirking responsibility, and even depending on public relations to set things right.

Beyond the immediate comparison between "small glitch" and "giant headache" lies a historical comparison. Brian had noticed it early on, but didn't know quite what to make of it and so left it out of his discussion. By parodying Neil Armstrong's words—"That's one small step for a man, one giant leap for mankind"—the cartoon asks the reader to look beyond the day's headline to a long-range view of the problems at NASA. In fact, the reference forces Brian to change the thrust of his entire thesis. The *Apollo* moon landing represents, at least in the public's eye, NASA's crowning technical achievement. But that accomplishment occurred well over twenty years ago. Favorable public opinion is what the boys in P.R. have been trying to maintain ever since. However, if we are to judge by the scientist portrayed in the cartoon and by the images on the television monitors, things have not gone well since.

What might Brian infer from all these new observations? He gives it one last try.

> Gorrell attributes NASA's decline since the moon landing to an over-reliance on public-relations image making that trivializes the technical failures encountered by recent programs.

Brian could go on fine tuning his assertion. In fact, you should always be ready to rethink and reformulate your position in light of new observations or unanticipated questions. In the next few pages, we'll discuss why Brian's classmates saw fit to argue with his latest interpretation. But for now, Brian is satisfied that he has a thesis he can defend.

Lending Shape to Insight

What Brian originally thought to be the cartoon's point—technical difficulties have created P.R. headaches—now becomes the occasion that sets up his new thesis. As to the reasons that would enable Brian to present a pointed defense of his thesis, a suitable place to start is the reference to the *Apollo 11* moon landing. With the historical context of the cartoon established and with its focus on long-term decline apparent, the analysis could then take up the implied comparison between the scientist and the P.R. boys. The final analytic category could well be the scientist's attitude as expressed in his own statement—an attitude that diminishes technical error and responsibility while magnifying the role of public relations.

Having already used the relationships among occasion, thesis, and reasons to test his inferences against observation, Brian found that his brief analysis virtually wrote itself.

(1) If recent technical difficulties have created public-relations headaches for NASA, Gorrell's cartoon in *The Richmond News* sets those headaches in a broader historical context. (2) He attributes NASA's decline since the moon landing to an overreliance on public-relations image making that trivializes the technical failures encountered by recent programs. (3) By parodying Neil Armstrong's statement upon first stepping on the moon, the cartoon uses NASA's former achievements as a yardstick by which to measure current failures. (4) Moreover, the implicit contrast between the scientist pictured in the cartoon and the "boys in P.R." relates technical ineptitude to a reliance on image making. (5) The danger inherent in such image making becomes clear in the scientist's very words, which minimize technical problems and diminish personal responsibility while magnifying the role of public relations.

With the occasion (sentence 1) and thesis (sentence 2) clear at the outset, Brian's analysis can focus on a coherent explanation and defense of his view. The reasons he provides (sentences 3–5) could suffice for a short analysis or could project the organization of a longer paper.

Analysis as Inquiry

Having looked over Brian's shoulder, you realize that analytic thinking and writing require patient and exacting work. But what should also be clear is that finding answers to readers' questions enhances your thinking and writing. By posing these questions early, Brian was able to test and refine his analysis even as he shaped his paper.

The gradual accumulation of observations might make Brian's analysis seem serendipitous. After all, he won his insights about the cartoon one at a time. But readers' questions provided a consistent method throughout the thinking—and writing—process. Such a method can prove invaluable when you are analyzing amorphous issues. Gorrell's cartoon has the advantage of providing evidence in the drawing itself. But what of topics that don't present themselves in a neat rectangular box—topics like race relations on your campus or social services in your community? When you tackle such topics, your ability to articulate the occasion at hand, the thesis you are advancing, and the reasons that justify your point can help you discover what you think and why.

When interpreting the cartoon, Brian did in fact use many traditional tools of analysis: definition, classification, comparison and contrast, and cause and effect. Yet no one kind of paper modeled after these tools—a comparison-and-contrast paper, for example—would have enabled him to write an analysis that developed his interpretation fully or defended it effectively. By answering readers' questions, he found a way of placing these individual tools in the service of his analytic project. These questions provided both a method for thinking through the analysis and a method for communicating and defending that analysis on paper. By shaping an analysis, you test your thinking so that you can express your best thoughts.

A Case in Point: Analyzing Baseball

Although the key elements of form are few in number and relatively easy to grasp, they can help you develop and sustain very complex essays. Consider the following excerpt from a speech entitled "Baseball and the American Character" given by the late A. Bartlett Giamatti, commissioner of baseball and former president of Yale University.

When Giamatti rose to give this speech before the Massachusetts Historical Society, he responded to the question implicit in the very title of his talk: What is the relationship between baseball and the American character? His answer, for all its intriguing detail, is simple: Baseball embodies American life. Giamatti devotes the first half of his speech to analyzing the origins and development of baseball as they reflect the growth of America itself. In the second half, excerpted here, he turns to the actual game and finds, once again, that baseball fits America.

Baseball and the American Character
By A. Bartlett Giamatti

(1) Genteel in its American origins; proletarian in its development; egalitarian in its demands and appeal; effortless in its adaptation to nature; raucous, hard-nosed and glamorous as a profession; expanding with the country like fingers unfolding from a fist; image of a lost past, evergreen reminder of America's best promises, baseball fits America. Above all, it fits so well because it embodies the interplay of individual and group that we so love, and because it conserves our longing for the rule of law while licensing our resentment of law givers.

(2) Baseball, the opportunist's game, puts a tremendous premium on the individual, who must be able to react instantly on offense and defense and who must be able to hit, run, throw, field. Specialization obviously exists, but in general baseball players are meant to be skilled generalists. The "designated hitter" is so offensive precisely because it violates this basic characteristic of the game. Players are also sufficiently physically separated on the field so that the individual cannot hide from clear responsibility in a crowd, as in football or Congress. The object, the ball, and what the individual must do are obvious to all, and each player's skill, initiative, zest, and poise are highlighted.

(3) Individual merit and self-reliance are the bedrock of baseball, never more so that in the fundamental acts of delivering, and attempting to hit, the ball. Every game recommences every time a pitcher pitches and a batter swings. But before a swing or not-swing can trigger the vast grid of mental and physical adjustments that must proceed with every pitch, there is the basic confrontation between two lone individuals. It is primitive in its starkness. A man on a hill prepares to throw a rock at a man slightly below him, not far away, who holds a club. First, fear must be overcome; no one finally knows where the pitched ball, or hit ball, will go. Most of the time control, agility, timing, planning avert brutality and force sport. Occasionally, suddenly, usually unaccountably, the primitive act of throwing or of striking results in terrible injury. The fear is never absent, the fear that randomness will take over. If hitting a major league fastball is the most difficult act in organized sport, the difficulty derives in part from the need to overcome fear in a split second.

(4) The batter is, they say, on offense yet batting is essentially a deeply reactive and defensive act. The pitcher is, they say, on defense, yet the pitcher initiates play and controls the game. ("Pitching is 75 percent of the game)." It is not clear, at least to me, finally who is on offense and who is on defense in baseball. Consider the catcher, who may actually control the

game. The catcher is the only defensive player in any sport I know of whose defined position requires him to adopt the perspective, if not the stance, of the player on offense. Part of what a batter must overcome, part of the secretive, ruthless dimension of baseball, is the batter's knowledge that an opposing player, crouching right behind him, signals wordlessly in order to exploit his weaknesses. Is it so clear who is the defense, who is the offense? I think it is clear that part of the appeal of baseball is that at the outset it focuses on the individual with such clarity in such ambiguous circumstances.

(5) If the game flows from the constantly reiterated, primitive confrontation of an individual with the world, represented by another solitary individual, nothing that ensues, except a home run—the dispositive triumph of one over the other, the surrogate kill—fails to involve the team. A strikeout involves the catcher and anything else brings the community, either on the bench or in the field, into play. And while the premium on individual effort is never lost, eventually the communal choreography of a team almost always takes over. Every assigned role on the field potentially can and often does change with every pitch, and with each kind of pitch, or each ball hit fair. The subsequent complexities and potential interactions among all the players on the field expand in uncalculable ways. When in the thrall of its communal aspects, hitting, stealing and individual initiative give way to combined playmaking, acts of sacrifice or cooperation, and obedience to signs and orders. Whether on offense or defense, the virtuoso is then subsumed into the ensemble. The anarchic ways of solo operators are subdued by a free institution.

(6) The ambiguities surrounding being on offense or defense, surrounding what it means to stand where you stand, endlessly recreate the American pageant of individual and group, citizen and country. In baseball and daily life, Americans do not take sides so much as they change sides in ways checked and balanced. Finally, in baseball and daily life, regardless of which side you are on and where you stand, shared principles are supposed to govern.

(7) Law, defined as a complex of formal rules, agreed upon boundaries, authoritative arbiters, custom and a system of symmetrical opportunities and demands, is enshrined in baseball. Indeed, the layout of the field shows baseball's essential passion for and reliance on precise proportions and clearly defined limits, all the better to give shape to energy and an arena for equality and expression. The pitcher's rubber, 24 inches by 6 inches, is on a 15 inch mound in the middle of an 18 foot circle; the rubber is 60 feet 6 inches from home plate; the four base paths are 90 feet long;

the distance from first base to third, and home plate to second base, is 127 feet 3 3/8 inches; the pitcher's rubber is the center of a circle, described by the arc of the grass behind the infield from foul line to foul line, whose radius is 95 feet; the distance from home plate to backstop, swinging in an arc, is 60 feet. On this square tipped like a diamond containing circles and contained in circles, built on multiples of 3, nine players play nine innings, with 3 outs to a side, each out possibly composed of 3 strikes. Four balls, four bases break (or is it underscore?) the game's reliance on "threes" to distribute an odd equality, all the numerology and symmetry tending to configure a game unbounded by that which bounds most sports, and adjudicates in many, Time.

(8) The game comes from an America where the availability of sun defined the time for work or play—nothing else. Virtually all our other sports reflect the time clock, either in their formal structure or their definition of a winner. Baseball views time as daylight and daylight as an endlessly renewable natural resource; it may put a premium on speed, of throw or foot, but it is unhurried. Daytime, like the water and forests, like the land itself, will be ever available.

(9) The point is, symmetrical surfaces, deep arithmetical patterns and a vast, stable body of rules designed to ensure competitive balance in the game, show forth a country devoted to equality of treatment and opportunity; a country whose deepest dream is of a divinely proportioned and peopled (the "threes" come from somewhere) green garden enclosure; above all, a country whose basic assertion is that law, in all its mutually agreed-upon manifestations, shall govern—not nature inexorable, for all she is respected, and not humankind's whims, for all that the game belongs to the people. Baseball's essential rules for place and for play were established, by my reckoning, with almost no exceptions of consequence, by 1895. By today, the diamond and the rules for play have the character of Platonic ideas, of pre-existent inevitabilities which encourage activity, contain energy and, like any set of transcendent ideals, do not change.

(10) Symbolic of this sensibility, the umpire in baseball has unique stature among sport's arbiters. Spectator and fan alike may, perhaps at times must, object to his judgment, his interpretation, his grasp of precedent and relevant doctrine. Such dissent is encouraged, is valuable and rarely, if ever, is successful. As instant replay shows, very rarely should it be. The umpire is untouchable (there is law protecting his person) and infallible. He is the much aligned, indispensable, faceless figure of Judgment, in touch with all the codes and lore and with nature's vagaries, for he decides when she has won. He is the Constitution and Court before your

eyes. He is also the most durable figure in the game for he, alone, never sits, never rests. He has no side, he is on every side. His sole obligation is to dispense justice speedily.

(11) So much does our game tell us, about what we wanted to be, about what we are. Our character and our culture are reflected in this grand game. It would be foolish to think that all of our national experience is reflected in any single institution, even our loftiest, but it would not be wrong to claim for baseball a capacity to cherish individuality and inspire cohesion in a way which is a hallmark of our loftiest free institutions. Nor would it be misguided to think that, however vestigial the remnants of our best hopes, we can still find, if we wish to, a moment called a game when those best hopes, those memories for the future have life, when each of us, those who are in and those out, has a chance to gather, in a green place around home.

Much of the pleasure we derive from Giamatti's speech comes from the elegance with which he raises and meets expectations and from the insight into our national character that he brings to back up his point. He justifies his view not by describing the game we all know but by revealing, through careful analysis, the character of the game as we may not have seen it before. Readers' questions help shape that analysis.

• The occasion for the talk, implicit in its title, helps Giamatti pose a question that literally occasions his reply. What is the relationship between an American sport (our national pastime no less) and the spirit of the American people? In replying, Giamatti does not merely hold forth; he reminds his audience of the question that prompts his response. The final paragraph, echoing the occasion, underscores the relevance of his words.

• The thesis for the talk, "baseball fits America," pulls together what would otherwise be random observations that compare baseball with America. Giamatti is saying something *about* that relationship, something worth hearing because it is not immediately apparent. He provides clarity by stating his thesis as a conclusion; he provides direction by following through on his claim and on our expectation that he has support for it.

• As an arguable opinion, Giamatti's thesis requires that he provide reasons. He projects the organization of his talk by announcing a plan that sets ideas in relationship. But Giamatti doesn't merely discuss "the interplay of individual and group" and "the rule of law," he relates them to his thesis. Not a one-time laundry list of things to talk about, this projected organization expresses logical relationships that underlie the entire presentation. In developing his talk, Giamatti expands on and justifies those relationships.

If Giamatti's speech helps us see baseball as an expression of the American character, we can see Giamatti's point all the better because he responds, elegantly and incisively, to questions that readers would themselves pose.

Argument: Evaluating Inferences at Issue

If analysis makes inferences explicit and credible, argument evaluates and defends inferences because they are under debate. Argument thus adds a new dimension to the already challenging task of analysis: the objections of your audience. Because argument addresses questions at issue, the audience debating the question helps shape your argument. In fact, you must make readers part of your argument rather than its passive recipients.

The distinction between analysis and argument is more gradual than absolute. When you analyze, you still must take into account your readers' questions and concerns. In turn, all argument need not be agonistic, a matter of black and white, pro and con. Even when you debate views close to your own, you still must meet objections posed by skeptical readers.

Argument heightens the implicit dialogue with your audience that all good writing should carry on. Although few arguments adopt the actual form of a dialogue, you must nevertheless write your paper with the dynamics of dialogue in mind. Point will meet with counterpoint. Your own voice will invariably contend with other voices, whose questions provide cues for your own lines. Rather than quiet this dialogue, an effective argument will, in fact, capitalize on it. Far from an inconvenience, dialogue is the source of argument's power and fascination.

Counterargument

A fourth element of form—the *counterargument*—helps you to account for and make use of the dialogue on which argument depends. In argumentative writing, this fourth element takes its place alongside the other three: your occasion, your thesis, and the reasons that can project your paper's organization. Although you may find the counterargument treated separately, it often influences or becomes an aspect of the other three elements.

• When specifying the paper's occasion, for example, you might call upon the counterargument to help you engage the issue and your audience. In fact, an opposing view or the actual point of disagreement can serve as your occasion.

• Likewise, your own thesis often implies a counterthesis, a competing claim against which evidence must also be evaluated.

• Finally, when you refer to reasons that justify your thesis, you must also acknowledge contrary evidence that may force you to qualify the nature and degree of your support.

You can only offer a persuasive defense of your thinking on a controversial matter if you account for counterarguments. By ignoring questions and objections, you make your case weaker and less coherent. Without an occasion sharpened by the edge of counterargument, your readers may not know that you are addressing a controversial issue, or even why you are bothering to write. Without a thesis that implies a counterthesis, readers may find your view one-dimensional and naive. Without reasons leavened with an honest appraisal of contrary evidence, your paper may do little more than pile assertion on assertion. The impression you create will be one of strident fanaticism, not fair-mindedness. Even if you intend your paper to be an argument that will persuade others, it will seem like a tiresome, strident monologue.

Your audience will press tough questions at every turn, so you must address them not once but throughout your paper. You might think that mentioning contrary evidence or opposing views will weaken your case. Actually, quite the opposite is true. Because your readers are skeptical from the start, they're apt to notice if you have ignored something that speaks against your point. You must also do more than note evidence that seems inconvenient; you must deal with it. If you treat your audience fairly, they will be disposed to give your views a fair hearing.

Fair-mindedness should also influence how you address your audience and present yourself. That your readers hold views different from your own should not turn them into ignoramuses or fanatics. If you argue too vehemently, you might find yourself sporting those very labels. Moreover, few controversial issues divide good guys from bad guys, however neat and tidy this moral division may appear. If you reach for the easy cliché or slogan, you so abbreviate your argument that readers may suspect that you do not care to discuss complex matters, preferring instead to recycle formulas. Argument asks you to inhabit two worlds—yours and your audience's—and draw them a little closer. By all means take a strong position and argue it well. But don't be so strident as to deny contrary evidence and opinion—or the human sympathies and common interests that make reasoned argument possible.

The shape you lend to your argument can improve how you think through and assess competing claims. Even in the early stages of argument, readers' questions ask you to evaluate the inferences that lead you and your audience to your respective positions. By responding to these questions, your thinking is apt to be more cogent, your case more persuasive.

Locating Disagreement

Let's return to Gorrell's cartoon, for in pursuing his analysis, Brian became aware of a host of potential arguments. Writing an analysis led him to see that he could write an argument as well. Indeed, only by writing argument could he address the disagreements that arose.

When Brian analyzed the cartoon, he was addressing an interested but skeptical audience that was saying, in effect, "Is that so? Really? Tell me more." He thought of his audience as if they were Missouri natives who at every turn would invoke the state's motto, "Show me!" But as Brian and his classmates tried to interpret what Gorrell was saying in the cartoon, they discovered that certain questions separated them from Gorrell—and from each other. The questions at issue marked where disagreement lay. To address those disagreements, Brian found he had to argue. Moreover, when arguing, Brian found himself addressing a different sort of audience, one that would say, "But no, to the contrary. . . ." To shape an argument that accommodates the needs of his audience and meets their objections, Brian once again seeks to respond to his readers' questions.

What Brian wants to blurt out is that Gorrell's got it wrong. But he quickly realizes that Gorrell doesn't have it all wrong, for some of Brian's own friends and classmates saw a lot of truth in the cartoon. Where, then, does disagreement lie? Brian takes an essential first step in argument by determining what specific question separates author and audience. We'll consider here the various sorts of questions at issue that can arise.

- questions of interpretation, including questions of fact and definition
- questions of consequence
- questions of value
- questions of policy

You can use these various questions to establish the point of disagreement. That point of disagreement, in turn, helps you articulate your occasion, hone an assertion that addresses the disagreement, and bring good reasons to bear that justify your position before a skeptical audience.

Questions of Interpretation

One kind of argument occurs when readers disagree with each other about what something means. And the cartoon surely represents an interpretation with which some readers may disagree. Brian, for one, objects to Gorrell's indictment of NASA's decline, an indictment the cartoonist achieves through the clever parody of Neil Armstrong's famous statement. But is NASA in decline? This is a matter of interpretation, to be sure. This point of disagreement readily provides an occasion for Brian to advance his own thesis: In parodying Armstrong, Gorrell's cartoon misrepresents NASA's current achievements.

To justify that thesis, Brian must marshall evidence that would meet the counterarguments implicit in Gorrell's cartoon. As Brian discusses the design that his argument would take, students in the class remind him that if he is to make a credible case, he cannot gloss over the problems depicted on the television monitors. To the contrary, he must engage Gorrell throughout in a sort of dialogue, always questioning his depiction of NASA programs. Only by doing so can Brian make his case that the Hubble Space Telescope and the Space Shuttle, despite their glitches, represent considerable technical achievements.

Many of the papers you write will engage questions of interpretation. The traditional texts you read, the cultural "texts" you encounter, and even the personal "text" of your own experience all oblige you to ask "What does it mean?" Like Brian, you must determine the specific point on which your puzzlement or disagreement rests. Because questions of interpretation often cannot be settled with absolute certainty, much depends on how you craft and justify your own case even as you answer questions and objections.

Questions of Fact

Brian's dispute with Gorrell is instructive because it shows how two other questions can underlie questions of interpretation. *Questions of fact* enter in because Brian must determine how well the Hubble Space Telescope is performing. Does the telescope really transmit only static? A quick scan of technical articles indicates that despite errors in the manufacture of the telescope's mirror, the telescope is still able to transmit better images than earthbound telescopes. Moreover, those errors did not affect numerous other scientific instruments on board. Although sometimes argued in their own right, questions of fact typically open up larger questions of interpretation—such as the one about NASA's supposed decline that Brian is now debating.

In your courses across the curriculum, questions of fact arise when there is an unknown to be determined—an unknown you hope to verify. Scientific and technical disciplines often pose such questions: Did my experiment replicate earlier results? Will this engineering design meet the stated load requirements? Questions of fact also arise in the humanities, where they often lead to larger questions of interpretation. In what respects does Shakespeare's depiction of the French campaign in *Henry V* depart from history? This question, in turn, begs another: What bearing does Shakespeare's editing of history have on our interpretation of the play?

Questions of Definition

Like questions of fact, *questions of definition* often underlie arguments about interpretation. They come up in Gorrell's cartoon as Brian ponders the lemon depicted in the television monitor labeled "Shuttle." Is the Shuttle really a "lemon," as Gorrell would have us believe? Is it unsatisfactory or defective? Like most questions of definition that are at issue, Brian cannot resolve this one by turning to a dictionary. He must set the question of definition in a larger context and argue whether or not the performance of the Shuttle warrants Gorrell's characterization.

Questions of definition can arise in virtually every field when the terms that allow us to share meaning become themselves a point of disagreement. Subtle distinctions among words (*liberal, moderate, conservative*), and the application of terms to specific cases (Bill Clinton, George Bush, II. Ross Perot) often spark such disagreements. You can pursue questions of definition in their own right. But such questions become especially relevant when they lead to broader questions of interpretation—that is, when they are not used neutrally but to advance a particular perspective or point.

The specific questions of fact and definition that underlie Brian's argument with Gorrell about NASA's decline remind us that questions of interpretation require more than Brian's own personal opinion. As in all arguments, he must test opinions in an implicit, ongoing dialogue with skeptical readers—among them Gorrell. Nearly all questions of interpretation involve judgment, not certitude, inference, not raw observation. All the more reason, then, to test and refine your ideas as you learn more about your subject, your audience, and yourself.

Questions of Consequence

Thus far Brian has been content to argue with Gorrell. Little does he realize that his own views might themselves generate debate. Some members of his class have begun to question whether his earlier analysis of Gorrell's cartoon can be justified. Their disagreement with Brian's analysis lies in a *question of consequence*—that is, cause and effect. What consequences has NASA's public relations had? Did public relations really lead to NASA's decline? With Brian's own interpretation of the cartoon now a point of disagreement, we can see once again how analysis enters the domain of argument when an audience no longer asks "Really?" but interjects "Not so!"

As you recall, Brian's analysis hinged on the role of public relations.

> Gorrell attributes NASA's decline since the moon landing to an over-reliance on public-relations image making that trivializes the technical failures encountered by recent programs.

Upon reflection, some classmates voiced strong reservations asking whether Brian could really infer a cause-and-effect relationship between NASA's decline and public relations. As with most questions of consequence, this one requires interpretation—of the cartoon and, by extension, of NASA itself. Few matters of cause and effect can be settled with absolute certainty; all the more reason, then, to think carefully about the conditions and variables that may cause something to happen or that result in some effect.

Given the dissent expressed by some classmates, Brian's cause-and-effect interpretation of the cartoon, once a matter of analysis, now becomes an occasion for argument. In pursuing this argument with Brian's analysis, his classmates can consider two options, each of which involves a dialogue with Brian. Most arguments take one or the other approach.

One option is to argue that Brian's analysis does not hold. To justify this assertion, classmates would have to demonstrate that, point for point, Brian's interpretation of the cartoon does not permit the cause-and-effect relationship he infers. Here, argument takes the form of *refutation*. Brian's own case shapes the *rebuttal* offered by his classmates; his reasons serve as counterarguments that they must answer.

Brian's classmates may also pursue another option. They might advance a *competing assertion*—one that would have to take into account the contrary evidence Brian is sure to provide. For example, classmates might argue that

> Gorrell exposes NASA's decline from making giant leaps for all mankind to making but glitches and PR headaches for itself.

No word here of cause and effect, no implication that an overreliance on PR image making has caused NASA's decline. The interpretation advanced by Brian's classmates is more modest than his own, but perhaps more in keeping with the evidence supplied in the cartoon. Nevertheless, because classmates have as their occasion a point of disagreement with Brian, they must account for the observations that led Brian to infer cause and effect.

With either option, classmates can pursue an argument only if they establish and then respond to a point of disagreement by engaging objections to their case. Without a countervailing voice, argument cannot take shape; without an implicit, ongoing dialogue it cannot be sustained.

Questions of consequence abound because inferences about cause and effect help us make sense of our world, no matter what discipline we study. When you write papers in scientific and technical fields, you hope to resolve such questions with some certainty. But in most disciplines—whether history, political science, or sociology—you must answer conditionally. You seek to find and justify a probable cause, given certain conditions and variables. Argument forms the basis of academic writing because it requires all of us to refine the reasoning that leads to sound judgments about matters that appear or remain uncertain.

Questions of Value

Questions of interpretation and consequence often hinge on a related *question of value*, one that addresses whether something is good, valuable, worthwhile, or right. For example, Brian's disagreement with Gorrell about whether NASA is in decline implicitly involves a question of value: Are NASA's recent projects—the Hubble Space Telescope and the Space Shuttle among them—worthwhile? Gorrell's cartoon makes some implicit judgments by using value-laden terms and icons, such as the lemon depicted on one screen, and the static depicted on the other. Brian's reaction to the cartoon likewise depends on value judgments, just as his reply to Gorrell will also call upon value-laden terms.

We can argue questions of value only by discussing the standards by which we determine value. That's why questions of value often involve questions of definition and interpretation. Unless we reach some agreement on standards, discussion about values tends to become merely subjective, a matter of personal preference. Yet it needn't be. We all assign value to works of art, to the consequences that follow from our actions, to the philosophical beliefs that guide our lives. We can discuss, even share those values when we invite inquiry into them. Because perfunctory declarations tend to cut off debate, college courses engage questions of value by asking you for careful, thorough discussion.

Questions of Policy

Yet another question can identify the point of disagreement, the *question of policy*. What action, if any, should be taken? Brian and his classmates were tempted to leap to this question almost immediately, for surely any thesis with a "should" or "must" boldly announces itself as quintessential argument. Some members of the class called for changing the method by which the government funds NASA projects, proposing that it receive long-term funding, thereby allowing it to develop projects without yearly budgetary changes and constant PR headaches. Others in the class objected, citing the need for close Congressional oversight and citizen involvement. A point of disagreement, to be sure. Yet as they considered how they would shape their respective cases, they quickly realized just how complex arguments of policy can be.

To debate policy, you must build your case by gathering together supporting analyses and arguments. In the end, the force of your recommendation—your "should" or "must"—is only as strong as the related analytic and argumentative cases on which your recommendation rests.

First off, you must establish that a problem exists, a task that involves the question of interpretation. For example, only by establishing that short-term funding is a problem for NASA can Brian hope to argue for a change in how the government funds NASA. By convincing readers that a problem exists, he establishes the common ground and goodwill that will encourage others to consider his recommendation. Moreover, only by interpreting the nature of the problem can he convince others that his solution will address it.

Questions of consequence also bear on the success of a policy argument. Brian must establish that, left unaddressed, short-term funding will have or continue to have unfavorable consequences. For example, he could argue that short-term funding leads to an unhealthy focus on public relations, for PR headaches or successes often influence Congressional budgetary decisions. In turn, he must establish that desired consequences would follow from his recommendation that NASA receive long-term funding for its projects. Perhaps long-term funding would insulate NASA from an unhealthy preoccupation with PR. What's more, Brian must pursue these arguments of cause and effect in the context of competing proposals or alternative solutions. Questions and objections abound: Is long-term funding feasible? Is it cost-effective? Would it maintain flexibility? Is there precedent for this action? Arguments of policy arise, after all, because readers face choices about what they should do. And rarely is there but one option for them to consider.

A further question often lurks undetected in arguments of policy, namely, questions of value. Is Brian's policy recommendation right or ethically sound? Thus, when Brian suggests that long-term funding would help insulate NASA from PR headaches, he is making value judgments about PR and its function in a larger system of values. As such, he must answer questions about competing values. When, for example, does being insulated from PR headaches begin to compromise the ability of Congress to oversee NASA programs, or undermine the citizen support essential to a civilian space agency? Answers to such questions depend on how Brian deals with questions of interpretation and on how he clarifies the standards by which he makes value judgments. Although questions of value can be argued on their own terms, they most often come up in the context of other questions under debate—interpretation, consequence, and most certainly policy.

Questions of policy may be uppermost in your mind because they influence behavior. Many college assignments ask you to consider policy; even if they don't, it's on your mind. Questions of policy turn argument into action, words into deed. Questions of policy lend inquiry immediate utility. But to act on your inquiry, you must first inquire into the questions of interpretation, consequence, and value that inform your actions. Because arguments of policy bring into play other questions, they challenge the writer who may otherwise presume that a boldly announced "should" or "must" thesis promises trouble-free argument. It doesn't. Policy arguments are notoriously complex. A more prudent alternative often lies in focusing on a question of interpretation or consequence that underlies policy. What we should or shouldn't do depends in the end on answers to these underlying questions.

Argument as Inquiry

Having looked over Brian's shoulder as he considered the various arguments he might pursue, or that others may pursue with him, you can appreciate the complexities of making your case before a discerning, skeptical audience. The educational value of argument lies not in winning—in pounding your opponent into the ground   but in exploring your own mind and the minds of others. Only by testing your ideas through shared inquiry will they become both credible and convincing.

The papers you write in college may reflect your disciplinary interests and stem from various questions at issue. But for all their differences, you can shape those papers by understanding the shape of inquiry itself. Like Brian, you must begin by establishing the question at issue. When you care deeply about an issue and the position you have adopted, as you must when writing argument, you need to consider the point on which disagreement rests. Because your audience will also care deeply, but differently, clarifying that point of disagreement is essential. By anticipating and responding to readers' questions, you can better grasp and respond to that debate. Their questions offer a method both for thinking through your position as you consider potential objections and for communicating your argument to others.

Like analysis, argument is both a way of expressing your point and a way of testing it. In argument, there is always something tentative about a thesis; it hangs in the balance, to be accepted, denied, or reconsidered. Thus, when you are shaping an argument, you are doing more than expressing your belief. You are also examining what to believe.

A Case in Point: Arguing Artificial Intelligence

A second, argumentative essay shows how attention to the shape of ideas can clarify the grounds of debate and thereby help writers offer a pointed defense of their views. John Searle, a professor of philosophy at the University of California, Berkeley, calls on readers' questions to help him keep the strands of a complex argument from becoming entangled. Here is the beginning of a long and detailed article that appeared in *Scientific American*.

Is the Brain's Mind a Computer Program?
No. A program merely manipulates symbols, whereas a brain attaches meaning to them.
By John R. Searle

(1) Can a machine think? Can a machine have conscious thoughts in exactly the same sense that you and I have? If by "machine" one means a physical system capable of performing certain functions (and what else can one mean?), then humans are machines of a special biological kind, and humans can think, and so of course machines can think. And, for all we know, it might be possible to produce a thinking machine out of different materials altogether—say, out of silicon chips or vacuum tubes. Maybe it will turn out to be impossible, but we certainly do not know that yet.

(2) In recent decades, however, the question of whether a machine can think has been given a different interpretation entirely. The question that has been posed in its place is, Could a machine think just by virtue of implementing a computer program? Is the program by itself constitutive of thinking? This is a completely different question because it is not about the physical, causal properties of actual or possible physical systems but rather about the abstract, computational properties of formal computer programs that can be implemented in any sort of substance at all, provided only that the substance is able to carry the program.

(3) A fair number of researchers in artificial intelligence (AI) believe the answer to the second question is yes; that is, they believe that by design-

ing the right programs with the right inputs and outputs, they are literally creating minds. They believe furthermore that they have a scientific test for determining success or failure: the Turing test devised by Alan M. Turing, the founding father of artificial intelligence. The Turing test, as currently understood, is simply this: if a computer can perform in such a way that an expert cannot distinguish its performance from that of a human who has a certain cognitive ability—say, the ability to do addition or to understand Chinese—then the computer also has that ability. So the goal is to design programs that will simulate human cognition in such a way as to pass the Turing test. What is more, such a program would not merely be a model of the mind; it would literally be a mind, in the same sense that a human mind is a mind.

(4) By no means does every worker in artificial intelligence accept so extreme a view. A more cautious approach is to think of computer models as being useful in studying the mind in the same way that they are useful in studying the weather, economics or molecular biology. To distinguish these two approaches, I call the first strong AI and the second weak AI. It is important to see just how bold an approach strong AI is. Strong AI claims that thinking is merely the manipulation of formal symbols, and that is exactly what the computer does: manipulate formal symbols. This view is often summarized by saying, "The mind is to the brain as the program is to the hardware."

(5) Strong AI is unusual among theories of the mind in at least two respects: it can be stated clearly, and it admits of a simple and decisive refutation. The refutation is one that any person can try for himself or herself. Here is how it goes. Consider a language you don't understand. In my case, I do not understand Chinese. To me Chinese writing looks like so many meaningless squiggles. Now suppose I am placed in a room containing baskets full of Chinese symbols. Suppose also that I am given a rule book in English for matching Chinese symbols with other Chinese symbols. The rules identify the symbols entirely by their shapes and do not require that I understand any of them. The rules might say such things as, "Take a squiggle-squiggle sign from basket number one and put it next to a squoggle-squoggle sign from basket number two."

(6) Imagine that people outside the room who understand Chinese hand in small bunches of symbols and that in response I manipulate the symbols according to the rule book and hand back more small bunches of symbols. Now, the rule book is the "computer program." The people who wrote it are "programmers," and I am the "computer." The baskets full of symbols are the "data base," the small bunches that are handed in to me are "questions" and the bunches I then hand out are "answers."

(7) Now suppose that the rule book is written in such a way that my "answers" to the "questions" are indistinguishable from those of a native Chinese speaker. For example, the people outside might hand me some symbols that unknown to me mean, "What's your favorite color?" and I might after going through the rules give back symbols that, also unknown to me, mean, "My favorite color is blue, but I also like green a lot." I satisfy the Turing test for understanding Chinese. All the same, I am totally ignorant of Chinese. And there is no way I could come to understand Chinese in the system as described, since there is no way that I can learn the meanings of any of the symbols. Like a computer, I manipulate symbols, but I attach no meaning to the symbols.

(8) The point of the thought experiment is this: if I do not understand Chinese solely on the basis of running a computer program for understanding Chinese, then neither does any other digital computer solely on that basis. Digital computers merely manipulate formal symbols according to rules in the program.

(9) What goes for Chinese goes for other forms of cognition as well. Just manipulating the symbols is not by itself enough to guarantee cognition, perception, understanding, thinking and so forth. And since computers, qua computers, are symbol-manipulating devices, merely running the computer program is not enough to guarantee cognition.

(10) This simple argument is decisive against the claims of strong AI.

Why is Searle's article interesting even to those who know little about computers and even less about artificial intelligence? For one, he makes his subject accessible and intriguing. Moreover, he takes pains to shape his argument and hone its persuasive edge. He doesn't overwhelm the reader with information but uses information to flesh out the issue, point, and support for his argument.

An awareness of form helps him lend clarity and persuasive force to what might otherwise be a dull treatise.

• Searle's occasion, apparent in the title and developed in the first two paragraphs, sets out the question under discussion, one that involves both definition and interpretation. In fact, the article itself opens with two questions that allow him to place his discussion in historical context and provide necessary background information for the general reader. Not given for its own sake, that information clarifies the question that prompts his discussion. Searle engages the issue at the outset, and in so doing focuses the debate that follows.

• Clearly evident in the explanatory subtitle to the article, Searle's thesis that "running the computer program is not enough to guarantee cognition" is itself announced at the end of paragraph 9. Once again we note how titles provide context and help orient the reader. Implied in the occasion and thesis is a counterthesis, an opposing view to which Searle responds. With the thesis established early on, the reader knows what is at stake, and can evaluate the details to follow not as so much bewildering information but as evidence and reasoning marshalled in support of a point.

• Paragraphs 3 and 4 articulate the counterargument to Searle's position. In these paragraphs we find the question posed in the occasion answered in a different way. By articulating the opposing view, Searle can acknowledge key assumptions and definitions held by readers who may disagree with him. He can also qualify, through the distinction between "strong" and "weak" artificial intelligence, exactly which view he is addressing.

• Paragraphs 5–8 describe the Turing test, on the basis of which advocates of strong artificial intelligence evaluate what constitutes cognition. You might think of the test as part of the counterargument, a test that advocates of strong artificial intelligence would themselves propose. Yet in performing a thought experiment according to the Turing test, Searle establishes reasons against the claims that advocates of strong artificial intelligence might advance. In fact, the thought experiment offers something of a projected organization, for in the remainder of the article Searle takes up first one and then another aspect of the experiment and answers various questions pertaining to it. Counterargument drives the argument, as Searle responds to strong artificial intelligence at its most decisive point.

As this excerpt from Searle's article demonstrates, readers' questions need not imply answers that produce formulaic writing. On the contrary, their questions are so basic that they invite creative treatment. What is more, these questions call for critical thinking—for discovering the essential conceptual relationships of an analysis or argument and for testing and communicating those relationships in the act of writing. The excerpts from Giamatti and Searle, so different in subject matter, tone, and style, both underscore that the shape you lend to your ideas enables you to analyze and argue.

Points
of Departure

4

How should you start writing an analytic or argumentative paper? If you are merely concerned with beginning, there is no one correct way. The writing process, particularly its first moments, is so individual and idiosyncratic that general rules and formulas seldom apply. Some of you may think through ideas well before you set down any words, while others may write pages to puzzle out those ideas. Detailed outlines will suit some; others may prefer rough notes.

As to the actual writing, individual temperament and habit prevail. Some writers feel at a loss if they can't set pencil to a yellow legal pad; others find themselves paralyzed unless they can sit down at a computer keyboard. Some eke out each word and don't dare to write a second paragraph before they are satisfied with the first. Others prefer to dash off drafts only to mark them up heavily when they revise.

In the end you must find your own writing process. But if you are interested in more than beginning, if you wish to find a point of departure that prompts analysis and argument, you must make strategic decisions that relate means to ends. This chapter will show you how.

We'll look over the shoulder of a student as she begins to write a short analytic paper. Jennifer shared her drafts with other students in her writing workshop as they each developed their essays. These students helped each other spot problems by seeing matters from a reader's perspective. We begin where Jennifer does, with the task of setting down ideas on an otherwise blank page. Through a series of introductory sketches to her paper, she gradually lends shape to her ideas. Along the way, she calls on strategies that enable her to

- assess the context in which she communicates,
- establish interest,
- achieve focus, and
- find patterns in her observations.

These strategies contribute to the ongoing challenge of testing and refining the emerging shape of ideas.

Jennifer's drafts underscore that writing analysis and argument is not a collection of random acts, nor is it a predictable sequence of specific activities. It is a process of problem solving that requires critical awareness and deliberate decisions. Although you may not encounter all of Jennifer's problems, or in quite the same sequence, you will deal with many of them as you write and revise your own drafts.

The Introductory Sketch

Jennifer's assignment left her a good deal of latitude: she was asked to write a three- to four-page analytic paper on a topic of her choice. That is, she was expected to advance and justify an assertion about a particular problem or concern. Jennifer liked the assignment because it allowed her to pursue her own interests. But as she would discover, that latitude also challenged her problem-solving skills.

Jennifer knew from the outset that she'd write about environmental problems. Volunteer work with a community recycling group and some outside reading of her own already provided her with a good deal of information. Writing the paper seemed rather straightforward—that is, until she sat down to work out ideas on the page. Jennifer discovered that information meant very little unless she found a means for establishing relationships. Facts, impressions, and half-formed convictions were only of consequence if she could set them together to highlight issues, assertions, and reasoned support.

Jennifer did so by developing a series of *introductory sketches*. She used her sketches to clarify her own thinking and to elicit comments from students in her writing workshop, who served as discerning, skeptical readers. We'll use those very sketches to highlight strategies that can help you launch your own paper.

An introductory sketch provides an overview of your case, rendered in a paragraph or at most a page. A sketch differs from an outline in that you are not merely categorizing information into topics, subtopics, and sub-subtopics. You are capturing your purpose by setting issue, point, and support into dynamic relationship. A sketch can help you clarify the question at issue, your thesis, and the reasons that make your position credible. As such, a sketch defines the conceptual architecture of your paper, much as an introduction orients the reader to your purpose, point, and plan. In fact, the sketch you develop and test can, in the end, serve as an actual introduction. But for now, think of the sketch as a design tool that allows you to develop and test the shape of your paper without resorting to time-consuming full drafts. It clarifies the shape of your analysis or argument before you construct it sentence by sentence; it's the abstract of the paper yet to be written.

The advantage of a sketch is that it is detailed enough for you to determine whether the shape of your ideas holds promise, but also preliminary enough to revise or even discard. With a sketch, unlike a full draft, you haven't yet committed the time or developed the emotional attachment that may dissuade you from making radical but necessary changes. The sketch allows you to scout out possibilities and can alert you to the consequences of your design decisions.

Writers, like artists, rely heavily on preliminary sketches. An artist will use paper and pencil to sketch and resketch in miniature the shape of a larger work. Writers, too, will find and test the key ideas they wish to express by stepping back from their notes and journals to capture, in a paragraph or page, the essential shape of their analysis or argument. These sketches head off major problems that the artist might otherwise encounter when actually applying acrylic to canvass— or that the writer might discover only when developing a full draft.

But sketches are more than tools for problem solving. They also contribute to the final work. In the artist's painting, now framed and hung, you can discern the sketch come to life and fleshed out. Likewise, you may find at the outset of a fully developed essay that the sketch has been revised into a polished introduction, one that orients readers to the shape of ideas that were themselves forged and tested in earlier versions.

Assessing Context

Confident that she wanted to write on the environment, Jennifer used her introductory sketch as a tool for discovering how she might tackle it. Here is her first effort.

(1) America, once beautiful, has become a garbage dump. (2) Tons of solid waste are discarded in landfills, which in turn leak toxins into groundwater. (3) Many parts of the country lack sufficient capacity to manage this trash. (4) Because pollution destroys our natural resources, it is important to examine wasteful habits. (5) We can cut back on the waste we generate, recycle what we do use, and protect the wilderness areas and sensitive wetlands that remain untouched.

When Jennifer brought her sketch to the writing workshop, she was a bit unnerved by the thought of live readers discussing her work. In fact, it hadn't really crossed her mind that her writing had a context. How was she presenting herself? Who were her readers? And why was she writing? Unexpected questions flooded her mind as she listened to the discussion.

When her classmates read the paragraph, they were puzzled by the many interests that she touched on. "We thought," they said, "that your occasion—the image of America as garbage dump—might set up a paper about solid waste or perhaps polluted groundwater. But before we knew it, you were off to wilderness areas and wetland conservation. What's the connection? Isn't the topic too broad? And don't you really have several topics competing for attention?"

A classmate added that although he could sense that Jennifer cared about these matters, he didn't know what she was saying about her topic. "Doesn't the main assertion—'it is important to examine'—in the end tell us very little?" he asked. "And what about that last sentence? Doesn't it promise three entirely different directions for the paper? Because the assertion is weak, it's hard to know whether the points mentioned in that last sentence are reasons supporting an assertion, or a list of entirely new subjects."

Jennifer realized that she would have to rethink her paper from top to bottom. She even contemplated changing topics, presuming that the problem lay in what she was writing on. You may find yourself tempted in this way. But in all likelihood you will encounter similar problems as you tackle your new topic. Focus instead on how you might approach your subject. Writers justify their topics by the manner in which they tackle them. In the end, the topic you choose may be less important than the angle or perspective you take on it.

The comments of classmates highlighted important issues that Jennifer would have to solve in her next draft. But the discussion also touched on three essential problem-solving strategies. Like Jennifer, you'll profit from calling on them. Together, they will help you assess the context in which you are writing and in which your words will be read. The following three strategies can correct the notion that you are writing in a vacuum. In so doing, they allow you to draw on resources that you might not realize were available to you.

Interpret Your Assignment

For all of your concern about choosing a topic, you may forget that words can only be used in context. Real-world, problem-driven writing does have a rhetorical context. When we write memos and progress reports, we generally respond to immediate issues or points of disagreement; we address specific individuals; we know our own role; and we write with a sense of purpose.

But what of college writing? At first, it seems to lack a rhetorical context, and thus can appear artificial. But if you look more closely, you'll find that the typical college writing assignment is a special case of context-specific, problem-driven writing. When you are given an assignment, you are in fact given a problem to be solved. In college, the assignment often *is* the context. Thus, to assess context, you must interpret the implications of your assignment. Start by distinguishing between your *topic* and your *task*.

Most students focus on the *what* of a writing assignment: "a five-page paper on More's *Utopia*," or "a ten-page paper on the function of enzymes." Yet there's far more to an assignment than topic and length. In fact, the most crucial aspect of the assignment may only be implied, or perhaps suggested in one key word. That aspect is the task that lies behind the topic.

The task defines what you are expected to do in your paper. The purpose of most writing assignments is to help you use content not for its own sake but for advancing and supporting your own analytic or argumentative point. If your professors were interested in content alone, multiple-choice or short-answer questions would more than suffice. But most professors are not interested in using writing to test factual information. They are looking for your ability to use, not repeat, information.

By interpreting the assignment to reveal the task, you can uncover the problem it asks you to solve. First look at key words, the words that ask you to do something. Jennifer recalled that some recent assignments in her other courses were relatively direct in their use of key words: "*analyze* the function of the storm scene in Act Two of Shakespeare's *Othello*" or "*argue* whether or not student fees should subsidize athletic programs." But many assignments only imply the task involved by pointing to the type of product desired, such as a "position paper," "critique," or "review." In such cases you must infer that the assignment asks not for description but for interpretation and evaluation if not outright argument.

Still other assignments leave much—far too much—unstated. They may simply ask you to "discuss" or "write an essay on" a topic. Here you must consider the assumptions that govern college writing. Because most college assignments require you to shape your ideas, your discussion should not resemble rambling cocktail chatter. The assignment's unstated criterion is that you take and justify a position, that you place your information and observations in the service of analysis or argument. If you are unsure of your task, ask your instructor for clarification.

If some assignments point you to a topic, others specify the task and leave the topic up to you. Such is the case with Jennifer's assignment in her writing workshop. The challenge extends beyond choosing a topic; you must find a problem or concern in that topic and respond to it. In other words, you must define for yourself and your audience why words are being written and read. Such "open-topic" assignments focus on your ability to define your own rhetorical context—to specify issue, purpose, audience, and your own persona. Even when a topic is announced, part of your task may be to establish or respond to the rhetorical situation in ways that serve your interests. Thus, our first strategy leads us a second.

Establish Your Rhetorical Situation

Unlike real-world rhetorical situations, the classroom context seems fraught with rather unsettling contradictions. In the real world, you often know to whom you are writing, and what issue or problem prompts the communication. Moreover, you write with a sense of your own role and expertise, and the authority they give you to press home your point. How different the college classroom seems. The assignment (not to mention the subsequent grade) places you in a subordinate position. As a student, you are exploring new ideas as you are initiated into the mysteries of an academic discipline. And yet you are expected to impress the professor with your command of the material. Some students respond to this situation by writing solely to the professor, an expert audience of one. Such papers often become an excuse to parade information and try on stilted academic styles. And when they do, they can make for the most dreadful reading.

When Jennifer reflected on the workshop comments, she found that no one really objected to her information as such. Instead, the relationships among her ideas had everyone puzzled. To forge those relationships, she had to look beyond content designed to impress and establish the context in which she was writing. College writing often asks you to discover and articulate your own rhetorical context. Only by doing so can you make the otherwise artificial classroom relevant, both intellectually and personally.

You can do so first by reaching out to readers—to your instructor, to be sure, but also to your fellow students, and even to readers off campus. The faces Jennifer saw in class were not that vague abstraction known as the general audience. The faces belonged to peers eager to hear what she had to say. Sheer information would not do. She had to come to terms with her audience by reflecting on their needs, on who she was when she wrote, and on why she was writing. What interested—yet still puzzled—them about environmental problems? What faulty assumptions might they have? The discussion in her writing workshop convinced her that only by subjecting her opinions to a reader's reasoned response could she understand what she and her audience already knew and what both still needed to learn. The assignment, in the end, asked her to establish context for herself—intellectually as well as personally. And in so doing, it asked her to speak not as a student to a professor but as an equal, a writer engaging readers.

To establish an intellectual context, you must know your subject well or, perhaps more importantly, be willing to explore it with an open and curious mind. In the process you'll accumulate a good deal of information. But information alone will not lend context. You'll need to discern the state of an ongoing discussion. Given what you've read and learned from others about the topic, what still puzzles you? What do your readers take as self-evident, and what still perplexes them? You establish your rhetorical situation by determining questions at issue and for whom those questions are a matter of concern or debate. You are then able to write in an informed context—informed not by information alone, but by your awareness of relevant questions.

In college, rhetorical situations don't necessarily come ready-made. They are for you to discover and shape through shared inquiry. To make your rhetorical situation concrete, you may find it useful to create scenarios—for yourself and your readers—that flesh out for whom you are writing, and why. Jennifer, for example, can sharpen her interest in the environment, and thus help shape her paper, if she bears in mind specific questions that she or her readers might have, and the contexts in which those questions would be relevant. College classes can help you craft rhetorical situations by having you place your own ideas and assertions before others to be tested, debated, and appreciated. Shared inquiry lends context to college writing.

Adjust Your Scope to Suit Time and Space

Deadlines and required page lengths are also part of the context in which you write. For Jennifer, the three-page limit on her paper seemed like a pleasant relief at first, but as she engaged her topic more closely it became a real burden. Constraints ask you to separate ore from slag. To this day I recall a history course I took in college that required a weekly paper on a reading we were discussing. Because the paper could only be one page long, I worked hard to narrow and focus my topic, define the issue I wanted to address, and articulate and support my own response. Constraints such as these force you to find purpose, point, and plan in your prose.

Because there is never enough time to explore the complete world of your topic, you must limit your field of interest. Broad topics invite superficial treatment. If your paper just skims the surface, you will learn very little by writing it, and your reader will profit little from having stayed with you. At best you can only recycle well-worn platitudes or make superficial observations. When it comes to your paper's topic, less is more. By focusing on a sharply limited topic, you can support your assertions with specific evidence and close observation. Good writing sparks interest because it engages details and uses them to make fresh sense of general notions. In choosing a topic, then, you become responsible for more than naming your subject; you also commit yourself to treating the topic responsibly and to rewarding readers for their interest.

You may shy away from narrow topics because you feel you simply don't know enough about the subject to sustain a five-, ten-, or twenty-page paper. This sentiment can mislead you from the start. If you limit your topic to what you know at the outset, you will never learn from writing, nor will your readers win new insights. What you know will change as you write the paper. That is, after all, one of the reasons for writing. What you thought was a frightfully narrow topic when you started may prove to have a reach you never suspected once you immerse yourself in the material. Instead of focusing on a topic, pursue questions that puzzle you and your readers. Unlike topics, questions can grow and mature as you explore your material and shape your case.

By using these three strategies to assess your context, you can discover clues that help you make conscious decisions about the shape your writing will eventually assume. Comments about her many topics and her weak thesis led Jennifer to take a second look at her assignment: "write a three- to four-page analytic paper on a topic of your choice." In hindsight, Jennifer realized she was taking on the world with her broad conservation topic, a concern far too vast for a short paper. Workshop discussion brought out that she was touching on several topics. Scanning her sketch, she now settled on solid waste as the topic. The requirement that the paper be analytic also reminded her of the task behind the topic. Her thesis would have to set ideas into clear relationship, one that wasn't apparent from the outset. No room here for mealy-mouthed statements that seem to say everything while saying nothing. Jennifer decided to reach her audience by avoiding big-think generalities and by orienting the question at issue to the role that each individual plays in creating and solving the solid-waste crisis. Inspired, she began sketching a new paragraph. She still didn't know what her eventual thesis might be, but she knew that by anticipating readers' questions she could already start exploring what she might make of her observations.

Establishing Interest

The second sketch that Jennifer brought to her workshop made it clear that she took earlier comments to heart. She narrowed the scope of her topic to solid waste and tried to say something about the problem. Moreover, by reading up on the subject, she sought to provide an informed context for her own discussion.

(1) America generates nearly 200 million tons of solid waste per year. (2) As this figure continues to rise, management of solid waste is reaching a crisis in the U.S., with over a third of all landfills expected to close in the next five years. (3) Part of the problem is that 75 percent of America's trash is buried in landfills, 10 percent is incinerated, with recycling accounting for only the remaining 15 percent. (4) Many U.S. businesses and government agencies are trying to increase the collection, processing, and marketing of recyclable materials to ease the pressure on landfills. (5) A drawback to these recycling efforts, however, is that after the materials have been separated, there is no guarantee that there will be a market for them. (7) An important and immediate impact on this garbage overload can be made by

creating less waste. (8) The amount of waste generated can be cut in half simply by shopping wisely, recycling, and reusing as much as possible.

Jennifer's classmates saw progress. They were impressed with her command of the material, and they liked the topic, which was now far more manageable in scope. But when they looked past the information, they didn't have a clear grasp of the implicit dialogue in which that information was being used. Nor did they feel engaged enough to participate.

"You do a fine job of providing us with information," they said, "but do we really need all of this right at the very beginning? We're looking for the specific issue that interests you—and should interest us. You may be writing on garbage dumps, but please do more than give us an information dump. If we bother to look closely, we find you are writing to us about the choices each one of us makes, but we're sorry to see you come off like a bureaucrat carrying an attaché case. Most readers won't be patient enough to follow you as you gradually funnel into your paper. You could capture our attention if you engaged the question at issue right away. The real shame is that you have something important to say, but you bury it in background."

One classmate, who had a way of reducing complex ideas to basic propositions, asked if Jennifer's thesis in sentence 7 wasn't simply saying that we can reduce waste by creating less waste. And if so, wasn't it all a bit obvious? Jennifer looked at her paragraph through her readers' eyes and saw that it held less than she had thought.

"But what about my last sentence?" she asked. "I'm mentioning three specific ways to create less waste."

"That's fine," the class replied, "but it all smacks of a shopping list. What can you do with it but describe how-to instructions? As to recycling, most of us have heard about it by now. What are you going to tell us in a paragraph or two that we don't already know?"

One classmate, puzzled by the reference to reusing, wondered aloud whether it was a useful category. "Wouldn't recycling already cover much of what you might say about reusing? And might the section on shopping wisely already address decisions to buy what one can reuse?"

"That all depends on what is meant by shopping wisely," someone added. Jennifer jumped in to explain. "Shopping wisely is sort of the mirror image of recycling. That's why some people call it precycling. It's a way to help consumers become aware of what they buy so that they generate less waste later on and can recycle more easily the waste that they do produce. When I volunteer with the community recycling project, I can't help but think that precycling and recycling go hand in hand."

The class was fascinated. They wanted to hear more. "Why not focus your paper on precycling," someone suggested. "It suits the question of individual action that you raise." The instructor added that if Jennifer could clarify the relationship between precycling and recycling, she might have a strong analytic thesis. A tightly conceived paper on precycling—perfect.

Look for Interests in the Information

Although Jennifer's topic—and yours—stakes out an area, it can mask something far more vital and productive: the relationship you and your audience have to the topic. Topics don't come to you neutrally, nor can you assume that audiences receive them neutrally. *Interests* are at stake. Whether you think of the word *interest* in terms of fascination, bias, concern, or motive, all of us know and interpret our world through our relationship to it, our perspective on it. The best way to approach a topic is not to attach names to areas of knowledge but to sort out interests that influence how we know.

Like Jennifer, if you try to narrow your topic, you may still find it difficult to deal with because it remains encyclopedic. By moving from topic to subtopic—from the environment to solid waste—you may succeed in narrowing the size of the encyclopedia, but covering information will still be your preoccupation and may still be your worry. Jennifer hoped her more narrow topic would help her find a stronger thesis. But information alone didn't help her lend point to her writing.

You can lend information relevance if you consider the interests that guide how you and your readers approach it. Classroom discussion helped Jennifer uncover that shared interest: precycling. Don't hesitate to ask yourself what readers are ready to ask you: "Why do you care?" For care you must if the paper is to have any vitality at all. Interests energize information; they set in motion what might otherwise be a museum-piece topic, labeled and listed but hardly alive. Moreover, only by committing yourself emotionally and intellectually to a topic can you establish a genuine relationship with your readers. If you do not care about your topic, why should they? As to your readers, what sort of interests do they bring to your topic? Do those interests differ from your own? What would it take to spark their interest? What does your audience know about your topic, and what concerns have motivated their understanding? Interests, not information, bring writer and reader together.

Find Meaning in Your Own Perspective

As the animated discussion about precycling brought to light Jennifer's specific interest, the class regretted that she had hidden herself from readers. "By writing yourself out of this paper," they said, "you are writing off your interests—your personal observations and experience. But the discussion we're having shows that personal perspective helps us see the specific problem you're addressing.

What's more, it would help us read your paper if we could hear your own voice on the page as you analyze the problem you see. By insisting on a neutral stance and the passive voice, you leave no room for yourself. We want to hear from you, not some nameless bureaucrat."

Confused, Jennifer replied that her own voice shouldn't have a place in an academic paper. But the class disagreed, and so did her instructor. A paper should grow out of your own interest, experience, and commitment. In that sense, what you write on should be personal. Academic writing does ask you to account for facts, observations, and experiences that you and your readers hold in common or that they can verify. For this reason, academic writing often seems more formal than personal reminiscence or narrative. Nevertheless, only by placing the stamp of your own imagination on information and observation can you ever hope to say anything that is distinctively your own. While your own self may not be the subject of the essay, the inferences you make and justify should nevertheless reflect your own intellect and sensibility.

By looking for interests in the information and by finding meaning in your own perspective, you can commit to a topic that you care about—intellectually and emotionally. Your own commitment will help you engage your readers even as you engage your material. Moreover, by examining specific interests you can reduce a seemingly overwhelming assignment to manageable proportions. In doing so you are already shaping your paper-to-be. The specific interest that motivates you and your readers to entertain a topic can provide the focused occasion that launches your actual prose. To lend your prose a point, derive significance for your readers by calling on, refining, and verifying your own perspective.

Elated about writing on precycling, Jennifer planned her revision. She'd be ruthless in cutting back her opening funnel, for she now saw her task as placing information in the service of an issue and a point. By evaluating interests, she'd establish an occasion—both for herself and for her readers. Yet the hardest, riskiest part of revision was writing herself into the essay. Could she craft an academic paper that granted a role to her own perspective and voice? Could she unmask herself without being trite, or speak without falling into her habitual "official style"? She decided to try.

Achieving Focus

When Jennifer submitted her revised sketch, she felt uneasy about her work. Had she understood the various suggestions that the class and instructor had made? And did she implement those suggestions well, or had she gone too far? She trusted that the response of her readers would highlight unresolved issues in her own text.

> (1) Each of us generates more than half a ton of solid waste every year. (2) Not only does this waste leak toxins into groundwater and pollute other natural resources, we lack sufficient capacity in many parts of the country to manage this trash. (3) To ease the pressure on landfills, my roommates and I recycle glass and newspapers each week by setting them out by the curb for pick-up. (4) It's a chore, but we like to think we are doing our part. (5) In fact, I've recently volunteered to serve as the recycling coordinator for our neighborhood. (6) This job has taught me that recycling is not the only answer. (7) By shopping conscientiously, or precycling, we can reduce the amount of waste we generate in our own homes. (8) By choosing products that are packaged efficiently and by avoiding throwaway products, each person can have an important and immediate impact on this garbage overload.

Jennifer's classmates applauded her progress. The precycling angle interested them, and they appreciated how the text now addressed them personally as readers. Jennifer had a reason to write, and they felt inspired to read.

But the very changes Jennifer made also brought to light new concerns. Her classmates found that revision does more than help improve a paper; it also improves their ability to ask intelligent questions. "We understand you're trying to connect recycling with precycling. And you bring in personal experience to draw that connection. But just as you are about to, you drop the ball. Look, your thesis doesn't even mention a connection; we're just back to 'shopping wisely can reduce waste.' As a result, the opening now seems merely personal."

Jennifer couldn't help but chime in. "I thought you wanted me to write myself into the paper." "We're glad you did," came the reply, "and doing so has made your writing more readable. But now it's time to edit a bit of yourself out."

To provide your own informed perspective on an issue, you need not write in the first person. An objective style, one that uses the third person, can still communicate your distinctive perceptions and sensibilities, and the human quality of your own voice. What Jennifer and her roommates did, and what she learned as recycling coordinator, would only matter if they helped her readers focus on the problem she wanted to address. Her readers still didn't have that problem in focus. "All you're saying is that there's more than one answer," Jennifer's readers told her. "Why not raise an issue that points to the recycling/precycling connection right from the start? Is recycling, by itself, bound to be incomplete, always less than an answer? If that's the question at issue, say so."

The comments helped Jennifer see the issue that her writing implied but never expressed. And with the issue now in focus, she saw how her thesis and reasons failed to say much of interest. Her classmates were quick to agree. "Your thesis promises little more than a description of precycling. And as for your reasons, they're really nothing more than a list of examples: if you buy this, you eliminate this waste; if you buy that, you eliminate that waste." And sure enough, Jennifer's plans for the development paragraphs of her essay were every bit as formulaic. Even as she was searching for a focused question as her occasion, she was clinging to familiar patterns and ideas.

Establish the Question at Issue

When you sort out interests, you become aware of the issues that lie behind the tidy one- or two-word tag you may give as your topic. Because you can't deal with all of these concerns, you must achieve focus by identifying the question at issue. That question may be

- an outright disagreement,
- a shared but unresolved concern or problem,
- a hidden contradiction, or
- a questionable assumption.

Perhaps the single most important step in moving from topic to thesis lies in the step from topic to issue. Without a question to answer, you will find it difficult to generate an analytic or argumentative reply. Indeed, you may be better off by starting not with a topic but with a question. By posing a question at issue, you avoid the agonizing search to "find something to say." You start instead with a concern that you and your audience share. The paper, in turn, becomes a process of shared inquiry, a search for a solution or appropriate assertion and the good reasons that such a position requires.

The questions you pose can help you discover why you are writing and what you have to say. Moreover, those questions can help you look for information and can accommodate the new expertise you will surely acquire about your topic. The strategy of identifying a question at issue enables you to focus your efforts as you begin to write. It also serves to orient your readers' attention.

The Advantage of Questions

As Jennifer's class discussed achieving focus through a question at issue, they found that the strategy has distinct advantages.

• Unlike narrowing your topic at the margins or chipping away from its edges, identifying a question at issue allows you to go to the heart of your concern. Once you identify the issue, extraneous concerns and material will drop away of their own accord.

• By identifying an issue, not merely narrowing your field of vision, you can avoid the tendency to be encyclopedic. The notion that you must cover a topic can often lead to mere description. Because an issue requires both a response and reasoned support, finding the question at issue will help you maintain an analytic or argumentative focus.

• A question at issue enables you to gather and read material in an intelligent and critical fashion. Passive consumption of information, mere note taking, will rarely prompt an analytic or argumentative reply. You'll profit from reading and research as you formulate and refine your questions.

• When you identify a question at issue, you are better able to find the reply that serves as your thesis. Questions elicit replies. Moreover, if you identify a question at issue, you help ensure that your response matters.

• A question at issue allows you to identify, understand, and write for your audience. After all, an issue must be an issue for someone. As you refine your sense of audience, how you articulate the question at issue may also change.

• By identifying a question at issue you spark interest in and lend energy to your writing. If the question is well known or controversial, you can tap into concerns already shared by your audience. If the question is not well known, you have the opportunity to create interest by revealing the question in a manner that would intrigue your audience.

Without a question at issue, you merely have a topic, perhaps a very predictable one. If you write on it without taking a distinctive angle, your readers' eyes may glaze over. Duty bound, your instructor will read the paper from start to finish, but with the impatience and disgruntlement that comes from taking in information passively, if at all, or from hearing well-worn ideas recycled still one more time.

When you achieve focus by establishing the question at issue, you are much more likely to discover your own ideas. Subject areas named by your topic may represent what you already know or what you have already read. Questions at issue, however, ask more of you. They resist easy answers and rehearsed positions. If those questions are genuine, they will prompt you to find out more about the material, to challenge accepted notions, and to explore your own mind on the matter. An issue or problem enables you to make the topic your own, even if it started out as generic or even if it were assigned to the whole class. When you achieve focus by framing the question at issue, you place the mark of your own experience, insight, and imagination on the material.

Comments about her sketch convinced Jennifer that she still clung to familiar ideas and prepackaged bundles of facts—patterns that no longer served her well. At first a matter of convenience, those old patterns were now plaguing her paper. She set about to question, gather, and sort anew with an eye to finding fresh patterns.

Finding Patterns

How do you find patterns in an otherwise bewildering thicket of details, observations, and facts? Creative insight and sudden inspiration lie behind many of those electrifying moments when you see patterns for the first time. Yet serendipity makes for poor strategy. Inspiration may not be there when you need it most. If shaping analysis or argument is not to be all hit or miss, you need a method for exploring your material that also helps shape your own case.

A strategy particularly suited to the demands of analysis and argument helps you find patterns in your material by *questioning*, *gathering*, and *sorting*. These three activities are simultaneous, not sequential. Your focus may shift from one activity to another, but you are at work on all three fronts. These activities, moreover, are mutually reinforcing; each enlivens and enriches the other two. Neglect any one and the other two suffer.

How do questioning, gathering, and sorting bear on the writing process? The activities reflect the very questions that readers ask when they look for and evaluate meaningful patterns. Both finding patterns as a writer and looking for them as a reader involve interpretation. The three activities also anticipate answers to readers' questions. An issue or concern provides the occasion for your writing, the information and observations you gather establish the evidence you need, and the possible assertions you sort through help specify the thesis that your essay seeks to justify.

With her topic now tightly focused on precycling and its relationship to recycling, Jennifer found she had to consider her observations and information anew. Half-formed convictions, random impressions, and unexamined assumptions could only get her so far. In addition to some very directed library work, Jennifer decided to contact the head of the local community recycling office. She soon wished she had done so earlier, for she came across firsthand information and insight that books couldn't possibly provide. She also decided to make an expedition to the local grocery, armed not with a shopping list but with a notepad. Interviews and field research were a pleasant change from musty books, and turned out to be far more helpful. In fact, the grocery store became for Jennifer something of a "text." As she looked at products on the shelves and read labels with consumer decisions in mind, she asked questions to uncover the central issue and gathered information that would serve her analysis. In the process, she hoped to sort out how precycling related to recycling. As she pursued these three inter-related activities, patterns began to emerge.

Questioning

Because analysis and argument do more than certify what is already known, you must risk asking questions about what you don't know. You must acknowledge and scrutinize your own uncertainty, your own bewilderment. Risk is essential to the essay form, and nowhere more so than when writing analysis and argument. You must test and articulate an interpretation that is not self-evident or justify a position that may be hotly debated. Analysis and argument thus make positive use of uncertainty, dissonance, and contradiction.

Experienced writers cultivate questions. Without questions, there is little point to pursuing an analysis or argument. Sometimes the question is given to you, as in an essay exam. The question may also be apparent from context, as when voters are asked to decide a ballot proposition. More frequently, however, interesting questions may not be apparent at the outset. As you consider those questions, you may find that you can answer most of them. Apparent questions can disappear upon closer reading or keener observation. But there remain the honest questions that resist simple answers. Those questions can help you discern patterns in your material, for the questions themselves require you to relate and support ideas as you pursue a response.

To cultivate questions, you need to develop a willingness to look closely. Abstract or big-think questions are seldom useful, for they have a way of dis-solving into vague assertions. Try instead to edge a potential question into a tight corner, where you can put your finger on it and say, "This is the problem; this is the question at issue." The more specific your question, the more pointed your reply. Also consider whether the question is trivial. Does the question matter, and is the pursuit of an answer worth your careful attention?

As you consider what you observe and know—or in the case of a written text, what you actually read on the page—try to articulate the crux of a question as follows:

• "It strikes me that the question is . . . , and it matters because. . . ."

As you jot down informal responses in a notebook, entertain different ways of seeing the problem. As you become better acquainted with the issue, reformulate your reply to make it more pointed, more penetrating. As you learn more about your topic, keep returning to this question, for questions have a way of changing right before your eyes. Some will answer themselves and disappear altogether, while more pressing questions may crop up unexpectedly.

Three techniques can help you uncover questions at issue that may otherwise escape your attention.

Question your material   Close reading and keen observation remain your best tools for uncovering insightful questions, so it is necessary to develop an eye for detail. Jennifer found that consumers who might otherwise recycle often chose goods in hard-to-recycle plastic containers, or favored elaborately packaged foods when the items were readily available in bulk. Note contradictions and questions that arise as you consider your topic. You needn't shy away from matters of uncertainty, confusion, or disagreement, for dissonance, when identified and clearly defined, can spark the most interesting discussions. Finally, favor the interesting detail over big-think generalities; engaging writing uses the concrete to rethink the general.

Question your audience   Might your readers see the material differently than you do? Jennifer paused to consider that her readers might see little connection between setting out newspapers for recycling and deciding whether to buy laundry soap in a box made of recycled fiber. Were the problems she found problems for them? What issues might they spot that ought to concern her as well? What motives and assumptions might her audience bring to the discussion? Take on and test out the perspectives of several audiences. In short, play the role of audience yourself. In the process you will discover concerns and problems that bear analysis and debate.

Question your own inferences   When you explore material, you are constantly drawing conclusions. Some of the most intriguing questions at issue arise when you consider what and how you infer. When Jennifer heard that the price paid for recycled newsprint has plummeted in the last several years, she inferred that it reflected the growing popularity of recycling. More newspapers were being set out at the curb. Yet when she cruised the aisles of the supermarket, she saw the matter in a broader context: perhaps low consumer demand for recycled fiber contributes to the low price. As you become aware of and question your inferences, you may start rethinking how you form concepts and relate ideas. Consider not so much the isolated insight but the patterns in which you place it. After all, we turn to analysis and argument when we are uncertain about how we perceive relationships.

As you question, you will also find that you can gather and sort more effectively. Questions orient you as you gather material, and lend purpose to your

To cultivate the habit of sorting out what you mean, you need to become conscious of the extent to which you are already making meaning. Although you may not be fully aware of it, you are already sorting through observations and experiences and drawing conclusions. Analysis and argument make the process more explicit and rigorous. Having posed questions and gathered material as you work your way toward possible conclusions, you'll find that college writing often asks you to invert the process. You must now state your position at the outset, and then defend it as would a lawyer before a skeptical jury. To become more aware of your inferences and the justification they require, articulate your hypothesis and keep on refining it in light of available evidence; for example,

- "My response to this issue is that . . . , and the reasons justifying this response are. . . ."

As you note your point, consider contradictory evidence and alternative conclusions. Try to formulate the question at issue in ways that will prompt different hypotheses. Above all, keep returning to the question "What is my response, my point?" As you learn more about the issue and become familiar with your material, you'll want to refine—or totally rethink—both your answer and the reasons that lend it credibility.

Three techniques can help you arrive at and sort out possible conclusions.

Consider what you might have left out   The tentative conclusion you arrive at may not reflect all of your observations. Early on, Jennifer thought of recycling in its own terms, as answer in its own right. But as she observed more closely, she found that she had left out the consumer side of the equation. Most preliminary hypotheses need revision because they are incomplete. They don't account for available evidence; they don't square with the facts. If you find that evidence can point you in a variety of directions, take another look at the question you have posed. By reformulating the question at issue, you can alter the grounds of analysis and argument and thereby prompt a slightly different reply.

Evaluate biases and questionable assumptions   What you find when you sort is often determined by the screen through which you look. Jennifer's own curbside recycling, and what she assumed about it, may have launched her paper, but when writing she soon found that she had to reenvision her experience. Biases and assumptions do screen what you see, hiding some aspects and making others visible. The screen will lead you to sort in a particular way. Although all analysis and argument proceeds on the basis of some assumptions, you should evaluate what those assumptions are and whether alternative assumptions might not lead you to different—more effective—conclusions.

Consider rival hypotheses   By keeping an eye out for alternative conclusions, you are asking yourself "What else might explain these facts, or what else might I conclude from them?" When Jennifer first examined the role of recycling in reducing solid waste, she thought that the success of recycling hinged solely on getting more citizens involved. Yet as she looked more closely, she recognized and adopted a different hypothesis: shopping decisions that consumers make can either further or hinder recycling efforts. Because more than one explanation might fit what you observe, try to generate rival hypotheses that push you to reconsider the validity of your own tentative conclusion. By weighing the merits of alternative explanations and positions, you can sort out a responsible answer to a question at issue.

As you sort out what you mean, you also gain a better grasp of what questions to ask and what material to gather. Since questions prompt replies, the conclusions you arrive at can help you rethink your questions. In fact, if you don't sort out what you think, there's little point to posing those questions. Likewise, a tentative hypothesis can help you gather relevant material and information. Actually, information can serve as evidence only when you have a possible conclusion in mind. If you wish to find patterns, be conscious of what you are concluding, and be ready to reconsider what you think.

You might think of questioning, gathering, and sorting as the three legs of a tripod. Neglect any one leg, and the other two offer little support or utility. Each of the three activities can help you find patterns and discern relationships because each reinforces the work of the other two. As you clarify your question, gather your material, and sharpen your point, you are already shaping your occasion and the reasons that might justify your thesis.

By checking the store shelves and thinking about shopping decisions, Jennifer refined the hypothesis for her paper: the decision to recycle comes too late to do much good; precycling decisions are necessary to make recycling work. Patterns for her paper began to emerge. With renewed confidence, she refined and tested them as she wrote out another introductory sketch.

> (1) In recent years, the United States has devoted much attention to recycling as an efficient answer to its waste management problems. (2) However, only 15 percent of America's trash is currently recycled. (3) By making a few wise shopping decisions, or "precycling," individuals can aid recycling efforts at the point of demand. (4) Consumers can purchase products

with minimal packaging, products packaged in recyclable containers, and products packaged in or made from recycled materials.

By enlarging and reenvisioning her own observations and experience, Jennifer found new patterns. Now she was ready to put them to the test.

Testing Relationships

When Jennifer wrote her first sketch, she was preoccupied with her own thoughts and impressions. But as she worked on each new sketch, she became increasingly aware of a different challenge: presenting ideas for the reader.

The strategies we have discussed can help launch your paper precisely because they contribute to actual writing meant to be read. In the end, you must justify your ideas in the public, goal-directed act of writing. The strategies introduced in this chapter culminate and find their utility in testing relationships among ideas before your readers.

Shift Roles from Writer to Reader

The best way to test relationships among your ideas is to examine them as would your most skeptical readers. Writing for yourself is by no means the same as writing to be read. To help you bridge the gap, you'll find that elements of form can serve double duty throughout the writing process. They provide both a way to generate shape and an analytic tool to test its coherence. Call on them whether you are the reader or the writer. Indeed, developing and testing your sketch actually require that you shift roles; if you play the writer shaping prose, you must also learn to inhabit the mind of the reader who discerns and evaluates its shape.

Introductory sketches allow you to know your own mind by explaining yourself to others. Random notes and journal entries can help you capture and reflect on your experiences. But the introductory sketch enables you to communicate to others the emerging shape of your ideas. In a sense, these sketches help you collaborate with your readers early on as you explore ideas and set them in relationship. Comments from these readers can help you discover how they construe your ideas so that you can then construct tighter, more persuasive relationships. Even if you are laboring alone on a paper, by asking the sorts of questions an intelligent reader might pose, you can become a perceptive critic and editor of your own work.

Like most writers, you can profit by adopting both roles as you draft and revise your work. Discussion in the writing workshop helped Jennifer do precisely that. As she commented on her classmates' writing, she began to see and develop strategies that would help her refine her own prose. When her new sketch came up for review, she was likewise eager to test relationships from a reader's perspective.

Confirm Your Own Editorial Hunches

Cheers went up when the class read Jennifer's latest effort. Special praise was accorded the thesis, which was much more analytic. Jennifer felt that if she could maintain that analytic focus, and draw clear relationships to it, the paper would write itself. Once so eager for a kind word, Jennifer now cut short the praise; she wanted to put her ideas to the test. With the final draft due in several days, she wanted to check her own editorial hunches against the response of her readers.

The class was ready to help with perceptive suggestions. They confirmed what Jennifer already suspected about her paper, for she was now learning to ask tough questions of her own writing from a reader's perspective. One classmate found that the phrase "point of demand" was especially helpful, but that Jennifer needed to set it up by suggesting early on its opposite. Perhaps "point of disposal" would do. Another friend suggested that the focus on product packaging, so clear in the final sentence, should be made more explicit in the thesis. The occasion might also focus on why packaging is such a problem. A third suggestion quickly followed: the reasons that project the shape of her paper aren't closely tied to the thesis and, moreover, they're tough to follow in one long sentence. Why not break that sentence up into manageable chunks? Doing so might give Jennifer a chance to suggest, if only briefly, why each shopping decision aids recycling.

Armed with helpful suggestions and buoyed with renewed confidence, Jennifer revised what was now becoming the polished introduction to her paper. By working through introductory sketches as she had, she was able to develop and revise the full paper with much greater confidence and ease. Only by putting each sketch to the test before readers could she see problems inherent in the shape she gave to her ideas. In turn, she was discovering creative possibilities for the paper that would otherwise have gone unnoticed. She needed successive drafts of the introductory sketch to find her way. But only now, with the full paper in nearly polished form, could she go back one last time and guide her readers on their way as they began to read.

(1) Americans may look to recycling as an answer to their waste management woes, but only 15 percent of our trash is currently recycled. (2) Of the rising mountains of solid waste, packaging accounts for half of the vol-

ume and 30 percent of the weight. (3) Whatever its virtues, recycling itself may be an inefficient answer because it emphasizes choices we make solely at the point of waste disposal. (4) By "precycling," that is, by making a few wise shopping decisions about product packaging at the point of demand, consumers can aid recycling efforts. (5) When consumers purchase products with minimal packaging, they decrease the total amount of material that must be recycled or disposed. (6) Moreover, when they buy items packaged in easily recycled containers such as aluminum or glass, they increase the percent of household trash they can recycle. (7) Finally, by purchasing products made from or packaged in recycled materials, consumers create a larger market for these goods and thereby help guarantee the success of the recycling industry.

Like all of us engaged in writing, Jennifer found it challenging to launch a paper. Beginnings can frustrate even veteran writers. But if Jennifer enjoyed some success, as I believe she did, she succeeded because she was not concerned solely with beginning. She was also not content to believe that each beginning was its own unsolvable mystery. She was interested in relating means and ends, in finding a point of departure and a problem-solving process that would lead to analysis and argument.

Jennifer's sketches provided more than a point of departure for her writing; they became a laboratory for learning and thinking. As she wrote, her ideas took shape. By calling on the strategies that were discussed in this chapter, you too can use your writing to discover and shape ideas.

Part III

Testing
Ideas

Troubleshooting Your Thesis 5

Once your paper is under way, you may be tempted to let it go its own way. But will your paper capture your best thinking and thus represent you well? Chances are it won't—unless you do some troubleshooting as you go.

As you develop your ideas, you'll want to refine them, to craft with growing precision the relationships you draw. This section will help you test the emerging shape of your ideas. And what better place to start than with the engine of your paper, your thesis? By noting how particular thesis statements can influence the shape of your paper, you can revise your way out of potential or real misadventures. Moreover, a bit of troubleshooting can help you pursue adventures worth your time and your reader's attention.

This chapter will help you understand why various thesis formulations can cause difficulties for an analytic or argumentative paper. I've grouped my recommendations under four headings, each addressing common concerns.

- launching the go-nowhere thesis
- strengthening the underpowered thesis
- sorting out multiple theses
- clarifying the cryptic thesis

Specific thesis types in each group will help you recognize the characteristics of a troublesome thesis and understand the consequences of leaving it unrevised. I can't mention all possible misadventures, nor are the categories I describe mutually exclusive. You may encounter a problematic thesis that is not listed, or find one that shares the characteristics of several types. The examples are meant to help you consider the adequacy and implications of your assertions regardless of type.

Throughout we'll consider some strategies for revising or otherwise rethinking a problematic thesis. These strategies will acquaint you with the conceptual moves that experienced writers employ when refining a thesis. As you become adept at reworking thesis statements, you will be able to spot the distinctive problems in your own prose and respond insightfully and creatively.

126

Before we begin, a few general tips for the novice troubleshooter. To make your work productive and enjoyable, you'll need to approach it with the right attitude. More than a means to find flaws, troubleshooting allows you to seize creative opportunity. Here's how.

• Treat your thesis as provisional, as subject to scrutiny and revision even through your last draft. By doing so, you can develop a capacity for intellectual play that leads to creative insight. The revisions you make lie not at the surface level but involve instead the basic thrust of your analysis or argument. For this reason, the work is ongoing and intellectually challenging.

• Anticipate problems and opportunities by considering where your thesis will send you and your readers, and what evidence or proof it might require. Your ability to judge what implications your thesis holds for your paper can spare you many false starts and time-consuming drafts. What's more, testing ideas without resorting to lengthy drafts can help you write and think well under pressure.

• Exploit your misadventures. Some rough drafts are crucial precisely because apparent misadventure has led you to unexpected insights. These insights, in turn, might help you reformulate your analysis or argument. No matter how well conceived, every draft is to one degree or another an adventure worth refining.

Launching the Go-Nowhere Thesis

If your thesis represents the conclusion you arrive at by reasoning from evidence, it ought to get you somewhere. If you sense that your thesis hasn't left home plate, you might have on your hands a version of the go-nowhere thesis—an assertion that is not an arguable opinion. Let's explore two typical varieties of the go-nowhere thesis and your options for launching a more rewarding adventure.

The Self-Evident Thesis

The need to fill up a blank page and the lingering fear that you don't have anything to say may tempt you to focus merely on what you already know, not on what you can discover. As a result, your thesis may offer little more than a statement of fact. Or, it may advance an idea so self-evident or widely held that any discussion would simply restate the obvious.

When I've asked students to analyze the architecture of a campus landmark built soon after the Civil War, some are content to assert the self-evident: "Built in 1875, Old Main reflects Civil War–era architecture." Literature students may likewise be tempted by self-evident plot summary: "*The Great Gatsby* traces the education of its narrator, Nick Carraway." Other students may, in turn, cling to fact: "The price of recycled newsprint has plummeted."

These writers will have trouble developing their papers because they can only restate the obvious. Sheer redundancy will stall these essays after little more than a page. At best, a self-evident thesis leads to a museum tour of examples— be they architectural details from Old Main or passages from Fitzgerald's novel. This tour remains essentially descriptive because examples are instances of what the self-evident thesis asserts, not an analysis or argument that justifies why a more penetrating assertion may be valid. A merely descriptive show-and-tell paper frustrates the reader's patience by compounding the initial problem: not only do you have a self-evident thesis, you also illustrate it with obvious examples. The self-evident thesis may be a quick remedy to the fear of the blank page or the anxiety that you may not have much to say, but it doesn't get you—or your reader—very far into a paper.

If you find yourself with a self-evident thesis, don't be too hasty to consign it to the waste basket. Although not particularly interesting in its own right, a self-evident thesis can help you with your next draft because it locates areas of agreement. Your analytic or argumentative task is not to restate agreement but to build on it, to use it, to move forward from it. Here are two revision strategies you might consider.

Place the self-evident thesis as a dependent clause in a new thesis   Completing the sentence will help you find an analytic or argumentative point that will engage readers; for example, "As an embodiment of architectural norms immediately following the Civil War, Old Main reflects the desire of a war-torn nation for renewed stability and shared patriotic symbols." Literature students can likewise use points of agreement to develop new insight; for example, "Because *The Great Gatsby* is really about the education of its narrator, Nick Carraway, his initial discussion with Daisy Buchanan must not be taken at face value. Nick would have us believe that Daisy is a simpering socialite, when in fact she is intelligent and sensitive." Whenever you find yourself with a thesis that you suspect to be weak, trite, or obvious, explore how you might push the thesis—and your thinking—one step further by using the existing thought to generate a further assertion. Here are some patterns you might bear in mind.

Although	[self-evident assertion]	,	[new thesis]	.
Because		,		.
By		,		.
If		,		.
When		,		.
As		,		.

A thesis can do more than state what you already know; it can also help you discover fresh insights.

Ask yourself for whom your thesis is self-evident, and then clarify the expectations of your potential readers   Some assertions may be obvious to one audience, yet far from self-evident to another. Revise your thesis as you become aware of your audience's interests and needs. For example, an analysis of the market forces that affect the price of recycled newsprint could be either self-evident or revealing, inconsequential or pertinent, depending on your audience. Are you addressing a home owner who sets out paper to be recycled, a client of a printing company who is choosing the paper stock on which to print a publication, or workers at a recycling company who must cope with a glut in the recycled paper market? If you start your paper by articulating a genuine issue that addresses the concerns of your audience, you are less likely to arrive at a self-evident assertion. The less artificial or generic your occasion, the less self-evident the thesis responding to it.

If you content yourself with a thesis that does little more than restate the obvious, your reader can't hope to fight off yawns after the first paragraph. The point of revising your thesis is to discover what you have to say that others may not yet have heard.

The Merely Personal Thesis

Although we all have tastes and hold opinions, it's difficult to analyze or argue such matters when the grounds of support remain merely personal. Why? Writer and reader cannot participate in a process of shared inquiry. You may like chocolate ice cream, while I prefer pistachio. You may find hang gliding challenging, while someone else might respond that breeding roses is every bit as tough. As the grounds of support do not extend beyond individual preference, it's impossible to establish that one flavor is better than another, or one task more challenging than the next. The discussion remains a matter of private assertion, not shared inquiry.

Left unrevised, a merely personal thesis can lead to two misadventures. First, because the criteria behind the opinion remain unclear or entirely idiosyncratic, you will find it difficult to develop your personal opinion into a full analysis or argument that will elicit the support of others. An assertion that rests on personal opinion or taste can only declare itself. You may be able to describe, through any number of examples, the challenging sport of hang gliding. But these examples may not be reasons readers can share. You will end up merely repeating the assertion and insisting—once more, with feeling—on the preference behind the examples. Although full of sincerity and conviction, your paper will lack analytic and argumentative cogency.

A merely personal thesis sends you on a second misadventure virtually from the outset of the paper: it divides your audience into two groups, believers and nonbelievers. When it comes to taste or personal opinion, you can say little as an author that will convince skeptical readers to abandon the attitudes they have. Likewise, you have little need to say much at all to readers who already share your preference.

To determine whether or not a thesis is merely personal, you must look beyond the immediate wording of the assertion to its grounds of support. "I feel that term limitations in Congress would reduce the influence of political action committees" may sound like a merely personal opinion if we focus on the opening qualifier "I feel." Yet the assertion can be the object of shared inquiry. On the other hand, a statement lacking a personal qualifier may seem more objective, even though it rests entirely on personal preference: "Cajun cooking is the most delicious of American cuisines."

Opinions whose support does not extend beyond personal preference remain nonstarters for an analytic or argumentative paper. But some opinions that give the impression of being merely personal actually harbor an arguable opinion. These are worth revising. To render such a thesis accessible to analysis or argument, consider one of the following three strategies.

Make terms that suggest personal opinion far more specific and clear   Simply by reconsidering your choice of words, you can make a thesis announcing itself as a sweeping assertion of taste or personal opinion far more specific and accessible to shared inquiry. In some cases a brief working definition can help you tie down a troublesome concept or word. For example, instead of reaching for a loaded or ambiguous phrase such as *inept writing*, specify what you mean. Are you pointing to writing flawed by numerous sentence-level errors, such as misspelling and incorrect syntax, or perhaps unfocused writing that wanders without making a clear point?

Shift the focus of your thesis from adjectives and adverbs to nouns and verbs   Instead of relying on adjectives and adverbs (qualifiers that often express personal opinion and taste), favor concrete nouns and robust verbs that clarify your assertion. As an added bonus, your thesis will become leaner and more precise. Instead of arguing that "multicultural education is *effective*," you may be better off asserting that "multicultural education *affects* certain students in a particular way."

Revise your thesis so that it focuses on shared grounds of support   Many of your opinions may combine personal preference with more objective grounds of support. If you were to assert that "Physics 100 was a lousy course," your readers would find some reasons more relevant than others: "I never do well in science courses, the lectures were boring, and the grading standards were inconsistent." By addressing support that readers can readily acknowledge, you can reorient your assertion to more solid ground: "The inconsistent grading policy in Physics 100 hindered students from improving their command of the material." Even the comment that the lectures were boring can lead to an arguable thesis if you assert, for example, that "By lecturing only on theory, not practical application, the physics professor failed to develop students' problem-solving abilities." By supporting a more narrow assertion, you still make the case that the course was "lousy," but without resorting to a thesis that smacks of mere personal preference.

Without personal commitment and perspective, writing would not be worth reading. Nevertheless, to justify assertions before your audience, don't analyze or argue solely from taste or personal opinion. If you wish to change attitudes and beliefs, work instead from a thesis whose grounds of support do not depend solely on the person making the assertion.

Strengthening the Underpowered Thesis

Even when your thesis seems to be going somewhere, it may be underpowered. With a bit of troubleshooting and revision, you can pep it up. The underpowered thesis dissipates whatever energy it has because it links ideas loosely, if at all. We'll discuss five varieties of the underpowered thesis. Because they share the same basic problem, we'll turn to a few revision strategies after introducing the various guises that the underpowered thesis might assume.

The One-Dimensional Thesis

Perhaps the worst case of lost power is the one-dimensional thesis, for it mentions just one concept or idea in isolation. In a sense, the one-dimensional thesis merely states the topic of the paper, not an assertion to be analyzed or argued. Here is an example.

> A situation not receiving as much attention as it deserves deals with the obstacles that women students face when pursuing an engineering degree.

Left unrevised, this thesis may engage the author in the rather hopeless task of arguing how much attention is enough attention. What is far more likely, the one-dimensional thesis will engender rather rambling, disjointed prose—in this case, a descriptive catalog of obstacles. Why? Not being anchored to one key assertion, the discussion will tend to wander; evidence will not support one point.

Not that you're unaware of the problem. Most writers seize upon the one-dimensional thesis because it performs a convenient place-holding function. The assertion says in essence, "This is where I'll put my thesis when I figure out what I have to say." Fair enough. Few writers, even experienced ones, know exactly what their thesis will be at the very outset of the writing process. The real problem lies in letting the one-dimensional thesis stand unrevised. It then signals not your core assertion, but rather your inability to come up with one.

The Umbrella Thesis

A promising adventure can turn into a misadventure if you try to fit diverse ideas under one general assertion. The attempt will produce a thesis that is little more than an umbrella covering a motley collection of points. Consider, for example, the following thesis.

> Race relations play a major role not only in national politics but also in campus life.

What is the core assertion? It is merely an umbrella statement, "Race relations play a major role." The thesis serves as a structural tie, a way to bring together two different topics or two as yet undeveloped theses. But as to the specific relationships among race relations, national politics, and campus life, we're not much enlightened. By providing at best a superficial structure, an umbrella thesis can inhibit the intellectual exploration that analytic and argumentative writing ought to encourage.

How might an umbrella thesis influence the shape of your paper? You'll be tempted to pursue several different paths—first national politics, then campus life, with race relations serving as a general thematic link. The paper will be easy to organize, but it remains distinctly underpowered. The more interesting questions remain unaddressed. What role, exactly, do race relations play in national politics? How have recent presidential elections treated the issue? In what respect do race relations influence campus life? How have discussions of race among college students changed over the last three decades? And what bearing do campus discussions have on national politics? In the absence of one strong, compelling thesis, all you have is a collection of discrete points. The result is vagabond prose that can disgruntle or bore your reader.

The List-Generating Thesis

A close cousin of the umbrella thesis, the list-generating thesis offers an easy but superficial way to fill up the page. While the umbrella thesis gathers diverse ideas under a weak common denominator, the list-generating thesis churns out reason after reason, but with little substance behind the apparent regularity and precision.

Consider, for example, the assertion "There are many benefits to holding a part-time job." At first glance, all seems well. In fact, you may already be thinking up benefits. But therein lies the problem with the list-generating thesis. Although it can churn out points to cover with the predictable regularity of a sheet-metal stamping machine, the reader is left in the dark about exactly why—and for whom—a part-time job would have these benefits.

You may be tempted to reach for the list-generating thesis because it is so reassuringly predictable. Crank up this thesis, and it churns out a paper with little effort or thinking on your part. The thesis can produce formulaic papers because the thesis formulation is itself very predictable. A list-generating thesis loosens the tie between topic ("holding a part-time job") and list generator ("many benefits"), thus shifting the energy and focus of the paper to the various items on the assembly-line list. In so doing, it sets for the author an essentially descriptive task. "Benefits" seem to march in rank and file, but the reader is left wondering what well-earned conclusions can be drawn about the relationship between part-time work and its benefits.

The Generic Thesis

The generic thesis tempts writers because it promises to be suitable for everyday use. It can be adapted to virtually any topic and offers a ready-made organizational plan—predictable, dreary, mindless. Consider, for example, the generic sports thesis "Basketball demands speed, skill, and endurance." The same statement could be made of cycling, or field hockey for that matter. The very adaptability of the generic thesis offers a shortcut to developing a paper, yet that shortcut eliminates virtually any thinking. If essentially the same thesis can appear in a variety of papers, what have you really said about basketball, cycling, or field hockey? Precious little. You have merely filled up the page with well-organized paragraphs.

Here are a few more generic theses that fail to engage their subjects, and thus fail to engage the interest of a reader.

> Jogging is healthy for both the body and the mind.

> Television entertains even as it instructs.

> In the search for a perfect mate one should consider appearance, personality, and intellect.

The first statement says nothing about jogging that couldn't be said about, say, karate. The second could be as true of books as of television. As for the desired qualities in the perfect mate, might not they also apply when hiring a sales-clerk?

By now you should be able to recognize the formulaic design inherent in the generic thesis—its reliance on a list of general attributes. The structure lends itself to interchangeable topics, yet the one-size-fits-all approach dooms the paper to vague, trivial generalities. True, the paper will virtually organize itself, one attribute per paragraph or section, but it will lack any incisive thinking. Why? The very structure that permits interchangeable topics also inhibits the writer from developing a close, analytic relationship between the subject and any one attribute.

By reaching for the generic brand-x thesis that can be cloned for any variety of paper, you don't permit yourself to respond to real issues. Left unrevised, a generic thesis will produce, if not a misadventure, then certainly an uneventful, predictable trip—one more walk around the same old block.

The Big-Think Thesis

The allure of the big-think thesis lies in the impression of intellectual mastery that the writer thinks it conveys. When compressed to one central assertion, an author's broad ideas and generalizations seem to carry a certain inevitability and authority about them.

> Erasmus's *In Praise of Folly* is a typical example of humanistic thought and expression in the Renaissance.

Although some readers will be impressed by this statement, the author tends to be even more impressed. And therein lies the problem with the big-think thesis. It gives the author an illusion of accomplishment while actually inhibiting inquiry.

As a writer, you may be tempted by the big-think thesis. Because this type of thesis relies on prefab concepts and distinctions, all you have to do is import them and stitch them together. A few examples from *In Praise of Folly*, a bit of cross-referencing to the Renaissance, and you've got your paper written. Or so you may think.

Although the terms may sound impressive, they are actually very hard to pin down. Scholars disagree about how to define the Renaissance, or for that matter Renaissance humanism; by importing global terms, you are actually making your case softer, not more solid. "Humanistic thought and expression" sounds weighty indeed, but what does it actually mean? Why the doubling of "thought" and "expression"? The most telling weakness, however, lies in the phrase "is a typical example of." Not only are the criteria for judging what is "typical" unclear, the phrase directs attention away from close scrutiny of the text. The paper may virtually write itself, but it will have precious little thinking behind it.

Where might a big-think thesis take your paper? Because the thesis relies on facile generalizations stitched together, it provides an easy way to begin your paper. However, those very generalizations will be difficult to develop, and as you try, the stitching will show. At best, a big-think thesis will resemble the list-generating thesis or the umbrella thesis in that it will produce but a list of examples or gather the most motley group of points under some sweeping generalization. Your paper about *In Praise of Folly* will become little more than a museum tour, where you point out first one attribute and then another. The big-think thesis will produce predictable results precisely because the thinking is not your own. In fact, it offers very little to think about.

Tune-Up Strategies for the Underpowered Thesis

If you're dismayed by the many ways in which your thesis can sputter along, take heart. Even experienced writers tune up their theses as they discover and refine their intentions. Because the underpowered thesis dissipates energy by drawing only very loose connections among ideas, your tune-up task requires that you discover or tighten those links. Four strategies can help you lend energy to your thesis and your thinking.

Link ideas more explicitly by recasting your thesis with an active, transitive verb Underpowered theses typically have a weak verb; for example, "There are many benefits," and "is a typical example of." They may also use indirect or formulaic expressions, such as "a situation not receiving as much attention as it deserves deals with . . ." or "plays a major role in." Underpowered verbs fail to draw vigorous relationships among ideas. You can relate concepts more easily if you choose a strong, active verb, especially a transitive verb that forces you to specify agent, action, and the object of that action. The strategy can help you move beyond single or loosely related concepts (for example, obstacles for women in engineering) to an actual assertion: "An engineering curriculum consisting of large, male-dominated lecture classes fails to recognize the different learning styles that would permit more women to succeed in the field." Powerful verbs like "fails to recognize" don't permit you to waffle or fence sit; they remind you of your obligation to say something *about* your topic. Moreover, they can spark new ideas. Forcing yourself to show your cards helps you discover what you actually have in mind.

Look behind "cover concepts" to draw finer distinctions   Because the underpowered thesis isolates ideas, you may not have looked closely at your key concepts. "Cover concepts" are vague generalizations and broad terms that sound more substantial than they are. To tune up your thesis, you'll need to examine these terms more closely. For example, look behind the cover concept "race relations" to determine what specific racial tensions motivate current discussions, and how those tensions influence the kind of discussion we carry on. Instead of contenting yourself with the generic statement "Basketball demands speed, skill, and endurance," why not look more closely? By recognizing that the endurance required in basketball is similar to that needed in soccer, you might analyze why soccer may be appropriate cross-training for basketball players. A high-powered thesis makes vigorous, specific distinctions. It won't permit empty generalization ("*In Praise of Folly* is a typical example of") but instead will ask you to look inside a book's cover and behind your own cover concepts.

Focus on just one aspect of your support to articulate far more specific relationships   The underpowered thesis offers assorted ideas only loosely related. To draw any link at all, you are forced to reach for a highly generalized connection, a weak common denominator. By selecting just one aspect of your support, you will be in a position to articulate specific relationships with your thesis that would otherwise remain hidden from view. In doing so, you are freezing the action of the list generator ("There are many benefits to . . .") that would otherwise force you to reach for general connections. Instead of relying on a broad umbrella ("plays a major role in") to cover all your points, pull out from underneath it just one concern. By focusing on that one point, you can explore and articulate a more specific relationship. Let's apply the tune-up strategy to the underpowered assertion "The bore, the brag, the flirt—these people typify most cocktail parties." A paper with this thesis could do no better than describe the three personality types, with cocktail parties providing the general setting for the paper. There's no real connection between cocktail parties and personality, for the same personality types could appear in other contexts as well. Pull out "flirt" for a closer look, and you're then able to draw tighter relationships and generate a far more interesting assertion: "The social dynamics of the cocktail party—its relative anonymity, its emphasis on small talk, its license for social preening—tend to induce flirtatious behavior."

Reconsider your occasion to define a specific question at issue or identify your audience   Your thesis may be under-powered because it fails to draw power from a specific problem you share with your reader. Consider whether your underpowered thesis, in its various guises, even has an occasion. A one-dimensional thesis merely states your topic because you may not have found an issue that prompts a more specific assertion. Likewise, the diverse points that you group under an umbrella thesis may represent your interests but not necessarily respond to a concern that matters to your reader. As to the generic thesis, it promises everyday use precisely because it is context-free. Most big-think theses don't have a clear occasion because you have started importing prefab concepts without first discerning what the specific problem is or why someone might be interested in it. Your best strategy? Clarify your occasion. If you focus your occasion on a genuine issue, you can tap its energy and interest to generate a high-powered thesis.

Because writing sets ideas in relationship, an underpowered thesis undermines your efforts from the start. Unless you establish those relationships, you cannot say anything about your topic that leads to coherent analysis or argument. The energy in any piece of writing—the spirit of inquiry itself—springs from the relationships you create, scrutinize, and refine. Moreover, the pleasure that readers will take in your writing comes from the guided discovery of those new relationships.

| Sorting Out Multiple Theses

The troubleshooting we've done thus far has focused on launching and strengthening your thesis. Yet finding a robust thesis is not your only challenge. You must also be aware how multiple theses can slip into your prose. We'll note two occurrences.

The Hydra-Headed Thesis

In Greek mythology, Hercules struggled to subdue Hydra, the many-headed water serpent. As soon as Hercules cut off one head, two new ones appeared. Only by burning the neck was Hercules able to vanquish the monster and rest from his labors. I don't necessarily recommend such drastic measures as you labor over your thesis. But the story suggests that finding a thesis may not be your only challenge. Pruning back the thesis, lopping off unwanted heads, may also be a part of your task.

A thesis can sprout heads in the form of clauses. You may have, for example, two separate clauses linked by *and*.

> Once an insurgent street music, rap has now entered mainstream pop and white audiences consume it under the guise of acquiring some kind of authentic black experience.

By offering two different assertions, you promise to support each one. Unless you draw tighter logical connections, the support you develop may lead you off in two directions.

Limiting your thesis to a single clause won't always stop heads from sprouting. If only it were that easy! Heads can also sprout in the form of subjects.

> Mahatma Gandhi and Martin Luther King, Jr., shaped American political thought in the 1960s.

This thesis will most likely launch a paper that describes the influence first of Gandhi and then of King. By settling for the simple conjunction *and*, the author fails to uncover and analyze the complex relationship between both men and the political thought of the 1960s. For example, did King influence American political thought by reshaping Gandhi's principles to suit a new context? Or perhaps Gandhi's influence on King is secondary to the impact of nonviolent principles and tactics on national politics? Might it be, then, that "Nonviolent protest shaped political thought in the 1960s"? With only *and* to go on in the thesis, and with a paper that will most likely be organized as two "parallel columns," we may never find out. What's more, by settling for a weak thesis, the author may not even broach such interesting questions.

Hydra heads can also spring up as adjectives. Multiple adjectives in a thesis not only point your paper in several directions, they also beg the question about their relationship to each other, as in the following example.

> Requirements that prohibit the National Endowment for the Arts from sponsoring exhibits with obscene material are unworkable and unwise.

If we prove "unworkable," do we need to prove "unwise"? In turn, "wise" or "unwise" in what respect? And might not the requirements still be unwise even if workable? Or workable even if unwise? Once again the "and" that connects the hydra heads may obscure relationships between terms that deserve scrutiny. You may reach for multiple adjectives out of habit or to smooth out the shape of a sentence. A series of two or three adjectives creates, after all, a pleasing, inevitable-sounding rhythm. But when it comes to your thesis, you need to trust more than your ear. You need to trust your brain.

Although conjunctions such as *and* can announce potential trouble, the hydra-headed thesis can sneak up on you with very little noise. Consider, for example, the difficulties that a simple comparative brings.

> Vietnamese who have sought to leave their country by legal means face more serious risks than the boat people.

The comparative "more serious than" obliges the author to treat both legal emigration and the plight of the boat people. Yet how can one set of risks be more serious than the other when those risks vary in kind? Who is to say what is more serious: severe ostracism on the job or hazards at sea? In this case, the author really wanted to treat the plight of Vietnamese who seek legal emigration, yet the thesis sends him and his readers off on a misadventure.

To subdue a hydra-headed thesis, some swift editorial action is in order. Consider these three strategies.

Use subordination to identify the core assertion   When you have two separate assertions that vie for attention as your thesis, examine their logical relationship. Independent clauses linked by *and* often mask that relationship, thereby misleading both writer and reader, or obscuring fundamental problems in the conception of the paper. By subordinating one assertion to another, logical relations come to the fore: "Only when white audiences began to consume rap music under the guise of acquiring some kind of authentic black experience did rap leave its insurgent street origins for mainstream pop." By using subordination as a tool for setting ideas in relationship, you will develop a firmer grasp of your key assertion. You may even discover some new ideas.

Consider whether one of the thesis elements properly functions as part of the occasion or as a reason supporting the thesis   The hydra-headed thesis can acquire its many parts when the thesis is not clearly distinguished from your occasion and reasons. The thesis about Vietnamese emigration provides a case in point. When the boat people become the occasion, the thesis becomes clearer and more logical: "Although the dangers endured by the boat people have captured our attention, Vietnamese wishing to emigrate legally face severe risks themselves."

Check whether multiple terms are necessary and consider what logical implications they carry; eliminate as many terms as possible   Restrain the natural tendency to add another noun, adverb, or adjective to your thesis, because each additional term carries with it obligations of proof. Each affects the logical coherence and thrust of your statement. Prune back your thesis statement. If you decide to keep terms linked by *and*, ask yourself whether they are needed and whether and how you are addressing their relationship. Consider alternative wording that replaces several terms with one apt term.

The hydra-headed thesis can lead to misadventures because it diffuses the focus of your writing. Each of several elements can send your paper off in a different direction, making it hard for a reader to see the originality or significance of your thought. By reducing various ideas to one core assertion, you show the relationships among them and thereby make them your own.

The Shadow Thesis

Despite your best efforts to formulate an effective thesis, readers may misunderstand or even miss your point. A frequent cause is that other statements elsewhere in your prose vie for attention as your thesis. When one or more of these shadow theses haunt your writing, it may become entirely unclear which of the potential candidates is your intended thesis. If we open the floor to nominations, readers may propose, to your chagrin, any number of assertions that might serve as the focus for your paper.

The following introductory paragraph reveals just how many statements can impersonate a thesis.

(1) Stories on television frequently portray an adopted child's search for his or her birth parents as a heartrending but entirely legitimate quest. (2) As these stories trace the painstaking detective work and the fierce legal battles that may be required to gain family information, viewers come to perceive the adopted child in heroic terms and the birth parents as virtual criminals to be tracked down. (3) Such stories do a disservice to the public and stations should also air stories from the birth parents' point of view. (4) Although many adopted individuals feel it is a birthright to have access to their entire adoption file, in fact it isn't. (5) Adoptees may have the right to obtain family medical history, but they don't have the right to violate a birth parent's privacy by acquiring family information without consent. (6) Adoption agencies need to implement a voluntary adoption program in

order to meet the needs of all parties involved. (7) Priority access to medical information, and the creation of a two-sided exchange process on family backgrounds will help accommodate both sides. (8) Adoptees must recognize the right to privacy and limit their own right to know because adoption agencies are themselves torn by conflicting obligations.

We encounter in these eight sentences as many as seven different assertions, each announcing itself as a potential thesis. The paragraph opens with a series of false starts. Comments on television coverage suggest first an analytic orientation and then a strongly argumentative one, with not one but two assertions vying for our attention in the third sentence. With sentence 4, however, television coverage virtually disappears from the discussion as access to adoption files emerges as the focus of still another potential thesis. Sentence 5 sharpens that focus by making the distinction between family information and medical history the subject of yet another assertion.

If at this point we have reason to believe that throat-clearing false starts may be over and focus now won, our hopes are dashed by the remaining sentences in the paragraph. Instead of supporting one particular claim, these sentences only add to the list of shadow theses. If the paragraph opens with false starts, it closes with the throttle wide open. Assertion piles on assertion, each vying for attention and calling for further development.

You can troubleshoot the shadow thesis if you understand why it can take enough shape to divert and ultimately confuse your reader's attention. Here are four revision strategies.

Sharpen your occasion so that it directly sets up your intended thesis   A shadow thesis can slip into your prose to haunt your intended thesis when your occasion is overly long or when it has only a tenuous link to your core assertion. The first three sentences in our example funnel slowly toward assertions made in sentences 4 and 5. The funnel tempts the author to make assertions about television coverage that bear no close relation to obtaining family information. Instead of setting up the thesis, the funnelled occasion sets off various other assertions. What's the immediate occasion for this paper? The presumed birthright for access to the entire adoption file. Eliminate the shadow thesis by allowing it no quarter; narrow the gap between occasion and thesis.

Consolidate an assertion split over several sentences into one core statement
Sentence 4 initially announces itself as a thesis (access isn't a birthright), yet becomes a shadow thesis when sentence 5 introduces the crucial distinction between medical information and family background. Because the core assertion is split between two statements, each shadows the other. Reformulate your thesis so

that you draw together scattered ideas: "Apart from family medical history, adoptees don't have the right to violate a birth parent's privacy by acquiring general family information without consent."

Revise your proofs so that they support your main assertion   As you articulate the reasons that should support your thesis, a shadow thesis can slip in if your proofs do not substantiate your claim. Sentences 6 and 7 do not address *why* adoptees lack the right to violate their birth parents' privacy. Such reasons may lie in the pain the disclosure can cause to birth parents or in legal arrangements that made adoption possible. The sentences assert instead, in a series of shadow theses, *how* or by *what* procedures medical information should be released. To answer the *why* question, you must do more than discuss the topic; you must provide reasons.

Review summary or concluding statements throughout your draft to ensure consistency and coherence   The final sentence in the paragraph becomes a shadow thesis because it seeks to round off the passage by echoing sentence 5. Yet the restatement departs from the earlier claim in that it fails to include the crucial distinction between family background and medical information. Moreover, it introduces an entirely new claim: conflicting obligations on the part of adoption agencies. By restating, rephrasing, or echoing an earlier assertion, you can introduce a new thesis that shadows and thus confuses your intended focus. Revise these statements to suit your intended thesis. Better yet, use these shadow theses to rethink your initial thesis. Conclusions to your essay often harbor a shadow thesis that rightfully ought to become the thesis that you announce at the very outset.

When shadow theses haunt the assertion you intend as your paper's focus, you're still working to sharpen that focus. Left unrevised, a paper containing shadow theses will have all the characteristics of vagabond prose; without a clear sense of purpose or destination, the writing will wander. To avoid such misadventures, learn from a shadow thesis even as you try to eliminate it. Treat it not merely as an error but as an opportunity to reconsider and refine your thinking.

Clarifying the Cryptic Thesis

We'll close with four instances of obscurity that can compromise even promising assertions. Each has a similar effect on your prose. Instead of launching your reader on a journey, the cryptic thesis requires the reader to circle back and have another go at your assertion.

Ambiguous Terms

Your reader may be forced to decipher your thesis if it contains vague or ambiguous terms. Quite often the problem can be traced to a failure to be specific, as in the following assertion.

> Altering forms of protest against sexism would help deter increasing harassment and victimization.

Altering which forms of protest? What are they now? How might they be altered? By "forms" does the author mean the *degree* of protest, or an entirely different *kind* of protest? Questions only multiply as you move past the first four words of the assertion. And as they multiply, the prose forces you to play sleuth, to ferret out meaning that has been concealed rather than revealed. If you impose this task on your readers, you only irritate them, undermine your credibility, and weaken the validity of your argument.

The revision strategy for this instance of cryptic writing may be obvious but is nonetheless indispensable.

Specify vague or ambiguous terms by taking on the perspective of your reader   The difficulty in revising your way out of trouble lies not so much in specifying those terms as in recognizing when and where you are vague. You can do so by taking on the perspective of your reader, who may come to your paper without impressive clairvoyant skills. Revise your thesis to address questions and possible misreadings; for example, "Women can only deter sexual harassment in the workplace if they become more vocal in their protests." Your best editorial tool can be the questioning attitude you bring to your own prose. You may also wish to seek out the advice of a trusted but honest and forthright friend, one who is prepared to offer candid comments.

Hidden Freight

While some assertions are cryptic because they lack specificity, others suffer from a surplus of meaning, as in the following example.

> Current bolting practices abuse the very structure that gives rock climbing much of its meaning.

The culprit here is the word "structure." The author intended that the term serve double duty, that it mean both the physical rock being climbed and the ethic or philosophy of rock climbing. By collapsing these two levels of meaning into one term, however, the author fails to distinguish points that call for their own specific treatment.

The added, hidden freight carried by this assertion forces the reader to unpack key terms. Meaning not elucidated by the writer can become a source of confusion for the reader. By imploding or collapsing inward, the thesis launches not so much an adventure as a debate about what the author might have in mind.

Limit the amount of hidden freight you ask your prose to carry by restating your assertion in simple, direct terms   Clarity can be compromised when you try to engage in verbal gymnastics with loaded terms. If your prose becomes cryptic due to surplus meaning, make your assertion simple and direct; for example, "By abusing the rock surface that climbers use, current bolting practices undermine the ethics of the sport." Don't equate simplicity with simplemindedness. A well-executed, straightforward thesis will, in the end, earn you more points than a triple-axle spin into opacity.

Contextual Reference

A thesis can also become cryptic if it relies excessively on its context for meaning. In this case, your assertion can't stand on its own. It won't be intelligible as the core statement of your paper.

Why should a thesis be able to stand alone? An independent statement provides both you and your reader with a clear sense of what you are asserting. Because a thesis sets ideas into relationship, those relationships must be expressed in a tight, coherent fashion. If strewn over several sentences or confused by vague pronoun reference, conceptual relationships lose both force and clarity. Context may help you infer what the thesis is, but considered on its own terms, the assertion may be entirely cryptic. When writing on research she was conducting with an engineering professor, a student of mine thought her assertion to be clear.

> Technology is transforming the arm. Once a simple tool, it is now developing it into a sophisticated device.

Yet for her readers, the assertion prompted puzzled looks. Moreover, readers had a poor point of reference when evaluating whether the analysis or proof actually justified that thesis. Here is a troubleshooting strategy.

Consolidate your assertion to one key statement that specifies obscure or unclear references   Consider your thesis apart from its immediate prose context to determine whether it can stand alone. If your thesis depends excessively on the surrounding prose for its meaning, it will not synthesize your ideas. To have your thesis perform the work it should, consolidate and clarify conceptual relationships; for example "Now mechanical engineering technology is transforming the artificial arm from a simple tool into a sophisticated replacement of the human forearm and hand." Only when your thesis pulls together your point can it generate the power to help you develop and substantiate your ideas in the full text.

By expressing your thesis as one tightly cast assertion comprehensible on its own terms, you're working from a conviction that the thesis, and the compression and rigor it requires, offers a laboratory for critical thinking and intellectual discovery.

Buried or Mixed Intentions

A fourth instance of obscurity occurs when you hide your assertion through improper subordination or when you confuse your rhetorical intent.

One student, for example, wished to convince the local city council that it ought to support the area's community access television (CATV) channel with tax dollars. Yet the thesis that he offered had a rather different focus.

> Community access television, when supported by city funds, would promote broader and more active citizen involvement in local community affairs.

The statement's core assertion concerns the relationship between CATV and citizen involvement, not the relationship between city funding of CATV and citizen involvement. To be sure, an analysis of the kind promised in this thesis statement could help support the argument for city funds. But the statement does not, in itself, put forth that argument. If you place the main thrust of your thesis in a qualifying phrase or subordinate clause, you run the risk of misdirecting your reader's attention, dulling the point you wish to make, and dissipating the force that generates shape for your analysis or argument.

Obscurity also results from unclear rhetorical intent. Your thesis not only makes a statement by saying something about your topic, it also performs an act. In other words, your thesis *does* something with what you are saying. A thesis can often become cryptic when your intent is unclear, or when you imply or announce one intention but fulfill another. A female ROTC student kept me guessing when she proposed the following thesis.

> Allowing women in the U.S. military to serve in ground combat units would eliminate the discrimination they now face when being considered for promotions.

Not one but two assertions lurk behind this statement: first, the proposition that women ought to be allowed to serve in ground combat units, now currently not the case; and second, the proposition that such service would end all bias that women face in career advancement. To comprehend such a thesis, readers must first labor to break its code—a burden you should not put on any reader. Remember that in writing analysis and argument your purpose is not to conceal but to reveal.

To avoid burying or confusing your intention, keep three strategies in mind.

Emphasize and clarify your assertion by placing it at the syntactic core of your thesis statement   A thesis can be cryptic if it remains unclear which of the several ideas raised in the thesis is the core assertion. Despite your best intentions, your intended thesis may lurk in a modifying phrase or dependent clause, or even in a parenthetical comment. To avoid misadventure, move your key assertion to the sentence's syntactic core (its subject-verb-object structure). By doing so, you will clarify the logical relationship between your core assertion and various modifying phrases and dependent clauses; for example, "The city council should support community-access television with public funds;" "If military officials were to allow women to serve in ground combat units, they would eliminate much of the discrimination women now face when being considered for promotions."

Use language that signals the rhetorical intent of your thesis   The most immediate way to clarify the rhetorical intent of your thesis (and thus the purpose of your document) is to use language that sharpens your point. Verbs often play a key role in signaling your intent. Note that by turning abstract nouns (*discrimination*) into verbs, you can lend an edge to your assertion: "Current restrictions that bar women from serving in ground combat units discriminate against them when they are being considered for promotions."

Use your occasion or possible counterarguments to help you highlight your intent   Because your thesis responds to the question at issue or other contending views, your occasion and potential counterarguments can set up your point. Here are two examples: "If we seek to involve citizens in community affairs, the city council should support community-access television with public funds." "Although military officials contend that gender plays no role in promotion, the restriction that women cannot serve in ground combat units hurts their prospects for advancement in the officer corps." Being coy about your intent is perhaps the surest way to confuse your reader.

The cryptic thesis obliges the reader to don a trench coat and play detective. Your job is to do the investigative work yourself and then make your case clearly. Few if any of us are purposely obscure. Often we simply lack a firm handle on our ideas or an awareness of our readers' needs. By checking for obscurity when revising your thesis, you can do more than identify the cryptic; you may also, in your pursuit of clarity, discover your true meaning.

Rarely does a writer come upon a thesis on the first attempt. Only by testing and refining your ideas can you discover your point. It's hard work, to be sure, but it's also fun. If you keep the spirit of intellectual play, your troubleshooting will lead to creative insight. That is the value of setting ideas in action; as you struggle to communicate a point, you can also discover what you think and why.

Sustaining Your Discussion 6

In this chapter you'll find answers to questions that nag at you as you write a full draft. Once you have sketched out the shape of your ideas, there remains the task of developing them. And as you write the full draft, questions flood in where you expected answers to lie.

Questions about how you might sustain your discussion can be disconcerting or, worse, disruptive. When producing a first draft some writers prefer to ignore intrusive editorial tugs at their sleeves. But the questions you've encountered during the drafting process deserve answers. You may prefer to return to these questions as you revise a quickly written draft. Or you may wish to respond to the questions as you encounter them. In either case, this chapter will help you address common queries.

Although varied, the eight concerns discussed in the chapter have as a common theme maintaining analytic or argumentative focus. They address problems you are likely to encounter as you try to sustain a cogent defense of your position.

- lending purpose to paragraphs
- handling background information
- calling on source material
- introducing and defining key terms
- using examples
- developing analogies and comparisons
- engaging counterarguments
- crafting the conclusion

Previous writing courses have surely introduced you to many of these same topics. This chapter will show how they relate to the central challenge of academic writing: making and justifying inferences to skeptical readers.

We'll begin with paragraphs, the building blocks of your draft. To use them effectively, you'll need to lend them purpose. Background information and source material, in turn, can make your case more substantial, yet they can also obscure your point if you don't integrate information into your own line of reasoning. We then take up three concerns that often trouble writers as they work to maintain their analytic or argumentative focus. These sections will help you introduce and define key terms, use examples, and develop analogies and comparisons—all in the service of your point. Counterarguments, however, seem to undo the very case you've worked hard to establish. We'll show how an honest treatment of opposing views and contrary evidence can only improve your thinking and strengthen your case. We'll close by looking at conclusions. That devilish end to your essay needn't be your last gasp. Conclusions invite you to lend significance to your point, perhaps even to reconsider that point as you refine your draft.

These eight concerns arise because developing ideas in a draft is simultaneously an invitation to rethink those ideas. As you write out a full draft, you are elaborating and expanding your initial sketch. The process allows you to match introduction with full development, promise with execution. A full draft renders visible the implications of what you are saying, and permits you to test the adequacy of your ideas and the sufficiency of your proofs. But your draft also permits you to discover new ideas as you articulate familiar ones, to sort out unforeseen relationships as you develop intended patterns. Only by working with the particulars of evidence can you discover what your claims ought to be. You may start your draft with one assertion in mind, but after several pages you may realize that you ought to advance a slightly different point or set your ideas in what now seems to be a more suitable pattern. By helping you sustain and sharpen your analytic and argumentative focus, the pages that follow enable you to write out what you know even as you write in what you are discovering.

Lending Purpose to Paragraphs

Paragraphs break up the text into manageable units. These units provide welcome relief to the mind and the eye, which might otherwise rebel against a long series of unbroken lines. Yet paragraphs do far more. They signal divisions, control pace, and suggest logical development. They enable you to lay out the substance of your case step by step, thereby earning the credibility that moves readers to grant your assertion. Paragraphs can thus contribute to your point.

Although writers today view the paragraph as the essential building block of an essay, it is in fact a modern convention. Only in the mid-nineteenth century was the paragraph codified as a textbook specimen: a short body of text marked by an indentation, whose first sentence announced a general proposition about a limited subject, and whose succeeding sentences developed that proposition.

But long before paragraphs became the staple of rhetoric handbooks, writers were grouping ideas together, signaling stages in logical development, and delineating key parts of a text. The term *paragraph* comes from the ancient Greek, meaning literally "a mark beside" the text. And indeed, for many centuries authors would place the paragraph sign (¶) at the head of a section of text to signal a noteworthy break in the flow of ideas. Thus, at root, the paragraph marks boundaries, both spatial and logical; it helps lend shape to ideas.

As you write out the full draft of an analytic or argumentative essay, you will surely build your text paragraph by paragraph. But if you are to lend purpose to those paragraphs, you must do more than resort to intuition or follow a rigid, mechanical model. Intuition may help tell you when a paragraph seems overlong (given the expectations of your audience) or when you seem to be touching on a new idea. But in a tightly conceived analytic or argumentative essay, you risk losing your audience, and your point, unless you paragraph to underscore the shape of your reasoning. At the other extreme lies the ideal model paragraph espoused since the mid-nineteenth century. But few experienced writers pour content into paragraph molds, as if the paragraph were a form to fill in. They work instead with the shape of their analysis or argument, and craft paragraphs to pursue their purpose.

To lend purpose to your paragraphs, consider their function in your analytic or argumentative project. Three aspects bear mention: the role and progression of paragraphs in your essay, the focus and development you achieve within each paragraph, and the cohesive connections that allow you to relate ideas.

Placing Paragraphs in the Service of a Point

Although paragraphs themselves are discrete sections of text, the work they accomplish extends beyond their immediate boundaries. And it is with their larger role that we begin.

In an analytic or argumentative essay, paragraphs should relate to your thesis, to the arguable opinion whose necessary support prompts the development you now provide. As such, paragraphs take their place in a line of reasoning. One way to clarify their function in an essay is to tie paragraphs closely to the reasons why you hold your opinion. Those reasons can clarify the function of paragraphs as you advance your case. If your essay is relatively short, each paragraph may correspond to a particular proof, or to one stage in the successive unfolding of your analysis or argument. In a longer essay, each proof or stage may consist of several paragraphs, each of which lends credibility to a particular aspect of your case. Whatever the length of your essay, paragraphs should serve your analytic or argumentative purpose. Don't think of them as self-contained sections of text about this or that subtopic. Use them to marshall ideas and evidence for your point.

Some paragraphs clearly serve special purposes. Introductions and conclusions come to mind, as do paragraphs that provide necessary background to your case. Writers also occasionally use very short paragraphs that serve an essay's logical development in particular ways, either by providing a transition or by emphasizing an important point. Most paragraphs, however, elucidate or develop points that justify your assertion.

Far from being independent minitexts, paragraphs mark progressive moments in the defense you provide for that assertion. They should unfold a logic so compelling that it wins the assent of your readers. For this reason, the links or transitions between paragraphs can help clarify the coherence of your case.

More than matters of local connection, transitions between paragraphs reflect and reinforce the overall logic of your analysis or argument. If you find yourself stuck for a transition, the solution may not lie in finding that right word or phrase but in rethinking broader questions of logical development. Transitions are not something you can tack on; they grow out of ideas set in relationship. As long as you are uncertain about the logical progression of your paper, transitions will remain a mystery, a matter of hit or miss.

To take the terror out of transitions, consider them as opportunities to rediscover your larger design. The following tips should help.

Ask yourself what you are connecting   Inexperienced writers tend to focus exclusively on the gaping hole between the paragraph they have just finished and the one they are about to start. But many transitions have a larger purpose; they signal shifts within or between stages in your analysis or argument. Because each stage may contain several paragraphs, you should be aware of whether you are bridging paragraphs within a particular stage of your discussion or whether you are linking the stages themselves. By understanding the purpose behind the transition, you have a better chance of establishing an appropriate link.

Check the reasons that project your essay's organization for clues on logical development   The organization you project in your paper's introduction should indicate, if only implicitly, how you are connecting ideas. If you find yourself at a loss for a transition as you write your full draft, refer back to your introduction. Links among the reasons you project in your introduction can suggest transitions in the body of your paper. Look closely at the following thesis and reasons that underlie a paper on Amnesty International's opposition to capital punishment.

> Amnesty International is stretching the truth in claiming that its opposition to capital punishment is derived from the United Nations' *Universal Declaration of Human Rights*. AI's citation of the Declaration as a source for its opposition is based mainly on two articles whose broad meanings quite possibly do not pertain to capital punishment. Moreover, the positions of the individual countries that ratified the Declaration are such that it is unlikely that they intended to repudiate capital punishment.

As you read the thesis and reasons, you can already imagine possible transitions the author might use in his full discussion; for example, "But what do those two articles of the Declaration actually say?" "If countries ratifying the Declaration intended to repudiate capital punishment, it only makes sense to consider their own legal systems." Likewise, as you discover suitable transitions in the body of your paper, return to your introduction to check and revise the organizational logic you projected.

Treat transitions as miniature occasions   Transitions look backward to what has come before and ahead to what follows. They act as miniature occasions in that they use established context to set up new material. Like occasions, transitions engage and focus the reader's interest by suggesting what motivates the discussion. So strong are these parallels that you should treat paragraph transitions as local occasions. Place a bridging word, phrase, or sentence at the very beginning of a paragraph (where you may have been taught to place your topic sentence). Many of the paragraph openers you have just read in this text demonstrate the technique. Let's look at them once more.

- Although writers today view the paragraph as the essential building block of an essay, it is in fact a modern convention.
- But long before paragraphs became the staple of rhetoric handbooks, writers were grouping ideas together.
- Far from being independent minitexts, paragraphs mark progressive moments in your case.
- More than matters of local connection, transitions between paragraphs reflect and reinforce the overall logic of your analysis or argument.
- To take the terror out of transitions, consider them as opportunities to rediscover your larger design.

Treating transitions as miniature occasions will lend lift to what might otherwise be a flat-footed statement of your main idea. When viewed as miniature occasions, transitions impart energy to your prose and momentum to your train of thought.

Consider alternatives to clear but heavy-handed transitions   Obvious transitional phrases—"a second reason is . . ."—may provide clear signposts to your reader, but they are also rather clumsy. They shout to your readers that they ought to brace themselves for a hard turn. Such phrases leap to mind when you're trying hard to link ideas whose relationship may not be clear. If you find yourself reaching for the heavy-handed transition, you may be ignoring problems in the design of your analysis or argument. Take a second look at the fit among your ideas; you may be fastening together sections of your essay that don't match. You can often find clear, graceful alternatives to the heavy-handed transition in the strategic repetition of a key word, phrase, or idea. You can also find them in an occasion-like link that suggests why you are taking your next step.

Focusing and Developing the Paragraph

Once you consider the logical progression of ideas in your essay, it's easier to make sense of focus and development within each paragraph. Most paragraphs have a two-part dynamic. Paragraphs raise and fulfill expectations. They make and respond to a commitment. They announce an idea and build on or flesh out that idea. Because too many expectations will be confusing and difficult to fulfill, it's best to establish in each paragraph only one central focus.

Expectations are set at the beginning of the paragraph, so the first sentence is crucial in establishing your focus. Many books on the "model" paragraph refer to this key opening statement as the topic sentence. You might think of the topic sentence as a particular assertion that supports your paper's larger point through the development and explanation that you provide in the paragraph. Found chiefly in writing that analyzes or argues, the topic sentence helps establish the focus or unity of the paragraph, and guides its development. Consider this student's paragraph on why spider silk may provide modern makers of synthetic fibers with their next breakthrough in technology. I've drawn lines from sentence to sentence to show how the author develops the expectations raised at the outset.

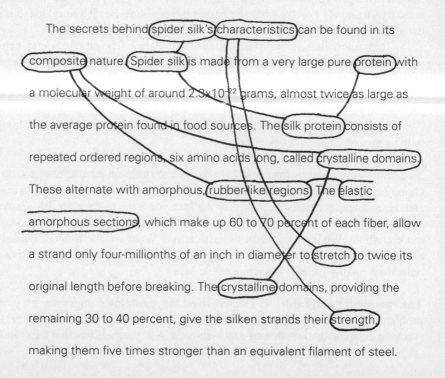

The secrets behind spider silk's characteristics can be found in its composite nature. Spider silk is made from a very large pure protein with a molecular weight of around 2.3×10^{22} grams, almost twice as large as the average protein found in food sources. The silk protein consists of repeated ordered regions, six amino acids long, called crystalline domains. These alternate with amorphous, rubber-like regions. The elastic amorphous sections, which make up 60 to 70 percent of each fiber, allow a strand only four-millionths of an inch in diameter to stretch to twice its original length before breaking. The crystalline domains, providing the remaining 30 to 40 percent, give the silken strands their strength, making them five times stronger than an equivalent filament of steel.

We could easily be overwhelmed by material in the paragraph if it weren't for its clear focus and for the connections that guide us through the paragraph as expectations are fulfilled.

Despite its usefulness, the notion of the topic sentence can be taken to an extreme. Perhaps you recall high school classes that forced you to write the most general, vacuous statements just to have the required topic sentence. What's more, much published analytic and argumentative writing (and virtually all writing that narrates or describes) does not have topic sentences that conform to textbook requirements.

For these reasons, I prefer to think of the topic sentence as a useful but special case of a more general approach to paragraph openings. This approach sees the writer setting down that first sentence as making a commitment to develop some word or phrase in it as the paragraph proceeds. The opening to the paragraph on spider silk would work just as well if the focus lay in a word or phrase, not a full sentence; for example, "A marvelous composite, spider silk is made from a very large protein. . . ." The word "marvelous" sets up expectations fulfilled as we learn about elasticity and strength; "composite" anticipates information on spider silk's two domains or regions. As you see, even a word or phrase can establish expectations that are fulfilled as the paragraph develops. Your first sentence in a paragraph is all-important. It needn't be a general, thesis-like statement that trumpets exactly what the paragraph is about. But it should establish the subject and direction for the sentences to follow.

To develop their paragraphs, writers particularize. They move from a general assertion or idea to specific, detailed support, and back again. In the process, writers justify their general claim by exploring its reach. They also examine the function of each sentence in the paragraph to ensure that they have supported their claim well.

Here are some strategies for addressing the two most common problems with paragraph focus and development.

The underdeveloped paragraph   If you seek to flesh out what is now a short, choppy, underdeveloped paragraph, explain yourself more fully by providing reasons, examples, or details that amplify the idea you wish to develop. It's always useful to play the skeptical reader yourself by asking what might make the point more credible. What else deserves clarification? What are the hidden implications? What objections to the point might arise? And in what ways might those objections qualify or limit the reach of the idea?

The rambling paragraph   If bloated, overlong, rambling paragraphs are your problem, locate the main sentence or idea in the paragraph (you may find several) and then examine the function of each sentence. Ask yourself whether a particular sentence supports or amplifies your main idea in the paragraph and thus maintains your analytic or argumentative focus. Revise for economy and relevance. In the process, you will surely find sentences that belong in other paragraphs, sentences that ought to become paragraphs in their own right, and sentences that you could do just as well without.

A paragraph gains closure when it fulfills the expectations it has aroused. Those expectations have to do with both the focus within the paragraph and with the service the paragraph performs in advancing your case. A paragraph is developed when readers understand how the discussion advances your point, how insights won substantiate an assertion. Writers can help by giving their leading idea the last word. Paragraphs can also close by suggesting, if only implicitly, why what you have said matters.

Creating Cohesive Connections

As you write out paragraphs in your full draft, you quickly discover that you have to write in connections that hold your material together. If readers mention that a paragraph flows, they are responding, albeit somewhat subjectively, to the dynamic of expectation and fulfillment realized in the paragraph's sentence-by-sentence movement. Cohesive connections help you create that flow by relating evidence to assertion, particulars to generalizations. The lines drawn in the paragraph on spider silk approximate the many connections that readers intuitively look for as they process paragraph development.

Connections matter in analytic and argumentative writing because you are building a case by developing a line of reasoning. Individual statements add up to a compelling essay as you shuttle back and forth between particulars and generalizations, evidence and assertion. As you move back and forth, you are creating and harnessing energy, building a point from evidence and then building on those points as you move through further material. If you leave out a step or fail to connect two steps, the line of reasoning quickly is broken, and the coherence of your case is substantially reduced. An essay does not convince us by its individual points of evidence. We are convinced chiefly by the connections that allow us to link parts to wholes and thus grasp the essay's compelling logic.

Writers help readers make cohesive connections by offering various hooks and nudges—small links and transitions that connect one sentence to the next. A variety of connecting words and phrases is available to you.

Logical Type	Examples
sequence	then, finally, above all
coordination	likewise, moreover, similarly

Logical Type	Examples
contrast	but, however, instead
causation	therefore, accordingly, thus
inclusion	for example, namely, indeed
alternation	or, another possibility, neither/nor
conclusion	in short, to summarize, on the whole

The list may seem overwhelming, but in reality it's only a very partial list. Still more effective are subtle devices, like the repetition of key words, the use of pronouns, or turns of phrase that contrast two points or set them in parallel.

But the sheer variety of possible connections can overshadow general principles. The connections you supply perform two functions.

- First, they *orient readers* by clarifying where they have been and where they are going. In so doing, connections place individual statements in broader context.

- Connections also compel your reader to *move forward*. Your goal is to keep your reader hooked by making your next sentence follow from your current one and by making your current sentence require the next one.

Connections, in short, place individual statements in the service of a larger project. Just as a good dancer will lead a partner, so too should writers provide hints on where their steps take their readers. The surest way to help your reader know where you are going is to provide a few directional signals. You need not be heavy-handed about it, but neither should you ask readers to double as clairvoyants.

If you have trouble making connections as you write, see your draft as an opportunity to test and refine the coherence of your ideas. Connections provide clues to your readers about your line of reasoning; in so doing they can also help you clarify your thinking. Remember: continuity doesn't just happen; you create it every step along the way. Those skilled in virtually any craft—from carpentry to weaving—follow the same procedure. If the details don't fit, they check the broader design. No amount of fudging to make local cohesion work can compensate for basic problems that may lie hidden in the overall coherence of your design. The connections you write in as you draft your paper can help you validate or revise your line of reasoning.

Paragraphs help you write out and develop the details of your case by making explicit the connections among your ideas. Early drafts allow you to write in ideas that may not have occurred to you. These new discoveries can, in turn, help you test and revise your essay's overall shape. It's not uncommon for a single paragraph to prompt you to rethink your essay's focus, or for that paragraph to open your eyes to what could be an altogether different essay. Treat paragraphs in an early draft as provisional structures that help you discover appropriate designs. Only then can you be confident that paragraphs in your final draft will help you construct an effective case.

Handling Background Information

When writing analysis and argument you cannot do without information. Readers need to know what you are talking about. Moreover, they need particulars if your points are to persuade them. Lacking a specific context, many written documents require that authors compensate by literally writing it in. Only when information provides some common ground can author and reader proceed. Information establishes that shared context.

Information also informs your context. Your own ideas take their place in a community of work done on your topic. If you remain unaware of that work, you will have little idea what questions are at issue for your readers. You will also be unable to test your ideas through shared inquiry or draw on the insights of others who have thought and written about these matters.

Yet for all its virtues, information can trouble writers as much as it can help. What do you put in? What do you leave out? The question can perplex the most experienced writers, especially toward the beginning of an essay or article. Raw information, you see, has a seductive quality. The more you present, the more substantial your case seems to be; quantity bespeaks your command of the subject. Information is all the more seductive because descriptive material is relatively easy to write. Yet information can exact a price. As you purvey information, the background you provide can obscure your case, rather than clarify your point. It can soften, even hide, the contours of your analysis or argument. Downloaded on the page like so much memory from a computer, undifferentiated information can overwhelm and disorient writer and reader alike. Vital material can sometimes appear pointless and the padding pertinent.

Consider how one student beginning an essay on oil drilling in the Alaskan wilderness soon became overwhelmed by the information at her disposal.

(1) North of the Arctic Circle in the state of Alaska lies the Arctic National Wildlife Refuge (ANWR). (2) ANWR lies on the border of Alaska and Canada, next to the Beaufort Sea. (3) Composed of 19 million acres of wilderness, ANWR represents about 13 percent of Alaska's 150 million

acres that have been set aside for conservation and recreation. (4) ANWR is covered with fragile arctic tundra that can bear the scars of a footstep or a vehicle's passage for as many as twenty years. (5) Caribou herds also use the coastal plain of ANWR as a calving ground, but elsewhere in Alaska researchers have documented the adaptive capabilities of the caribou. (6) ANWR lies adjacent to the Prudhoe Bay oil fields. (7) The reserves at Prudhoe Bay are estimated at 11 billion barrels; the reserves in ANWR could be as much as 10 billion barrels. (8) By opening much of the coastal plain of ANWR to full oil exploration and development, the US could tap these reserves. (9) The technology and equipment for exploration, drilling, and transport of oil on the tundra are already present.

The challenge you face when providing information lies in discriminating between background and foreground. Here the writer fails to make this distinction. As a result, the reader can become as disoriented as someone caught in an arctic blizzard. Details obscure issue, point, and support.

Four Strategies

How, exactly, might you render information in your essay, especially in the opening pages? Experienced writers often invoke the following strategies.

Resist the temptation to tell all   Just because you have access to a large amount of information is not sufficient reason to provide it. To judge by the extraneous information that often clutters a paper, you'd think we were all being paid a dime a detail for our labors. Put information to a functional test; if it doesn't serve the needs of your reader or the development of your case, chances are you don't need it. When in doubt, delete.

Highlight the point and shape of your essay   In the introduction to your paper, provide information that helps your reader grasp the question at issue, the point you are making, and the essay's logical development. All else can wait. Let other details recede into the background, where they can serve those relationships, not compete for attention. Your first obligation on page 1 is to engage and orient your readers. Do so by rendering the essential point and shape of your essay with clarity and force.

When necessary, provide a coherent body of background information   As you frame your analysis or argument to highlight its purpose, you may find that your readers require a coherent body of information before you can proceed with the details of your case. If this is so, consider providing a paragraph or two of background information immediately after your introduction. But remember, background only helps your reader once you have put into the foreground the essentials of your case. Also be sure that what you provide is really needed in the discussion to follow.

Relate information to your purpose   If you can offer your readers the information they need as you actually make your case, so much the better. Although necessary from time to time, a section of background information can be clumsy, a piece set apart from the dynamic of your paper. Information becomes relevant when you put it to use, and where better than when you are marshalling evidence to establish a point? By folding in background information when you need it, you are better able to determine what and how much to include.

The Strategies Applied

How would you apply these four strategies when revising the paper about oil drilling in Alaska? First determine how ideas relate to each other. Define the question at issue, the thesis, and the individual proofs. After all, for information to become relevant, it requires some point of reference. As you place these key points in the foreground, you are able to restate descriptive material so that it clarifies the shape of your argument. The occasion for the argument, now only implied, deserves explicit and early mention. The thesis, now so hesitant that it borders on a statement of fact, can then carry an argumentative edge. Counterarguments, in turn, come to the fore: adverse effects on the tundra and caribou herds. And support for the thesis, once mere nuggets of information, now assumes its function as reasoned proof that projects the essay's argumentative shape. Here's the result.

(1) In a report to Congress in 1987, Secretary of the Interior Donald P. Hodel recommended opening the Arctic National Wildlife Refuge in Alaska to full oil exploration and development. (2) By opening the refuge to development, the U.S. would be able to tap reserves estimated up to 10 billion barrels. (3) But questions about the environmental impact of the exploration fill the arctic air. (4) What of the fragile tundra? (5) And what of the caribou herds that use the refuge as calving grounds? (6) Because the effects of exploration and production will be minimal, Congress should open the refuge to oil development. (7) By using equipment and technology designed for the tundra, oil developers will have but a minimal impact on this sensitive region. (8) Moreover, prior studies of caribou in drilling areas suggest that herds can live in harmony with oil drilling and production activities.

By using information to highlight the occasion (sentences 1 and 2), counterarguments (sentences 3–5), thesis (sentence 6), and proofs (sentences 7 and 8), the author has placed data in the service of debate. Now readers have a framework for understanding whatever background information remains necessary. Because the specific location and vast expanse of the refuge are pertinent to the entire argument, a background paragraph on these matters is now appropriate. Other information—about drilling equipment and arctic tundra, caribou migrations and calving activity—is best integrated into the proofs that seek to win the reader's assent.

How, then, do you inform as you analyze or argue? By not appearing to do so. When information serves the case you make, it becomes not information given for its own sake but evidence to support a point. If, however, information appears to be merely that—description untethered from the line of your reasoning or the needs of your audience—you can be sure that you need to shake out data from your draft. Should an assignment or a required format call for a section on background, don't think of it as an excuse to tell all. See it as an invitation to place in the foreground information that clarifies your paper's issue, point, and plan.

Calling on Source Material

To make their own case, writers often enlist others in their cause. The analytic or argumentative essays you write in college often have you use published material to help you evaluate and justify your point. Inquiry, after all, is a community affair. Yet the difficulties of integrating source material into your own case are everywhere apparent. Far too many essays stitch together material without advancing their own claim. Or, if they do make a claim, the material marshalled in its support fails to speak on the author's behalf. Used inappropriately, source material can dull the very edge that the analytic or argumentative essay seeks to sharpen.

The problems stem from the allure that source material holds for writers. That allure can lead you to forget that different contexts and purposes are involved as you draw on existing material and put it to your own use. If you wish to use source material effectively, you must shift contexts and harness material to new purposes in a responsible fashion. To that end, I'll highlight potential opportunities and errors, inventory a few tools available to you for using sources, and suggest a two-part strategy for integrating sources into your own work. In the process, you may find yourself considering source material in a new light—not as a repository for information, but as a tool to sharpen your own thinking.

Opportunities and Errors

All writers use source material, and for two good reasons. We use the work and ideas of others as a base from which to proceed. Because we write and read in a community, we needn't start with a blank slate. The acquired knowledge available in source materials allows us to stand on the shoulders of others. But if source material provides a base from which to proceed, it can also justify the new conclusions we reach. Sources help make new ideas credible; they allow us to develop and defend our own original points.

Yet published source material can also seduce the unwary writer to commit two fundamental errors. Because published material is ready at hand, often expressed with an eloquence that you may envy, it's tempting to cite or quote plenty of it. This first error can result in papers that resemble a cut-and-paste job where information and quotes are assembled into a collage. In such a paper, the writer is more tour guide than author, reciting this point, referring to another, with perhaps a bit of commentary thrown in for good measure. Given its array of sources, such a paper often fails to establish and sustain its own line of analysis or argument.

The authority that we tend to vest in published material—if it's printed, it's got to be true—can also lead you to commit a second error. When you wish to provide evidence and support for a point you are making, it's tempting to enlist the help of an authority. What could be more convincing? Yet when you are about to drive a point home, you are not well served by pulling up short and plugging in a quotation that you hope will finish the job for you. It rarely does, for the point you need to make is not someone else's but your own. Do not assume that borrowed eloquence will necessarily speak to your own distinctive point. However pertinent your source material may be, it can never speak for you but only in your behalf. To ask your source material to do anything more than that is to dabble in ventriloquism. When you throw your voice by trying to speak through the borrowed authority of your sources, you risk surrendering what you can least afford: the authority and credibility you can win only by speaking in your own voice to make your own point.

Both errors—that of the tour guide and that of the ventriloquist—stem from a lack of awareness that source material has its own original context and serves another author's distinctive purpose. We need only recall the familiar phrase *taken out of context* to understand that source material cannot be disassembled and reassembled like so many interchangeable parts. It's a point that inexperienced writers tend to forget, and a wealth of secondary source material cannot compensate for the lapse. To use sources well, you must shift contexts responsibly and harness material to serve your own distinct purpose. Moreover, you must judge whether you are abusing the accuracy of your source material or the intent of its author. You can integrate sources into your analysis or argument only by articulating their place in your own line of reasoning.

Tools for Calling on Sources

To place sources in the service of your own ideas, you must know what tools are appropriate to your purpose and what strategies you can call on to link material to your point.

First, the tools, with a few caveats about their use. Writers can introduce secondary material into their own text in four main ways.

Factual or statistical reference   As you develop your case, you may have occasion to refer briefly to specific factual or statistical data. Unless your reader considers the information to be common knowledge or easily accessible, you should cite its source. Beware, however, that the meaning of data can change as you shift contexts and use the material to develop your own point. For example, we learn from "Harper's Index" in the January 1992 issue of *Harper's* that one American out of fourteen is an immigrant—apparent confirmation that the United States is still a melting pot. That is, until we consider our neighbor to the north, where one out of every six Canadians is an immigrant. Might it be, then, that current U.S. immigration policy has made the melting pot a thing of the past? It all depends on your line of reasoning, and on the responsible use of sources in your own analytic or argumentative context.

Summary   A summary reports your understanding of another body of source material. It condenses the point of that source by extracting its main ideas. Some summaries can extend to a paragraph or more, especially if you are reporting another author's line of argument. For the most part, however, summaries are relatively brief, often no more than a sentence or two.

> Writing in the January 1992 issue of *Harper's*, Lewis Lapham addresses the issue of national identity in an essay entitled "Who and What Is American: The Things We Continue to Hold in Common." There Lapham argues that the current politics of blame and difference hides something far more fundamental: our complicity in a shared act of the imagination whereby we invent our own distinctive identities.

When you discuss this or any other text, you often need to orient your reader by providing a brief description of its contents and main ideas before you can engage that text by analyzing or arguing with it.

Summary plays an important role in analysis and argument because the credibility of your own case often depends on your ability to report and appreciate another person's point of view. Be careful, however, to distinguish between summary and your own analysis or argument. If readers can't make this distinction, your own writing may have lapsed into description. Likewise, your summary may have colored (even distorted or misrepresented) your source to suit your own analytic or argumentative ends. You can best harness the energy of summary by maintaining the integrity of your own line of reasoning.

Paraphrase   In a paraphrase you the writer restate point-by-point another author's ideas in your own words. More detailed than a summary, a paraphrase enables you to give your readers an accurate and comprehensive account of another person's specific ideas. Consider Lapham's original prose from his article in *Harper's*.

> Among all the nations of the earth, America is the one that has come most triumphantly to terms with the mixtures of blood and caste, and maybe it is another of history's ironic jokes that we should wish to repudiate our talent for assimilation at precisely the moment in time when so many other nations in the world (in Africa and Western Europe as well as the Soviet Union) look to the promise of the American example. The jumble of confused or mistaken identities that was the story of nineteenth-century America has become the story of a late-twentieth century world defined by a vast migration of peoples across seven continents and as many oceans. Why, then, do we lose confidence in ourselves and grow fearful of our mongrel freedoms?

And now a paraphrase.

> Lapham considers it ironic that America should wish to renounce its ability to assimilate differences among its citizens. Unlike virtually any other nation, America has been able to deal with its racial and economic disparities. Yet we wish to renounce this ability at a time when many other nations seek to follow America's lead. Considering that the century-old image of the melting pot, long realized in America, has now become fact worldwide, Lapham laments our loss of confidence and our distrust of the many and diverse freedoms we enjoy.

Because a paraphrase follows the design of the original very closely, you should use it only if you wish to explain, analyze, or argue with specific facets of the author's case.

The proximity of paraphrase to original statement makes it both a powerful and dangerous tool when analyzing or arguing. Unlike Lapham's essay, many of your source materials may not be authoritative or eloquent enough to merit direct quotation. Some will be so riddled with jargon that translation into your own words will help your reader appreciate the import of the passage. Paraphrase allows you to integrate important material into your paper without disrupting your prose.

Yet the very virtues of paraphrase can also become a vice in your analytic or argumentative paper. Paraphrase makes sense if the material you present is germane to your own discussion—if, in other words, you intend to do something with what you paraphrase. Yet all too often, one paraphrase is followed by another, and yet another, thus dissipating the focus and force of your own case. Moreover, because paraphrase represents another person's specific ideas in your own words, it can be a crutch or, worse, an invitation to plagiarize. To avoid these problems, distinguish between the source you are using and the use to which you put it, between what you are talking about and what you yourself are saying.

Direct quotation   Quotation represents the most easily recognizable way to use source material, for you are literally incorporating part of another text into your own. Writers quote because the material provides crucial support for their case; establishes key terms; lends ideas vivid, memorable expression; or offers an opportunity to comment on the passage cited. Because quotation announces itself so clearly and interrupts your own words, be sure that you have good reason to quote; otherwise, turn to paraphrase or summary. Nevertheless, precisely because quotation calls for the spotlight, a crucial phrase or a memorable statement can electrify your essay and lend force to your point.

Yet for most writers, quotes are rarely so successful. When overused and poorly integrated into your own line of analysis or argument, quotes can distract your reader's attention and undermine your own analytic or argumentative purpose. For these reasons, quote sparingly and quote as little of the passage as you can. Frequent long quotes suggest that you yourself have nothing to say. Moreover, long quotes can disorient readers, who may not know exactly what to focus on in a quoted passage. Cultivate an ear for the decisive phrase, and the skill to lend it an emphatic position in your own prose. Here's some analysis of Lapham's article—analysis that is possible because quotes from Lapham become an occasion for comment.

> Lapham places our anxiety about national identity in historical perspective. The end of the cold war no longer enables us to construct our own "monolithic virtue" by pointing to a "foreign demon." Now, instead of casting our gaze abroad, we "search our own neighborhoods for fiends of con-

vincing malevolence." By invoking history, Lapham uncovers both the common imaginative act that has formed our sense of identity through the years and the source of our current discontent: we now trade on our differences, and on the resentments that inevitably spring from them.

Once you quote a phrase or a passage, be sure to use it; interpret its meaning, analyze its relevance to your case, argue with it. To do so, call on strategies for integrating sources into your own line of reasoning. You needn't restate the quote in your own words. But you also should avoid the opposite extreme: dismissing the quote altogether once you've introduced it as you move on to other concerns.

Strategies for Integrating Sources

Whether you use these four tools individually or in combination (as most experienced authors do), they pose a common challenge to your analytic or argumentative paper: if you do not integrate sources into your line of reasoning, they can fragment the coherence of your paper. The following two-part strategy can help you integrate sources so that they serve your purpose.

Prepare for mention of source material   Examine the shape of your analysis or argument to determine what information or material the reader needs. For source material to be relevant, you must have some occasion for introducing it. Let your reader know why you are turning to the material that you employ. In the following quote, note how Lapham himself prepares for a remark by John Quincy Adams.

> We were always about becoming, not being; about the prospects for the future, not about the inheritance of the past. The man who rests his case on his color, like the woman who defines herself as a bright cloud of sensibility beyond the understanding of merely mortal men, makes a claim to special privilege not unlike the divine right of kings. The pretensions might buttress the cathedrals of our self-esteem, but they run counter to the lessons of our history.
>
> We are a nation of parvenus, all bound to the hopes of tomorrow, or next week, or next year. John Quincy Adams put it plainly in a letter to a German correspondent in the 1820s who had written on behalf of several prospective emigres to ask about the requirements for their success in the New World. "They must cast off the European skin, never to resume it," Adams said. "They must look forward to their posterity rather than backward to their ancestors."

If you use sources for their own sake—to impress your reader with numerous citations or to cover what you may feel to be weak ideas—you're not doing yourself a favor. Source material not called for by the requirements of your own analysis or argument will always fit poorly in your paper.

Follow up on your use of source material   However eloquent or pertinent the source material you introduce may be, it rarely speaks for itself. Instead, see source material as providing an occasion for *you* to speak. Lapham does exactly that by following the Adams quote immediately with his own comment on the expectations of the early Pilgrims.

> We were always a mixed and piebald company, even on the seventeenth-century colonial seaboard, and we accepted our racial or cultural differences as the odds that we were obliged to overcome or correct.

If you do not use the material you introduce, you have either wasted an opportunity to drive home your point, or you have introduced extraneous material that points your reader in directions you have no intention of pursuing. Unless you actively use your source material by linking it to your line of reasoning, you run the risk of having sources take control of your essay. You can avoid that risk by having sources serve your own ideas.

A final word   Sources can lend credibility to your essay only if you use them responsibly. Be sure you have represented source material fairly. In turn, be sure that you have not misrepresented yourself by plagiarizing the ideas or words of others. Documentation for your sources can help you accomplish both tasks. As a courtesy, citations allow readers to follow up on an essay's information, either to check for its accuracy or to pursue research of their own. As a duty, citations enable you to acknowledge your intellectual debts. But citations are more than a way of covering yourself; they fulfill a larger persuasive purpose and carry their own persuasive force. They suggest that you take seriously the opportunities and responsibilities of writing in a community—of writing for readers.

Introducing and Defining Key Terms

Terms matter because words are not always what they seem. Definitions help you clarify what you mean—in your own mind and in the minds of your readers. It's tempting to think of definitions as a way to tame pesky terms so that you can get on with the real business of writing your paper. But definitions don't so much put problems to rest as they orient you and your readers to the problem at hand. In this respect definition goes to the heart of your paper's design. Analysis and argument help you sort out answers precisely because they ask you to identify and engage a problem. Thus, the need for definition—for appropriate distinctions— is always with you.

The dictionary, surprisingly enough, may be less helpful than you think. It records definitions by offering a generalized description of how people use a word. But definitions do not themselves originate in dictionaries. Definitions merely reflect the ongoing social process of sorting out distinctions to accomplish certain ends.

Inexperienced writers often appeal to a dictionary definition because it lends authority to what they say. The mere phrase "According to *Webster's*" seems to promise clarity and consensus, for a definition classifies the world. It places a word (*carrot*, let's say) in a class of similar things (biennial herbs) and then proceeds to distinguish it from other members of its class (a biennial herb with a usually orange, spindle-shaped edible root). Such definitions seem to establish authority. Who, after all, can disagree with *Webster's*?

Yet you quickly lose whatever borrowed authority you may acquire if you don't know the *purpose* that motivates you to make distinctions. If your readers are already familiar with the definition, they may resent your condescension. If they are not, they gain little from a standard definition they could look up themselves. In either case, the definition you cite is likely to be so bland and general that it may do little to advance your essay. The only reason to present a definition is if people have used the same word in different ways, or found that it holds different connotations. Definitions are distinctions motivated by purpose. Your own purpose brings them into play and lends context to their use. To know when you should introduce and define terms, you must first look to your purpose.

Let's consider three common problems that come up as you link definition and purpose.

When Definition Risks Becoming Your Purpose

In choosing a topic and formulating your thesis, you may mistakenly assume that all of your readers agree on the meaning of a key term. Explaining that term may become more trouble than it's worth, only diverting you from the focus of your paper.

Some essays, of course, explicitly offer themselves as essays in definition. An essay in the summer 1991 issue of *Southwest Review*, for example, pursued the meaning of one intriguing term—the personality type known as "the crank"—by considering its various dimensions and connotations. Definitions also play a role whenever you are asked to classify, as with the essay exam item "Explain why Stephen Crane is considered one of the foremost exponents of realism in American fiction."

But most essays are not explicit exercises in definition or classification. Let's say you wish to assert that "a national health insurance plan will end up socializing American medicine." If you are to support such a sweeping generalization, you must first pin down exactly what you mean by *socialized medicine* or, for that matter, *socialism*. Economists, political scientists, and, yes, doctors and politicians have argued endlessly about the nuances of the term and the diverse interpretations it has been given. You may intend your topic to be national health insurance, but the problem of defining "socializing" risks becoming your actual focus. Here, definition no longer advances your purpose; it has, unwittingly perhaps, *become* your purpose.

If you find that definition threatens to overwhelm your stated intention, apply the following strategy.

Avoid terms that resist adequate definition   Even if the term sounds impressive and has gained widespread currency, develop a healthy reluctance to call on it. You may find that it is not only abstract but insubstantial. Reorient your paper so that it asserts a far more concrete thesis. For example, consider one specific proposal for national health insurance and examine how it might affect a particular sector of the medical community, such as family doctors in private practice.

When You Need a Working Definition

Even when your topic is not burdened by terms that resist definition, you may still need to define a term that is central to your analytic or argumentative project. Consider, for example, an essay question in a linguistics course—"Do infants acquire language through imitation?" To answer this question well, you must establish what you mean by "imitation." If you do not, your answer may imply competing (but unstated) definitions at various points.

To define imitation, you need not pull a dictionary off your shelf and give a verbatim rendering of that entry. In fact, the dictionary entry may not suit your purposes well at all, for the definition you need to provide should apply specifically to language acquisition and should reflect how researchers in the field use the term. What you're after here is not a formal definition but a working definition, one where you stipulate, for the purposes of your discussion, what *you* mean by imitation.

When you reply to the essay question, you might, for example, address whether imitation refers to the literal repetition of sounds, words, and longer phrases. If imitation isn't, for the purposes of your discussion, direct repetition, perhaps it is a more complicated process of modeling, where children seek to incorporate the language they hear into their own changing strategies of language use. As this example suggests, the borrowed authority of *Webster's* will not get you far. Instead, you must sort out the term yourself, according to your purpose and current usage in your field.

If you wish to stipulate a definition, bear in mind two points.

Be sure your definition is reasonable   Although a working definition allows you to stipulate what a term means, your latitude is constrained by the problem you're addressing and what your readers will accept. You may wish to consult specialized dictionaries and encyclopedias that discuss terms within a particular discipline or problem. If you stray too far from a term's generally accepted meaning or if your definition is slanted to such a degree that it becomes biased, you risk losing your reader's goodwill.

Use your working definition to define the grounds of debate   By determining the shape and size of your conceptual playing field, you can emphasize one aspect of the discussion or deflect certain objections as being out-of-bounds. Thus, even the modest latitude you enjoy when offering a working definition can help orient your analysis or argument. Interestingly enough, according to its Latin origins, the word *define* means "to establish limits." In stipulating a definition, you are doing precisely that—articulating boundaries that help shape your ideas and your prose.

When Technical Terms Overwhelm Your Point

The link between definition and purpose also becomes decisive when you must deal with an avalanche of technical terms, each calling for definition. You are likely to encounter this situation when you are writing for readers who may know less about your subject than you do. This situation may be a rare occurrence in college, where papers, it's sad to say, tend to be written for professors only. But the situation is exceedingly common in professional life. What and how much you need to define depends on the expertise and interests of your audience. What is technical for one audience may not be for another.

Consider, for example, the plight of a chemical engineering student who wishes to analyze for an intelligent but nontechnical audience the atmospheric chemistry of chlorofluorocarbons—the CFCs that produce the greenhouse effect. The complexity of the information and the number of terms requiring definition may not be her most formidable challenges. She must also ensure that readers understand how individual definitions figure in the broader shape and point of the discussion. Simply defining terms may not be enough; you also have to help readers use the definitions you provide. When the larger purpose behind your definition becomes unclear, no amount of careful, local explanation can help your readers make their way through the labyrinth of technical information.

If you find yourself in such a predicament, keep the following strategies in mind.

Link definitions to your line of reasoning   You need not dumb down the discourse to explain technical terms. Your lay reader may not need a refresher course in high school science, merely a clear indication of what is at stake when you introduce technical terms. If you clarify the shape of your discussion—its issue, point, and support—you offer readers a context in which to place technical details.

Integrate definitions into your prose   You need not interrupt your discussion with each new technical term by pulling your reader aside to provide a formal definition. Slip in definitions by using a short explanatory phrase, a synonym, or a lay term.

> Global warming, commonly termed the "greenhouse effect," threatens the stability of the earth's climate. Halogenated hydrocarbons, also known as chlorofluorocarbons or CFCs, contribute significantly to the greenhouse effect and thus pose a serious risk to the survival of all life on earth. A result of man's influence on nature, these gaseous compounds accumulate in the stratosphere (the portion of the atmosphere between 20 and 50 kilometers above sea level), where they effectively inhibit the planet's ability to irradiate energy into space.

Consider other alternatives to the usual X = Y definition   Work into your discussion a functional explanation, an example, a comparison, or an extended analogy.

> What is the life of a CFC molecule like under constant exposure to infrared radiation? Infrared radiation contains less energy than light, its visible counterpart in the electromagnetic spectrum. Therefore, it cannot be seen with the naked eye, yet it can be felt as heat upon the skin. Most atoms, including those that make up skin tissue, respond to infrared energy by vibrating back and forth about their bonds like balls linked with a rubber band. The halogen atoms (fluorine or chlorine) that, along with carbon, make up the CFC molecule possess the ability to absorb and trap greater quantities of infrared energy than other molecules. Thus, much like skin that becomes uncomfortably hot by continued exposure to infrared light, CFC molecules get "hot." The cumulative effect of millions of tiny molecules getting "hot" is a giant body of molecules, like the stratosphere, heating up. In effect, CFCs create a stable, hot portion of the atmosphere that blankets the earth.

This blanket also traps the infrared radiation the earth regularly attempts to eliminate. After collecting energy from the sun by day, our planet needs to cool itself by night. The earth accomplishes its task by reemitting excess infrared energy into space at day's end. Unfortunately, CFCs obstruct earth's natural cooling process by scavenging this discarded radiation as it passes through the stratosphere. The earth becomes infinitesimally warmer with each rising and setting of the sun, resulting in perpetual warming: the greenhouse phenomenon.

If the task of defining terms preoccupies you, remember that definitions should serve the purpose of your writing. Don't let them overwhelm or become your point. By integrating definitions into your line of reasoning, you can help your reader arrive at your conclusion, not stumble over every new term. Because they offer appropriate distinctions, definitions can help you find and sustain your analytic or argumentative focus.

Using Examples

As you sort through experience or marshall material, you may develop your ideas in terms of examples. We all do. And it's a good thing, for without examples our ideas would collapse. Examples are the stuff out of which we create ideas. They lend poignancy to what might otherwise be an abstract point; they are the vivid pictures and stories by which we remember and interpret our world.

But when you write an analysis or argument that seeks to justify an assertion, examples may not speak for themselves. That was the case when a student offered an early draft of a paper on bathroom graffiti. She organized the paper as a string of examples: graffiti in classroom buildings and in dorms; graffiti on first one subject and then another. And her examples were indeed engaging. But for all the details she provided in her discussion, she was surprised to learn that her readers didn't recognize how the examples supported her thesis.

She wished to assert that bathroom stalls offer a distinctive forum for women to discuss, by way of graffiti, such sexually charged issues as abortion and date rape. The hidden rationale for this assertion was that women choose this forum for two reasons: it offers a private, anonymous opportunity to air views about personal issues that have now become matters of public debate, and it provides an opportunity to seek advice and comment from an exclusively female audience. But the connection between her many examples and the two reasons behind them was not apparent. Like this writer, you may have to step in and clarify how your examples provide reasons for your point. Although detailed examples may be essential to your case, they do not in themselves make your case.

The distinction between an example and a reason is important because you may be tempted to design your analytic or argumentative paper around a handful of examples: "Here's my thesis, and now let me give you several examples." Examples of graffiti helped this student group what she had to say in manageable chunks. What's more, the chunks were relatively easy to write, for the issues and emotion behind the now angry, now humorous, but always poignant comments etched on the stalls readily lent themselves to vivid description and narration. Examples, in themselves, are ready tools for telling *what*.

And therein lies the problem. Examples may provide a painless way to organize your paper, but that organization may not help you justify your point. When you analyze or argue, you must answer the question *why*. "Why is my point well taken?" Examples in themselves do not answer this question. Examples may point to reasons or they may help convince readers to accept reasons, but they are not themselves reasons. Examples can support, emphasize, illustrate, or clarify. They can, in a word, exemplify. But unless you state the reason behind the example, you leave the better part of your work undone. When you organize an analytic or argumentative paper around examples, not reasons, you risk having your paper lapse into description and narration.

Three Strategies

How can you harness the energy of examples without sacrificing your analytic or argumentative purpose? To sustain a line of reasoning, place examples in the service of reasons. Three strategies can help.

Determine how an example relates to your thesis   Look at examples in terms of their function in your reasoning process. What reason lurks behind the example? For instance, if you wish to discuss several examples of graffiti, ask yourself *why* they help you justify your point. Highlight those reasons, not just the examples. By relating examples to your point, you can evaluate whether your reader might find the example to be clear or problematic, whether it supports your thesis or implicitly asks you to qualify your assertion. Also consider whether the example is typical or representative. To what extent can you generalize from one or two examples of graffiti? Might some aspect of the example undermine the very point you wish to make? Might your own examples invite troublesome counterexamples? Offering examples, then, is not enough; you also have to focus on how and why you might use them, and on what implications they hold. See examples not as pictures or stories in themselves but as tools in a process of inquiry.

Mine examples for the reasons that they contain   As you unearth an example, don't be content to see it in its own terms, as if there were a simplistic one-to-one correlation between an example and a reason. Several different examples may actually point to the same reason. Graffiti from the library, the dorms, and classroom buildings may address different topics, yet together they may illustrate one particular reason: the need for a private, anonymous opportunity to air views about personal issues that have now become matters of public debate. A single example, however, might also bear on several reasons. An extended graffiti dialogue among several women about date rape may demonstrate not only the need for a private, anonymous forum but also the desire to seek advice and comment from an exclusively female audience.

Write in explicit signals to help your readers know how to use your examples   Review the logical shape of your paper to ensure that you project its organization on the basis of reasons. If you find yourself mentioning examples as your organizing principle, recast the projected organization in terms of reasons that underlie your examples. As you write out your full draft, be aware that examples don't necessarily speak for themselves; you need to give voice to the reasons they suggest. Readers should know what it is that your examples illustrate, emphasize, or clarify. If they become interested in an example for its own sake, you haven't focused enough attention on the function served by that example in your line of reasoning.

Examples have an eloquence of their own, a power to persuade that abstract reasoning can never match. Yet for their eloquence to be heard and their power to be felt, you must harness their energy as you advance your own line of reasoning.

Developing Analogies and Comparisons

Examples help you analyze and argue because in them you can perceive similarities and differences to your own case. As you write out a full draft, you may find yourself reaching for an analogy or comparison—two ways that writers express similarity and difference. Yet the matter of judging similarity and difference is not always easy, nor is the application to another case always straightforward. Once again, let's revisit a topic familiar to veterans of writing courses—analogy and comparison—with a special concern in mind: maintaining your analytic or argumentative focus.

Forming Analogies

Whenever you perceive similarity, you are already well on your way to forming an analogy. Analogy underlies inductive thinking, where we link individual observations into a pattern that suggests a tentative hypothesis. If we recall that warm-up stretches help us jog better, we may be tempted to practice our scales at the piano before launching into a Chopin étude.

Analogy expresses similarity in that you find A to be like B, at least in certain respects. In drawing the analogy, you implicitly extract a rule or principle from one term, and declare it applicable to the other. By establishing likeness, analogies help us make sense of our world.

Basic though they may seem, analogies can guide even the most sophisticated thinking and scientific research. Cancer tests conducted on mice, for example, suggest the degree of risk to humans, in so far as there is a basic similarity between rodent and human physiology. Analogies can also help you clarify one term by seeing it in relationship to another, usually more familiar or concrete term. Earlier in this chapter we saw how a student used the analogy of a blanket to explain the effect that chlorofluorocarbons have on our upper atmosphere.

Yet analogy is more than an explanatory tool. It is an implicit form of reasoning, and thus carries persuasive force. When you set two situations in an analogous relationship, you are implying that what holds for one situation also holds for the other. A key to inductive reasoning, analogy thus can also serve as a tool when you defend propositions. Consider the extended analogy New York Governor Mario Cuomo used when nominating Bill Clinton as the Democratic candidate for president in 1992.

> The ship of state is headed for the rocks.
> The crew knows it. The passengers know it. Only the captain of the ship, President Bush, appears not to know it. He seems to think that the ship will be saved by imperceptible undercurrents, directed by the invisible hand of some cyclical economic god, that will gradually move the ship so that at the last moment it will miraculously glide past the rocks to safer shores.
> Well, prayer is always a good thing. But our prayers must be accompanied by good works. We need a captain who understands that and who will seize the wheel, before it's too late. I am here tonight to offer America that new captain with a new course.

In offering this analogy, Cuomo is doing more than presenting us a choice; he is persuading us of his choice. Persuading us quite inappropriately, the Republicans would surely say. And to convince us, they would question at each turn whether Cuomo has accurately characterized matters.

However eloquent, Cuomo's rhetorical move is hardly uncommon. Whenever you put forward and justify an assertion, you are more than likely engaging in analogous thought at some level. For example, our entire legal system, with its emphasis on precedent and common law, is based on drawing analogies between one case and another. In building a case and persuading judge and jury, an attorney is analyzing and arguing with the help of analogies. You may not think of yourself as an attorney, but most of the analytic and argumentative writing you do in college shares with legal writing the obligation to articulate and defend a position.

Unless you use analogies carefully, however, they can undermine your case as much as they can advance it. Many analogies are so covert you may be hardly aware of the persuasive force that lies within them. Just consider the word "lies" in the previous sentence. Does persuasive force "lie within" an analogy, ready to be unpacked, or might not that force *spring* to the minds of readers who interact with the author? Seemingly innocent choice of words can reveal root metaphors that guide—even persuade—how we construct meaning.

The suitability of the terms in the analogy can also influence its persuasive force. When you analyze and argue solely on the basis of similitude, you may find the two situations less similar than you make them out to be. Don't rest your case entirely on an analogy, for resemblance provides in itself little proof. Nevertheless, appropriate analogies can orient and clarify your discussion so that readers will be more disposed to accept the reasons that you do offer.

To use analogy appropriately, be sure to ask yourself the following two questions.

How apt is the analogy?   If you try hard enough, you can find similarities between virtually any two situations or things. The results can be ludicrous, if not fallacious. Is premarital sex like test-driving a car? Hardly, for the similarity on which the analogy rests is slight at best. To determine whether an analogy is apt, consider not only the similarities but also the differences between one term and the other. Moreover, ask yourself how relevant the similarities and differences are to the discussion at hand. An analogy may look reasonable in one context, but entirely unreasonable in another. Arguments based on similitude can border on the unethical for this reason. Just because a witness lied once does not mean he is lying now, yet this argument of implied similitude is a favorite tactic of attorneys when cross-examining a witness. Moreover, if you point out that two situations or two people are alike in some respects, you cannot argue that they are alike in all respects. Political campaigns thrive on just this sort of distortion; a liberal record on environmental concerns need not imply radical left-wing allegiances on matters of fiscal or foreign policy.

What purpose does the analogy serve?   Before you apply an analogy that you think to be apt, consider whether it is relevant to the question at issue and serves the point you wish to advance. Most analogies break down if pushed far enough; the question thus becomes whether an analogy is appropriate to a particular context and purpose. Ask yourself whether you have sufficient occasion to use an analogy. What purpose does it serve? The question of purpose is crucial because analogy inherently carries some motivation. Analogies cannot be used neutrally, for they come loaded with interpretive freight. They reflect, if only indirectly, certain purposes and values and already point readers to a conclusion. Try to recognize that implicit conclusion before you apply what seems to be an appropriate analogy.

The question of purpose becomes doubly complex because the analytic or argumentative point to which you apply an analogy may not square with the hidden persuasive appeal that the analogy carries. For example, among the many analogies about writing, one of the most famous was coined by the eighteenth-century poet and essayist Samuel Johnson: "Language is a dress that thought puts on." Johnson draws a likeness between the concrete act of putting on clothes and the abstract idea of using language. But I would be misguided to invoke Johnson's likeness, stunning as it is, for it runs counter to the argument I am advancing in this book. (Indeed, it is contradicted by Johnson's own style, which is never merely decorative.) We don't create finished thoughts in our heads and then find words in which to dress them. We discover and refine ideas as we shape them on the page. Thus, an analogy may point in one direction, your stated intention in another. The problem is more common than you may think. It lurks whenever an analogy—explicit or hidden—diverts attention from the focus of your paper or whenever it raises troubling concerns that seem tangential to your stated purpose. Once you recognize that analogies are themselves hidden persuaders already burdened with some degree of interpretation, you realize how alert you should be when using or reading them.

Drawing Comparisons

Comparison enters the picture when similarities end and differences also become relevant. Comparison highlights what remains covert in analogy—that is, comparison requires you to account for both similarity and difference. In fact, you may be more familiar with the term *comparison* when it is linked explicitly to the term *contrast*, as in that favorite essay-exam phrase *compare and contrast*. The phrase is actually a bit redundant, for in comparing you must necessarily contrast.

Comparison is a tool that writers use to express one of the most fundamental of mental acts: the ability to distinguish, to classify by sorting out similarities and differences. We draw comparisons at many levels of writing. A single sentence (this one, for example) need not isolate one idea but can draw an apt contrast. A paragraph or an entire essay can likewise develop a comparison by drawing out resemblances and differences.

Whatever the context or level, comparison is seldom an end in itself. You generally compare two or more things to address a specific problem or to advance a particular point of view. Thus, issues of relevance, motivation, and purpose once again enter our discussion. The questions you must ask yourself when using comparison resemble those for analogy, but with the added twist that you must now account for differences as well as similarities.

Three questions can help you harness comparison as you pursue an analysis or argument.

What motivates the comparison?   Although you can compare virtually any two objects or situations, it only makes sense to compare them if they share a common frame of reference. You can compare Homer's *Odyssey* with Twain's *The Adventures of Huckleberry Finn* or Wordsworth's *Prelude* with Milton's *Paradise Lost*, but the comparison makes sense only if you can articulate a question at issue that draws together both works. Otherwise, the comparison may remain gratuitous. Virtually any two things can be compared, but comparison itself is not the point. Comparison is only worth pursuing if you can identify a problem or concern that generates the comparison and is illuminated by it. If you can't, you risk having your readers ask, "Why bother?"

If you are faced with the task of comparing and contrasting, as you often are in college, your first move should be to uncover why the comparison has been drawn. Don't simply dive in and start reporting this similarity and that difference. You'll only confuse yourself and your reader. Begin by articulating a question at issue that engages and draws together two works or situations. Any two things worth comparing share an occasion. Ask yourself what that common occasion is and what is to be gained by the comparison.

What structure is appropriate for the comparison?   The task of drawing out both similarities and differences may unnerve you at first, for it seems that you must do several things at once. The solution is to find a structure that encompasses both tasks but lets you focus your energies on just one aspect at a time. This question boils down, then, to one of procedure; how should you organize a comparison to suit your purposes?

Two basic alternatives present themselves. You might think of the first alternative as a block pattern, where the comparison is divided into two halves. You first discuss item A fully, and then you move on to item B, as shown by this pattern.

A1 A2 A3 / B1 B2 B3

This pattern is useful if the comparison is relatively straightforward or if an overall perspective is more useful to you and your readers than detailing individual similarities and differences.

Your second alternative is to structure the comparison by individual characteristics. You might think of this possibility as a point-by-point comparison, where you alternate between both items as you take up specific aspects of each, as shown by this pattern.

A1 B1 / A2 B2 / A3 B3

The point-by-point is a bit more complicated, but it has the advantage of providing a tighter, more rigorous comparison, especially if the items you are comparing are involved and your discussion lengthy.

Which pattern should you choose? It all depends on your purpose, which brings us to the third and most important question.

What's the point of the comparison?   If you treat comparison as an exotic formal exercise or isolated task, it will hold little value for you and your readers. Comparisons should prompt conclusions. If a question at issue motivates the comparison, then your paper should throw some light on that concern.

The danger that you face when comparing is that the process can overwhelm the point. I recall reading a paper by a student who compared, in glorious detail, two computer programming languages, Fortran and Pascal. He became so preoccupied with the comparison that he failed to link it consistently to the question at issue: which language should the college of engineering choose in developing an introductory computing course suitable for all of its majors? Like this writer, if you focus on a mechanical inventory of similarities and differences, you may even neglect to draw a conclusion. Readers may miss the purpose of comparison if you merely ask them to follow its back-and-forth movement. Don't let your point get lost as you compare, for comparison above all requires a point. To avoid this pitfall, analyze or argue from your conclusion and use comparison as a means of support. Treat every aspect of the comparison as an opportunity to advance your point of view. If you merely report a comparison like an accountant recording figures in a double-entry ledger you're sure to be as dull.

Comparison can serve your analysis and argument precisely because it requires you to highlight purpose and sharpen your point. It can enlarge your vision and that of your readers, but only if you clarify what you see in it. To make use of comparison you must first make something of it.

Engaging Counterarguments

As you write out your draft, writing in counterarguments to your own case may seem, at best, an unwelcome obligation and, at worst, a perverse way of sabotaging your own efforts.

It's not hard to understand why. In defending a thesis, you usually find complicating questions, opposing viewpoints, and rival hypotheses lying in ambush. Counterarguments can assault what you thought was a secure position or can distract you as you try to develop what may already be an uncertain and tenuous point. Not wanting to add to your difficulties, you may prefer to avoid counterargument altogether. Why draw attention to problems readers ought to discover for themselves? Why weaken a case about which you already feel insecure?

You won't be able to dispel these hesitations and misgivings by sprinkling your prose with an occasional "Granted" or "To be sure." A perceptive reader will recognize token, halfhearted references to another viewpoint as counterfeit counterargument. Furtive glances at unanswered questions will not build your credibility, nor will they bolster your confidence. Moreover, if you are unwilling to look troublesome issues in the eye, you won't be able to strengthen your case as you refine your draft.

Instead of being coy about counterarguments, try being forthright and fairminded. The strategy will amaze your severest critics and convert fence sitters to your cause. To help you with this approach, let's consider why, where, and how to address counterarguments in a manner that turns obligation into creative opportunity.

Why Should You Address Counterarguments?

When writing analysis and argument, you should expect that your views and those of your readers may differ. In fact, you ought to be worried if they don't. An analysis or argument that doesn't engage a question genuinely at issue probably isn't worth writing. When you analyze, your counterarguments will take the form of questions and perhaps rival hypotheses. When you argue, the counterarguments will likely become more pointed and challenge more directly your point of view or the adequacy of your evidence. In both cases, counterarguments are more than a matter of polite deference to your audience; they are risks inherent to analysis and argument. You can't disregard your reader's capacity to disagree, because that very capacity also provides for the possibility of assent. By ignoring counterarguments, you alienate your audience and weaken the very basis for agreement.

If analysis and especially argument oblige you to treat counterarguments, that's no reason not to take creative advantage of them. Although you may think of counterarguments as a defensive measure, a way to forestall problems, they can also carry positive persuasive force. When my students tackle controversial issues, they are regularly amazed that an honest, respectful treatment of opposing views can help their case. When you acknowledge that opinions other than your own deserve a hearing, your own opinions generally find a more willing audience. Likewise, by engaging counterarguments seriously, you show yourself to be reasonable, fair-minded, and well informed. Most of us turn a deaf ear to the one-dimensional dogmatist or the insistent fanatic, and we shouldn't be surprised that readers do likewise. If you write as if those who disagree with you merit little consideration, you are only inviting the same treatment. You can turn counterarguments to your favor by exploring them fully and dealing with them fairly.

Counterarguments can serve as positive persuasive tools if you are confident that your case has merit. But what should you do when counterarguments readily dismantle whatever case you're trying to build? Consider these counterarguments as tools for discovering and refining a case that merits your confident support. As you write out a draft, it's imperative that you write in and explore points that call what you say into question. If you don't, you deprive yourself of an essential learning tool. A dogmatic, one-dimensional case in a final draft usually reflects an unwillingness to explore early on. The sooner you raise counterarguments, the more likely you can revise your way out of simpleminded assertions. As you explore questions that seem inconvenient to the case you are building, you may even find some of your most persuasive support. Your own assertions gain credibility, after all, if you can answer probing questions regarding them. Once you look on counterarguments as ways to test the limits of your case and even to find good reasons for it, you'll pursue them as doggedly as your severest critic. And your own case will be stronger for your effort.

When you confront counterarguments, you force yourself to *think*. You're challenging—and enhancing—your own reasoning by asking, "Is my opinion or hypothesis *really* the best way of accounting for all the evidence? Why exactly is my opinion better than other opinions that could also be argued with some force?" When you confront counterarguments in your paper, you have to answer these questions. When you do so, you are engaged in serious thinking, thinking that is both rigorous and creative.

Where Might You Address Counterarguments?

You should alert readers to counterarguments early in your essay, preferably in the introduction. By mentioning counterarguments at the outset, you can clarify the issue that occasions your essay. Moreover, you can forestall questions that your reader may wish to pose by indicating that you will take up points of controversy in the body of your paper. If readers sense that you are aware of concerns that complicate your case, they will be more willing to grant you a hearing and not beset you with immediate queries.

As you set up dynamic relationships among occasion, thesis, and reasons in your introduction, you will find three ready opportunities to address counterarguments.

• A counterargument can serve as your occasion, especially if the counterargument presents a view to which you respond in your essay.

• You can also introduce a counterargument in conjunction with your thesis; such a counterthesis suggests you are aware of rival hypotheses and conclusions.

• The reasons that project the organization of your essay also allow you to engage counterarguments, especially if the questions readers are likely to pose concern specific aspects of your evidence.

By introducing counterarguments at the outset of your paper, you are signaling your intent to deal with them in the body of your discussion. You have three basic ways to make good on your promise as you develop your full draft.

You can address counterarguments all at once before you move on to your own case   This strategy works well if you believe that your reader needs to have a set of questions answered immediately or if you must set aside a series of reservations before you move on to your own point. In setting up her argument that life imprisonment should replace the death penalty, this student saw the need to address reasons for capital punishment straightaway. This first paragraph promises she will do so early in the essay.

> Today on the death rows of 37 state prisons, 1,788 offenders await the courts' decisions on their death sentence appeals. If, instead of the courts, present public opinion decided the fate of these criminals, they would surely die, since 75 to 84 percent of the population supports capital punishment. Although the reasons for supporting the death penalty vary, the two most commonly cited are that it is the only fitting punishment for some crimes, and that it deters other people from committing the same crimes.

I am not convinced by these arguments. The one is based on a simplistic view of the penal system, the other on statistical misinformation. Because there is not acceptable justification for capital punishment, I believe that it should be abolished in the United States. Life imprisonment, rightly conceived, would be a more fitting punishment, a more effective deterrent, and a lesser drain on the public purse.

You can engage counterarguments as you present the reasoning behind each of your proofs   When counterarguments relate to your own specific evidence, you are best served by engaging opposing views and contrary evidence as you advance your own proofs. When writing to expose the hazards of shipping radioactive waste to the proposed Waste Isolation Pilot Plant in New Mexico, one student found that counterarguments lay in the details. Here's how she set up one of several proofs for her argument, this one pertaining to the safety of the roads on which the nuclear waste would travel.

When New Mexico originally agreed to host WIPP, the Department of Energy indicated that it would secure federal funds for the road improvements and bypasses necessary to transport the waste safely. The federal government now states, however, that the funds are unnecessary at the present time because New Mexico's interstate highways have recently been upgraded with federal money. Although portions of the interstate have been improved, highway conditions remain a central concern. The waste-disposal route takes trucks through downtown Albuquerque on I-25, where heavy congestion persists despite nominal improvements. Moreover, the secondary roads that could be used to avoid congested areas remain in poor condition, as they have not been upgraded in recent years.

In succeeding paragraphs she then elaborated on each aspect of her rebuttal to the counterargument that roads are now adequate. By addressing counterarguments early in each paragraph or section of your paper, you can anticipate questions before your reader poses them. Moreover, early mention of those questions allows you plenty of opportunity to respond.

You can organize your paper as a refutation   Some argumentative essays reply to the reasons given in support of another position. The approach is useful if you are responding to an already articulated position; reasons for that position then become counterarguments to your own view. By answering arguments already set forth, you may be able to show that the other case is unreasonable or a proposal unworkable, as illustrated in the following example.

Tipper Gore, spokeswoman for the organization Parents Music Resource Center (PMRC), contends that a great many song lyrics, such as "My true love is Satan, riding in a phaeton," are harmful to children. The PMRC wants to protect children from lyrics that glorify violence, obscenity, drug use, and satanism by having the music industry place warning labels on records, print song lyrics on albums, and renegotiate contracts with "offensive" performers. The PMRC's plan, however, is unworkable. First of all, it would be impossible for a group of people to come to an agreement about the proper label for 25,000 songs a year. Second, the record industry could not print the lyrics on all album covers because they don't own the rights to most of the lyrics. Third, children cannot be protected from offensive on-stage performances because the record industry has no control over the performers.

How Should You Handle Counterarguments?

Most papers treat counterarguments inadequately not because they don't mention the other side at all or do so at an inappropriate time; they come up short because they don't engage counterarguments seriously. Afraid that they may undermine their own case, students often accord questions, contrary evidence, and opposing views the briefest of mention. Merely pointing to counterargument becomes a way of keeping confusion at bay. Satisfied that they have done their duty in what is often no more than a phrase, they then pick up where they left off, as if nothing had been said. And if the truth be known, not much has been said. When you fail to take a counterargument seriously by considering its merit, probing its implications, and answering its concerns, your gesture—dismissive at heart—is more likely to enrage than mollify the skeptical reader.

A cavalier attitude carries a further cost: your readers may not understand exactly how those counterarguments figure in your discussion. Mentioning counterarguments makes little sense unless readers know how you respond. You must therefore integrate the concerns you acknowledge into your own line of reasoning. The task calls for subtle discernment, for questions at issue necessarily vary and the psychological disposition of your audience can be rather fickle. Stock replies are inherently unpersuasive. Nevertheless, you may wish to keep in mind three general strategies for engaging counterargument.

Strategic concession   Because few arguments reduce themselves to black and white, be ready to acknowledge the merit in other views. Spirited debate in Congress about the wisdom of launching military action in what became the Persian

Gulf War pitted intelligent, well-meaning people on either side of the issue. Many were surely tempted to characterize proponents as militaristic yahoos or opponents as wimps unwilling to support their nation's interests—but at the price of losing respect and goodwill. Inexperienced writers often undervalue the persuasive effect of concession: by acknowledging competing views and contrary evidence you own up to legitimate disagreement. In doing so, you present yourself as fair-minded, as someone willing to earn conclusions responsibly. Moreover, strategic concession can help you set up your own strong arguments to follow. Should you find yourself conceding too much, however, you may wish to reconsider the position for which you are arguing.

Refutation   If you can meet and refute the challenges posed to your case, so much the better. Be careful, however, not to gloat over victories concerning minor objections, while you leave major reservations unaddressed. For example, in a paper lauding court rulings that give police more latitude in searching automobiles for suspected drugs, it makes little sense for the author to discuss at length matters of convenience and inconvenience, while leaving aside the far more central objection of search and seizure without a warrant. You are best off tackling the strongest counterarguments, or readers may believe that you are missing key points.

Irrelevance to the matter at hand   If you frame the issue carefully and qualify your own thesis appropriately, you can demonstrate that some counterarguments may not be germane to the discussion. For example, instead of arguing that all gun owners should be required to take a class in gun safety, you could focus on a more narrow assertion: that such a class would reduce the likelihood of accidental death or injury. By carefully establishing the grounds of debate, you can treat some apparent objections as out of bounds. Troublesome questions central to requiring the class (such as cost or enforcement) are no longer germane to the revised assertion on which the broader thesis nevertheless rests—the likely effect of such a course on firearm accidents.

As helpful as these three strategies may be, you cannot handle counterarguments unless you first see them as tools for refining your own thinking. Engage counterarguments not merely to acknowledge or refute them, or to dispense with them as irrelevant, but to *learn* from them. If you approach each question or objection as an opportunity rather than an obligation, you will develop subtle, colorful shades to your thinking and your prose. Reasoned nuance persuades far more readily than the simplistic black-and-white contrasts to which most arguments are reduced. Questions and objections ought to find a place in your analysis and argument as you write out your final draft. But long before that, be sure you write them in as tools for discovery.

Crafting the Conclusion

If concluding were simply a matter of stopping, writers wouldn't agonize over their final paragraphs as they do. Nor would readers expect much from them. As you near draft's end, you may be tempted merely to stop. Your energies are flagging; you've said what you set out to say. But you know that just stopping is inherently unsatisfying. Readers appreciate a sense of closure; writers, in turn, appreciate one last chance to press home and lend significance to their point. A memorable conclusion appeals to us intellectually and emotionally, for it clarifies at once meaning and relevance.

Writers find conclusions difficult to write because they are so multifaceted and, what is more, so idiosyncratic. They resist the easy formula. One reason is that they are both integral to and yet somewhat separate from the text. On the one hand, they depend on and are determined by what has already been written. Conclusions are as specific as the different essays they conclude. Yet conclusions are also undetermined, up for grabs as it were. They offer a final moment of inventive freedom, an opportunity for panache.

The strange double life that conclusions lead becomes particularly apparent when writers focus on one aspect to the neglect of the other. A conclusion that merely repeats what has already been said belabors the obvious, and will only bore or insult your readers. Resist the transparent summary ("In conclusion, I have now shown . . ."), for it merely duplicates the text. At the other extreme, a conclusion that raises entirely new issues obscures your essay's focus, and will only confuse your reader. It initiates a new, slightly different text. If conclusions don't work, it's usually because writers have isolated one or the other of these double strands, taking each to an extreme.

Two strategies can help you harness the energies inherent in a conclusion's double role. The first provides a way to write a conclusion by seeing the relationship it bears to your introduction. The second enables you to use the conclusion you have written as an opportunity to initiate further revision.

Conclude by Relating Text and Context

Think of your conclusion as looking in two directions: back to the text and forward to context. In this regard, conclusions are analogous to introductions. Indeed, your conclusion should reflect the concerns raised in your introduction. Both provide framework—the introduction does so prospectively, the conclusion retrospectively. They literally frame the body of your essay and provide a field within which you can develop it. At the same time, they place your essay within larger contexts; the introduction announces the issue that occasions your essay and the conclusion underscores the awareness or potential for informed action that readers take with them from your essay. Your conclusion is, then, not so much final as pivotal. It echoes the meaning of your essay while pointing to the purpose it must accomplish, the action it might inspire.

Let's consider first the opening and then the closing paragraph of an essay that a student wrote about her own engineering education.

> The attrition rate in our College of Engineering is much higher for women than for men. While approximately one in five freshmen students is a woman, the number drops to fewer than one in seven for seniors. It is easy to treat this statistic as a reflection of competence related to gender. After all, men and women are subject to the same curriculum. I suggest, however, that the statistic reflects another reality: a hidden, largely unintentional bias against females in engineering, one that becomes apparent in the typical college classroom. Because women have a style of learning different from men's, they find themselves at a disadvantage in the typical male-oriented engineering class. Moreover, inadvertent but widespread sexism among professors and students drives all but the most determined women from the study of engineering.

> Women are able to succeed in engineering. But, because invisible barriers are placed in their way, they remain a minority in the field. If we are to increase the number of female engineers, we must not only increase enrollment but also improve retention. The latter can be accomplished only with fundamental changes. Smaller classes, better teachers, active and personal support of all students by faculty and administrators—these are the radical transformations that engineering education must undergo. Good intentions and lip service can accomplish only so much. Until such measures are introduced, engineering will remain predominantly male, and the discipline will be poorer for it.

By summarizing or synthesizing her discussion, the conclusion looks back toward her text. In a short essay of several pages, such backward glances should be swift. There's no need for a prolonged stare, for readers have just read the analysis or argument. If you have identified reasons for your point along the way, the shape of your ideas should be sufficiently fresh in their minds. Your job, then, is to echo, to recall the focus and salient support in a sentence or two, or perhaps only a phrase. Look back at your introduction for help, especially your thesis and reasons. Note that "invisible barriers" recalls the author's point and her essay's plan. Likewise, desired changes in engineering education reflect the difficulties her essay uncovered. The need for synthesis grows as your discussion becomes longer and more complex. In essays of fifteen pages or more, a synthetic look back helps your reader gain perspective and distinguish essential from subsidiary ideas.

The author's conclusion also sets her text in a larger context—her readers' context—by answering the question uppermost in their minds; "Why should this matter to me?" If you don't, your essay has little point. Your meaning becomes memorable only when your readers know why your message is important. For the writer's audience (faculty and administrators in the engineering college), the essay's relevance hinges on the issue that launched her essay: difficulties in retaining women engineering students. At the end of her essay, readers are looking for the significance, implication, and urgency behind its leading idea. Like this writer, you can place your text in context by looking once again at your introduction, particularly at your occasion. Use the question at issue to bring out the implications of your essay's reply. By returning to or echoing the concerns raised in the occasion, you help your reader appreciate how your discussion has advanced understanding. In so doing, you provide a sense of closure.

A final word about writing your conclusion. Graceful exits tend to be swift. Most conclusions diffuse the forceful impression they try to create by belaboring obvious points. Reward your reader with incisive answers about the essay's broader significance.

Use Your Conclusion to Introduce Revision

Because conclusions are written last, you may think of them as your final word. They shouldn't be. Conclusions offer one last chance to get things right, to make the point you've been searching for. As a result, they often produce your best and most cogent thinking. Eleventh-hour clarity may be gratifying to you and your readers. It's all but wasted, however, when your essay has not capitalized on it from the start, or when your essay may even confuse or contradict your belated revelation.

To make the most of your final words in a full draft, consider whether they might initiate another round of revision. I recall an early draft of a paper on eating disorders, written by a student who was herself a recovering bulimic. In her five-page ramble, she touched now and again on her relationship with her father and mother, and more generally on male and female personality traits. Only in the conclusion to her rough draft did she articulate her point with electrifying clarity: "Far from being a 'personal problem,' eating disorders are family affairs." Take the advice I gave to this writer: consider starting your next draft with a tightly reasoned defense of an insight won in the concluding moments of a lengthy ramble. When you analyze and argue, you are, after all, searching for and working from conclusions. Because the writing you do in college typically asks you to state your point up front and then justify it with a pointed defense, your conclusion on a question can literally serve as your introduction. By spotting the conclusion toward which you drift in an early draft, you can revise the destination you announce at the outset and reach it more directly.

You may think of your conclusion as determined by what you have already said, but the double life it leads enables you to capitalize on the freedom it provides. By harnessing the energy inherent in closure, you can turn your conclusion into more than a point of arrival; it can also serve as a creative point of departure. Because conclusions are, in one sense, up for grabs, seize them as opportunities to reconsider and sharpen your case. In a moment of panache, you might find your point.

Revising by Argument   7

Revising, rewriting, rethinking—the terms all suggest belated attempts to set things right. They speak of one more go at the paper, one last chance to correct what you have already written.

Nothing could be further from the truth. Experienced writers view revising, not composing, as their greatest challenge and their most creative opportunity. Not something to be left to the night before, revision, properly done, consumes far more time than writing a first draft. Veteran writers will take three, four, or even five cracks at a paper. Each revision might differ radically from the previous one as they shake out irrelevancies and explore new angles of approach. Each serves as a further opportunity to find an appropriate design, to clarify the line of thinking, to reach the reader intellectually and emotionally. To hear them speak of their work, you'd think that nine-tenths of what they write is revision. And it is.

Why, then, the bum rap? Revision evokes images of drudge and dunce work because it has long been seen as a process of correcting details—grammar, spelling, and the like—instead of as an opportunity to explore new possibilities that may call for global change. Students tend to see revision as addition or subtraction: a chance to stick in what's missing or throw out what doesn't fit. Rarely is the entire project reconsidered, the appropriateness of the design to which "correct" words are added and from which "wrong" ones are deleted.

This chapter will help you gain a different perspective on revision—appropriately so, as revision itself requires not so much one more look at a paper as a fresh perspective on it, a re-vision. More transformative than repetitive, revision doesn't ask you to have another go at your text; it encourages you to acquire a different take on it. It is not so much one specific stage as an approach you can adopt throughout the writing process. Although writers may emphasize revision once they have a full draft, they reenvision their work whenever they wish fresh perspective. A writer's ultimate wisdom lies in recognizing that a long, diffuse draft may yield only one idea that can then be built into an interesting essay.

How can you look at an old text with new eyes? Revise by argument. We do our best revising when we argue with ourselves, when we try to pick apart our own paper as would our most skeptical readers. All good writers do that;

inexperienced ones seldom make the effort. This chapter will help you revise by argument. It will also give you some specific strategies for arguing with your writing and for responding creatively should your text come up short in the discussion.

Revising by argument encourages you to develop the skeptical, experimental habit of mind so appropriate to analysis and argument. The approach asks that you take on a questioning, even adversarial, attitude toward your own prose. It helps even very accomplished writers check their work for intellectual loopholes. Rather than accepting what's on the page simply because it is there, you look for missing evidence and hidden assumptions. You question whether information that you present may be irrelevant or the logic misleading. The strategy asks, in short, that you become a critical reader of your own work, that you quarrel with your own words. By extension, revising by argument can engage you in dialogue with actual readers. Collaboration with readers—be they instructors, classmates, or trusted friends—can turn revision into what it ought to be—a creative, often collective, act of problem solving.

Why revise by argument? The reasons extend beyond personal improvement, although that is surely reason enough. If you take your responsibilities seriously, you'll want to clarify your point and find the best reasons to support it. But there is also a more public motivation to revise by argument. If you don't, your readers will. As lawyers will quickly confess, it's much better to find and revise the flaws in your own case than it is to wait until opposing counsel does the work for you by refuting your case before a jury. Although you may be the one presenting your case, analysis and argument are not your tools alone; readers can make ready use of them when considering your own work. The very tools of analysis and argument that can lead readers to accept your point also permit them to test the coherence of your thinking.

As well they should. Your purpose in writing is not to put one over on your readers but to justify your point with cogent reasoning. Because it provides a reader's perspective, revising by argument can help you to hone your own critical-thinking skills. The questions that a skeptical reader would likely pose provide a point of reference from which you can gain fresh perspective on your work. Revising by argument asks you to think like a reader.

Adopting the Reader's Stance

Thinking like a reader won't be foreign to you if you have acknowledged the concerns of your audience from the very start. Because the principles for shaping ideas that underlie this book grow out of questions that readers pose, revising by argument is a natural extension of the book's techniques. Revision nevertheless requires that you adopt the reader's stance in a more explicit, more persistent manner. Questions on the part of your readers may have guided your writing, but revision requires that you question what you have actually written. Here are five tips on how you might achieve a reader's perspective and use it to your advantage.

Approach Your Own Writing with a Reader's Fresh Eye

To do so, you must first gain some distance from your writing. The greatest obstacle to revision is self-absorption. Set aside your writing for a few hours, preferably overnight. (In a famous passage, the Roman poet Horace recommends seven years.) With a fresh eye, you'll be better able to experience your work as a reader would. You will also recognize discrepancies between what you think you've said and what you've actually put on the page. As you collaborate with actual readers (your instructor or classmates) during the revision process, bear in mind how you might anticipate their comments. Doing so can help you recognize and develop your own editorial voice, your own internal reader. Comments from readers make objective the inklings and intuitions you may have felt as you were writing. Use these comments as a way to train and trust your own editorial sixth sense.

Look Ahead to Productive, Creative Change

Comments from readers can put you on the defensive if you focus on the work you have already done. You can lessen the sense that revision comments are personal attacks by putting the purpose of revision into perspective: more important than the draft you have finished are the changes you can make to it. Although you may sense some safety in having committed words to the page, your greatest risk lies in resisting change.

Summarize Your Paper to Understand What You Have Written

Before you can contemplate changes to your work, both you and your readers need to clarify what is already on the page. Midcourse corrections may only confuse matters unless you and your readers can locate where your text currently stands. By asking yourself and your readers to summarize your paper, to put it in a nutshell, you can match deed with intention. Do the words you have written fulfill your purpose? What is that purpose? Where and why might your readers misread your intentions? Can your readers identify the issue, point, and plan that generates the design of your paper? Does the design that your readers discern match the design you intend? By evaluating any discrepancies, you lay the foundation for revising by argument.

Ask Specific Questions that Generate Analytic Replies _____

General reactions to your paper can be so vague that they don't render the help you need. When you ask broad questions of your readers—"Do you like the paper?" or "Is it okay?"—you elicit comments that, whether positive or negative, remain essentially dismissive and evasive. To get feedback you can use, ask questions that generate specific analytic replies. For example, instead of asking whether a transition is effective, ask what effect the transition has. Instead of asking whether a paragraph seems useful, ask what function the paragraph serves. Be willing to pursue vague comments by pressing your readers for specifics. Only when you know what readers see in your writing, or why they respond to it as they do, can you know how you might improve it. Likewise, when you comment on someone else's paper, ground your reaction in the text. Specify what prompts your response. Then propose an action the author can take or an alternative that he or she might consider. Criticism becomes constructive when you help each other resolve the problems you uncover.

Give Top Priority to the Point and Shape of the Case _____

As you offer or receive comments on a paper, focus first on concerns that affect the entire project. Such concerns include the issue that prompts the paper, its thesis, the means and design by which it justifies the thesis, and the manner in which it takes into account the concerns and attitudes of its audience. Pause before you chase down run-on sentences; let the modifiers dangle. First see to the merits of the case. After you adjust the case, those troublesome sentences may no longer be in the next draft. Local problems, whether at the sentence or paragraph level, are often symptoms of more fundamental design problems. After you address global concerns, you can then resolve whatever local issues remain. If you wish to make noticeable improvements to your paper, do more than tinker with the first design you latch onto. If you consider fundamental questions of form, you're more likely to make the changes that matter most.

These five tips can help you adopt and profit from the reader's view. By providing a second perspective on your work, the reader's view enables you to question and argue, to consider options and make conscious decisions. The reader's view can become objectified when you work with actual readers, or internalized as you develop your own editorial awareness. In either case, revision can help you see readers as more than recipients of your writing; they also become collaborators in your thinking.

Revision brings you freedom and control—opportunity, not merely obligation. By revising, you realize that you can choose differently, that your current design isn't the only one you can have. Revision can and should empower you. It can help you become aware of options and should encourage you to make conscious decisions. Revision does demand that you control your writing, but it also helps you to assert control. By asking you to take responsibility for what you write, it develops your sense of authority.

Clarifying Conceptual Relationships

Revising by argument should begin with questions that readers themselves are likely to pose.

- What is the question at issue?
- What is the author's point?
- Do the author's reasons elicit my belief?

These questions have helped you shape your paper around an occasion, a thesis, and reasons that justify your position before skeptical readers. Now the very same questions that helped you write your draft can shape the process by which you revise.

Revision needn't be a mysterious alchemy. Transforming leaden prose into gold requires skill and hard work, but the process is far from inscrutable. Don't expect a hidden hand to move words and ideas around the page, and don't rely on eleventh-hour inspiration. Revision begins when you first adopt a reader's stance. It becomes easier when you base your design from the outset on questions uppermost in the reader's mind. By understanding and posing reader-oriented questions, you can lend method and focus to your revision.

First, ask yourself whether your writing responds to or ignores readers' questions. Then determine whether your replies are on speaking terms with each other. Does your thesis turn a deaf ear to your occasion? Might your reasons fail to answer the concerns of your thesis? Have you left counterarguments out of the discussion altogether? Simply having formal elements in your paper is not enough. You need to do more than plug in an occasion, a thesis, and an organizational plan. They must work together to create a web of meaning. Readers' questions do more than help you inventory structural elements; these questions can clarify the relationships that shape your thinking.

Probing with Questions

Proceeding from these basic questions, you can pose further, far more specific questions.

• Do you interest your reader by engaging a specific issue or concern, one your reader cares about? Or do you hide the question at issue in an avalanche of information, or edge toward it as you funnel in from broad generalities? Does your occasion set up your thesis? Does your occasion suggest that you can answer the question "Why bother?"

• Do you have a clear thesis or one that is buried in information and merely implied? Does the paper wander in search of a thesis? Is the thesis that you announce analytic or argumentative, or does it promise but a descriptive recitation of facts? Does your thesis adequately represent your point, or do other interpretations vie for attention?

• Do the reasons that project the conceptual organization of your essay remain loyal to your thesis? Or do they wander away from the thesis to address other concerns, thereby compromising the support you intend to give or contradicting the very point you wish to make? Do you distinguish between observation and inference, and account for the latter based on evidence and reasoning? Do you support generalizations with particulars, opinions with facts?

• Do you acknowledge evidence inconvenient to your thesis, or do you simply ignore contrary evidence and counterarguments? Do you answer possible objections to your case and thereby qualify it appropriately so that it is neither under- nor overstated?

As tough as these questions may be, they shouldn't take you by surprise if you have been willing to shape your paper from the outset with your reader in mind. Revising by argument enables you to ask these questions before they occur to your reader. If your reader does ask them before you do, you'll have a hard time salvaging your case or earning back the credibility you have lost. All the more reason, then, to press yourself hard on these questions. Unfavorable replies commit you to revise.

Dramatizing an Implicit Dialogue

To suggest how a few basic questions can generate a variety of queries, let's follow one student—Audrey—as she revises an introductory paragraph through several drafts. We'll pay special attention to the questions that her classmates pose—questions that help her revise by argument. Experienced writers revise by engaging in a dialogue with their own ideas. By discussing essays in a workshop setting, you give voice to what would otherwise be an internal dialogue. Probing discussions can help you, like Audrey, learn to revise more effectively. Here's how she begins.

(1) Due to the inability of current laws to prohibit the use of marijuana and the lack of medical evidence showing that marijuana is dangerous, the U.S. government must act. (2) The possession and use of marijuana should be made legal in the United States. (3) An examination of the benefits will show that legalization of the drug would make it safer to use, provide economic advantages to the government, and allow "hard" drug laws to be rigidly enforced.

Audrey's opening seems competent enough, if you content yourself with a cursory inventory of parts. Classmates quickly noted that the three sentences present, in order, the occasion, thesis, and reasons for her case. Revising by argument, however, looks beyond the naming of parts to interrogate their relationship. It uncovers missing links and identifies links that mislead. It dramatizes the implicit dialogue that occurs whenever a reader examines a piece of writing critically. This dialogue is essential to analysis and argument, for both seek to win the informed assent of skeptical readers.

Yet dialogue is precisely what is missing from Audrey's own draft. Revising by argument would supply plenty of that. Classmates remarked that her thesis asserts an arguable, indeed controversial opinion, but they would hardly know it judging from the dull, ho-hum tone she assumes or the reasoning she lays out. As Audrey adopts a reader's stance, she notices that her case fails to engage skeptical questions or, for that matter, to stifle the yawns of her audience.

Treating diction and style for the moment as symptoms of larger problems, her classmates pointed out that she lacks a counterargument that would help set her case in an intellectual context and a genuine occasion that would give her a reason to write and compel others to read. As fellow students considered her opening, Audrey discovered that she needed to acknowledge other views and clarify her occasion. "How can you say," classmates replied, "that we don't have medical evidence that marijuana is dangerous? And what, exactly, do you mean by dangerous?" They also questioned whether the inability of laws to prohibit certain behavior was reason enough to abandon them. What about murder? People continue to kill each other in spite of the laws against murder, but we wouldn't, for that reason, legalize murder.

The discussion convinced Audrey that she had better invite her readers into her prose. By ignoring them, she was not making her case as clearly as she might; her monologue, moreover, succeeded only in irritating some readers and boring others. Learning that revising by argument rests on dialogue helped Audrey over the first and most fundamental barrier to revision—self-absorption. Revising by argument reveals the social implications of communicating with others.

Pondering Connections

In her second draft Audrey began to reach out to her readers intellectually and emotionally.

> (1) A sixteen-year-old high school student can obtain an ounce of marijuana more easily than she can purchase a bottle of whisky. (2) Although many critics feel that marijuana is very dangerous, the United States should legalize the drug. (3) An examination of the benefits will show that legalization would make marijuana safer to use, provide economic advantages to the government, and allow "hard" drug laws to be rigidly enforced.

Classmates appreciated Audrey's new opening (one that appealed to their own experiences) and her first, if hesitant, acknowledgment that they as readers might hold views other than her own. But they still found much to argue with in this second draft. Missing links and misleading links caught their attention. "Your opening example about marijuana and whisky is interesting," said one student, "but I'm puzzled about its implication, its link to your thesis." Another commented that the link between the counterargument and thesis misleads the reader; each half of sentence 2 talks past the other. "If we take the 'although' clause seriously," the student went on, "the second half of the sentence should answer the critics, but it doesn't." A third classmate pondered the reasons that project the essay's organization. "Because you indicate the reasons you will use to justify your thesis as a brief list, I'm not sure how each supports or even relates to your thesis. Take your reference to 'hard drug laws.' As it stands now, it seems like an unrelated tangent. And how would legalization be economically advantageous?" Still another student pleaded with Audrey to do more than wave from afar at opposing views. "You admit in one sentence that critics question marijuana's safety, yet in the very next you assert without any clarification that legalization will improve its safety. Aren't some steps missing?"

If the first round of revision opened Audrey's eyes to the presence of skeptical readers, this second round helped her become aware of missing and misleading links in her case. Armed with advice from her fellow writers, Audrey became even more engaged in critical dialogue with her own work. The fruits of that discussion became more apparent in her third revision.

> (1) A sixteen-year-old high school student can obtain an ounce of marijuana more easily than she can purchase a bottle of whisky. (2) Clearly, the laws against the possession and use of marijuana aren't working. (3) Some people, as a result, are urging the government to increase its law enforcement efforts. (4) But a better course by far would be to legalize the drug. (5) If marijuana were legalized, its purity could be monitored, so that it

would be safer to use; the government could save the money it now wastes in trying to control a relatively harmless drug; and the law enforcement agencies could redirect their efforts to controlling truly dangerous drugs like heroin and cocaine.

Reading Between the Lines

As Audrey worked out the implications of her argument, put in missing links, and adjusted misleading signals, her paragraph gradually achieved greater form and focus—not only for itself but also for the paper that it introduced. But as the thinking and writing became more clear, concrete, and lively, her classmates were also better able to spot remaining weaknesses in her case. Each successive draft allowed her readers to pose more incisive questions.

The third draft sparked a lively discussion about hidden assumptions. To find them, you have to read between the lines. The question of marijuana's safety had been haunting Audrey's paper from the start. Her classmates noted that it still received inadequate treatment; although safety is assumed, it is never defined. They encouraged her to make safety a central part of her case, and thus answer questions that, if left unattended, would reduce her credibility and undermine her point. The suggestion helped Audrey clarify another muddled point—marijuana's relationship to drugs sanctioned by society and to harder drugs such as heroin and cocaine. Here's how Audrey applied this round of discussion to a fourth draft.

(1) A sixteen-year-old high school student can obtain an ounce of marijuana more easily than she can purchase a bottle of whisky. (2) Clearly, the laws against the possession and use of marijuana aren't working. (3) Some people, as a result, are urging the government to increase its law enforcement efforts. (4) But a better course by far would be to legalize the drug. (5) After all, the medical community has failed to present convincing evidence that marijuana is significantly more dangerous than other drugs now sanctioned by our society. (6) Moreover, if marijuana were legalized, its purity could be monitored, so that it would be safer to use. (7) In turn, legalization would allow the government to save the money it now wastes in trying to control a relatively harmless drug, thereby enabling law enforcement agencies to redirect their efforts to controlling truly dangerous drugs like heroin and cocaine.

Revising by argument helped Audrey adopt and profit from the skeptical attitude that readers bring to analytic or argumentative writing. You might say she tried her case before friends prior to delivering it to a jury. Her fellow writers weren't trying to change her mind or sway her opinion; they were helping her examine and tighten the conceptual soundness of her case. The work of revising by argument is rarely done before the paper is due. Such was the case with Audrey's paper; although improved, it's hardly perfect. In fact, we'll return to her paper shortly to uncover problems that lurk as yet undetected. Nevertheless, the most important improvements may not be immediately apparent in one paper, or even in one semester. Revising by argument develops and confirms Audrey's own editorial hunches. In the process, she's discovering an internal reader to whom she can turn for a fresh perspective and a bit of friendly argument.

Because revising by argument addresses the actual writing in front of you, it resists the easy formula. Each paper, not to mention each draft, requires and deserves its own nuanced response. Because readers' questions are so fundamental, they actually encourage varied application. Nevertheless, some common conceptual problems recur. By looking out for them, you can make your revisions both more efficient and more precise. The rest of this chapter will help you spot and deal with the following problems.

- hidden assumptions
- misleading links between assertion and support
- distractions from the question at issue
- inappropriate appeals and dodges as you engage audience and opposition

As we address these problems, you will become acquainted with the logical fallacies that I've found to be most common in student writing. Perhaps previous writing courses have acquainted you with them as reference-book curiosities—lists of inadequate steps in reasoning to which writing instructors will point a warning finger and add a red pencil mark. This chapter takes a different approach. Fallacies are far more than local errors in thinking. Here you'll discover how fallacies relate to the practical demands of shaping ideas as you write and revise a full paper.

Hidden Assumptions

Revision requires close, critical reading because there's more to analysis and argument than meets the eye. What you see on the page is not all that you get. Both analysis and argument rely on unstated ideas that connect the visible elements of your case. These unstated ideas are called assumptions. They remain hidden when writers and readers take them for granted.

Most—but not all—assumptions deserve to be taken for granted. If your friend, for example, tells you that she needs to go to the store because she's out of milk, you can safely assume that she uses milk in her home and that the store would have milk to sell. There's little point to specifying all hidden assumptions because most of them are trivial. The example reminds us that it's both normal and necessary to make assumptions. What matters is the quality and credibility of your assumptions.

If your readers do not share your unstated assumptions, then the visible or explicit aspects of your case quickly fall apart. Unexamined assumptions are potentially deceptive because they can act as blind spots. They hide from view both the weak foundations of your case and options for revising it into something far more substantial.

Revising by argument requires that you examine these hidden yet questionable assumptions. To do so, you'll need both skill and a skeptical frame of mind, for assumptions by nature do not announce themselves. You'll need to read between the lines to uncover them. An analysis or argument may make sense at first glance yet fall apart when you give it a close look. Here are some tips to help you along.

Where Do Assumptions Hide?

Virtually everywhere. When writing and reading, we make assumptions all the time. But the assumptions with which you most need to concern yourself tend to hide in the gaps between the visible structural elements of your analysis or argument. That visible structure includes your occasion, thesis, and the reasons that project your essay's organization. Questionable assumptions that affect this basic structure can weaken the credibility of your entire case. Here are two places to look.

- *The occasion/thesis connection.* If you make questionable assumptions about the issue that occasions your paper, readers may question the relevance of your thesis and proofs.

- *The thesis/reason connection.* If you make faulty assumptions as you move from thesis to reasons or from reasons to thesis, you sacrifice your credibility and weaken the glue that holds ideas in relationship.

Assumptions matter because the relationships among structural elements, not the elements themselves, hold your writing together.

What Kinds of Assumptions Should I Look For?

To help you recognize the kinds of assumptions you need to be aware of, let's pursue Audrey's case a bit further.

One kind of assumption is immediate or *descriptive* in nature. One of Audrey's reasons for legalizing marijuana was that if its purity were monitored, it would be safer to use. As she develops her case, she will need to establish that purity can, in fact, be monitored efficiently and effectively, and that purity does have an important effect on safety.

A second kind of assumption concerns relationships among or implications behind stated reasons; let's call them *analytic assumptions*. When Audrey makes her case for legalization, she assumes that smoking marijuana is akin to socially sanctioned drugs like the bottle of whisky the teenager cannot buy. She assumes, likewise, that marijuana will not lead users to try or become addicted to "truly dangerous" drugs. Moreover, she assumes that monitoring purity will not cost the government more money than it would save by abandoning efforts to prohibit marijuana use.

A third kind of assumption concerns *values* and value conflicts. They are assumptions about which reasonable people frequently disagree. When Audrey argues for legalization, she assumes certain values or ethical frames of reference, among them that the government should not control an individual's personal behavior and that smoking marijuana, unlike murder or even heroin addiction, is indeed an entirely personal matter.

The distinctions among these three kinds of assumptions are far from airtight; treat them as informal tools to help you recognize that various assumptions can come into play as you develop an analytic or argumentative case.

How Can I Find Hidden Assumptions?

By knowing where assumptions hide and what they look like, you are already on your way to spotting them. Here are some essential self-questioning strategies to help you flush assumptions out of hiding.

How do I get from here to there?   Because assumptions connect two visible elements in your case, they represent a third or middle term. Think of them as stepping-stones. To find an assumption, you must uncover the middle term. If the stated reason is true, ask yourself what third element must be true for the conclusion to follow. In turn, ask yourself what third element would make the conclusion false, even if the stated reason is true. For example, the statement that legalization would save the government money assumes that the feds are spending money on marijuana control beyond what they already spend on controlling "hard" drugs. By checking for the middle term, you are considering what makes the reasoning plausible or implausible.

Can I find alternative conclusions?   Remember that one reason may support more than one conclusion. For example, Audrey's first reason—that marijuana is not unlike other drugs now sanctioned by society—might just as easily serve, in a different context, as a reason to prohibit or drastically curtail the use of alcohol. Legalization of marijuana is not the only conclusion one might draw. To reveal hidden assumptions, consider rival hypotheses. Could stated reasons be used in a different line of reasoning?

What larger interests are at stake?   Many assumptions—especially value assumptions—derive from fundamental preferences or judgments that people express. To uncover these assumptions and know how people will react to them, consider the backgrounds of your readers. Put yourself in their roles. What values are important to them and which are they willing to sacrifice? What hidden criteria influence their decisions? For example, legalizing marijuana may hinge on larger questions: What's the relative importance of collective and individual responsibility? Where should or shouldn't the government act?

　　As you look for hidden assumptions, you may come across sketchy, undeveloped reasons that look for all the world like assumptions but are actually meant as support for a conclusion. If you do, the reason needs to be developed further before it becomes credible. On the other hand, you may find assumptions that deserve to be turned into full-fledged reasons. Such was the case when Audrey turned vague assumptions about the relative safety of marijuana into an explicit reason for legalization: "The medical community has failed to present convincing evidence that marijuana is significantly more dangerous than other drugs now sanctioned by our society."

What If Readers Question My Assumptions?

Once questioned, assumptions become stumbling blocks, not stepping-stones. Questionable assumptions act as miniature unsettled arguments within your larger case. Until you settle them or mutually agree to set them aside, they will distract attention from or even undermine your case. Here are two basic ways you can make productive use of questioned assumptions as you revise.

Clarify your assumption   Readers often object far more to murky thinking or the clever dodge than to the assumption itself. If you clarify your assumption, readers may be willing to grant it. Consider the questioned assumption as a cue that you need to explain yourself more fully. What seems to be an unreasonable assumption often turns out to be an assumption that lacks a reasoned explanation. Even if readers do not accept your assumption, they may still be willing to entertain a case that follows from a clearly stated point of departure.

Recast your case   Some assumptions are so questionable and yet so fundamental to your case that they render further refinements pointless. Here, you're better off redesigning your analysis or argument so that you need not make those assumptions. Although it can be disheartening to find your paper in pieces on the cutting room floor, arguing with your assumptions can help you clarify the focus of your case or the manner in which you define the issue that occasions your discussion.

A final point: if you find yourself making questionable assumptions *in* your writing, you may be making some misguided assumptions *about* your writing. You may be assuming, for example, that readers share your interest and enthusiasm and needn't concern themselves with small imperfections. You may be assuming that you and your readers define the issue in the same manner. You may be assuming that an idea clear to you will necessarily be clear to others. Finally, you may be assuming that interest translates into agreement. When you address an issue about which your audience is concerned and familiar, be aware that they are likely to have their own ideas and possibly a skeptical attitude toward yours.

If you view questionable assumptions as more than isolated false steps in your thinking, they can teach you about the shape you have given—or might yet give—to your ideas and your writing. Assumptions may even reveal how you are approaching the task of forming and communicating ideas.

Misleading Links Between Assertion and Support

Even when they are not hidden, faulty connections between assertion and support can easily mislead both you and your reader. Misleading links can occur virtually anywhere in your paper. But perhaps the most crucial place lies in the connection between your thesis and the reasons that project your essay's organization.

Revising by argument requires that you pay attention to the rigor with which you relate assertion and support. Here are some common problems you should be aware of. Although you may have come across them before as isolated errors in reasoning, consider here how each affects the general shape you lend to your paper.

Irrelevant Reasons

Reasons become irrelevant to an assertion when they address a concern different from the one you announce. In such a case, the conclusion you advance based on your reasons is a *non sequitur*; it literally "does not follow." An irrelevant reason claims a logical relation between assertion and support where none exists; for example, "He'll be a good mayor; he's so very handsome." Most irrelevant reasons are not so obvious.

(1) Chlorofluorocarbons, found in many everyday items such as styro-foam packaging, may significantly alter our future daily activities as their en-vironmental effects become pronounced. (2) All skin exposure to the sun must be drastically limited, and people will have to cut down on their out-door exercise.

Sentence 2 does not give reasons why the contention about CFCs may be valid; it specifies instead how daily activities would change.

A special but common instance of the irrelevant reason occurs when you fail to maintain your analytic or argumentative focus and fall instead into de-scription and narration. An analytic or argumentative thesis like the one about CFCs requires reasons that answer the question of *why*. If you end up answering that question with a descriptive *what* or a narrative *how*, the discussion might eas-ily become irrelevant to the thesis you must justify.

If you wish to analyze, for example, why college deferments to the draft made Vietnam a poor man's war, you cannot content yourself with a description of deferment requirements or with a narrative about the debate regarding their fairness. If you do, the connection between thesis and reasons no longer follows. Strictly speaking, you are not giving reasons *why* the draft made Vietnam a poor man's war. You may be providing information or narrating events, but you are not justifying an assertion. If you don't catch yourself before you pursue an irrele-vant reason, your paper will digress or even wander.

Circular Reasoning

Circular reasoning, also known as *begging the question*, obliterates the difference between assertion and support. It does so by taking for granted the very thing that needs to be proved; for example, "The panda may become extinct because its fu-ture existence is in jeopardy;" or "Bicycle helmets should be mandatory because no one should be out on the road without one." Political and other emotionally charged arguments frequently use *slanted language* that contributes to circular reasoning; for example, "Abortion violates a baby's freedom of choice when that baby's life is cut short based on the dictatorial whims of its mother." References to the fetus as a baby capable of free choice and to the mother's dictatorial whims assume as given ideas that first must be carefully established.

The shape of your prose can suffer should you find yourself reasoning in circles. When the reasons that should support your thesis are little more than the thesis in disguise, your paper goes nowhere. Instead of proving an assertion, you end up repeating it. You merely insist when you should support. As you revise by argument, check to see that your occasion, thesis, and reasons are related but not identical. An occasion should set up your assertion, and your reasons should support it. A paper that reasons in circles, repeating but never justifying its thesis, can quickly become a one-dimensional monologue that denies the reader's need for proof. Along with your logic, you are apt to lose your reasonable tone as persuasion gives way to intolerance.

Cause and Effect

When you analyze or argue, you must often establish causal relationships as they occur over time. Although temporal sequence provides many clues about cause and effect, both are easy to misread. Here are several problems you might encounter as you shape a paper that handles cause and effect.

To start with, you might incorrectly infer cause from a temporal sequence. An example might be "I win my swim meets only when I eat oatmeal in the morning." That a good race time often came after eating oatmeal may not be sufficient reason, however, to conclude that oatmeal alone improved performance. The Latin term for the fallacy describes the problem well; *post hoc ergo propter hoc*, or "after this, therefore because of this." Bear in mind that just because two events are associated with each other does not mean you can conclude that one caused the other.

Why might you fall into post hoc problems? Two related and somewhat more general problems can lead writers astray.

It's tempting to claim too much for one cause. In an effort to convince readers about the certainty or significance of your point, you may overstate your case by claiming more than your evidence warrants. When you uncover a causal relationship, keep it in perspective; you're better off supporting a modest claim well. Even if the morning oatmeal didn't cause you to win the swim meet, it could still contribute to a good performance.

It's also tempting to simplify causes. Writers simplify causes when they assume fewer causes than are actually at work. Should you uncover one cause, don't leap to the conclusion that it is the only one that accounts for a given effect, any more than your morning oatmeal may have accounted for your winning swim times. Especially in human affairs, it's common for not one but several factors to influence the outcome of events. Because it is often impossible to consider all causes, use your occasion to help you focus on those germane to the discussion. Unless you can account for or control variables, however, be ready to revise by argument anytime you find yourself claiming the one and only cause.

Analytic and argumentative papers tend to bring out problems associated with cause and effect, for in writing them you are trying to sort out complex relationships. Because such papers call for a claim, it's tempting to claim too much. And because the scope of these papers is invariably more narrow than the world you try to make sense of, it's equally tempting to oversimplify causes. Finally, the linear nature of the written word may tempt you to treat complex causal relationships as a one-dimensional temporal or narrative sequence. Revising by argument can help you meet these challenges. It prompts you to qualify or limit your claim, to consider contrary or complicating evidence, and to maintain your analytic or argumentative focus when narrative beckons as the easier option.

Generalizations, Hasty and Sweeping

To justify the thesis that you assert, you must bring to bear evidence that will support your claim. Because you cannot account for every shred of evidence (nor would your reader have the required patience were you to try), you must generalize. We all do. We never have all the evidence on hand before we must interpret its meaning. Likewise, we never fully understand how new or different situations relate to those we know well. Generalizations, by definition, remain incomplete and uncertain; they needn't, however, be hasty or sweeping.

The *hasty generalization* is one in which you jump to conclusions too quickly. You may know something about a particular case, but you misuse that case by drawing from it conclusions that extend to most or all cases; for example, "Carl had to attend an extra semester just because of poor advising. Faculty advisors are ill informed." Carl's experience may be relevant to the conclusion, but it is not sufficient by itself to warrant the conclusion drawn. Hasty generalizations draw a conclusion based on too few or on atypical examples. Stereotypes and evaluative statements about groups frequently involve hasty generalizations; for example, "Asian-Americans don't need tutoring help in calculus; they're such whizzes when it comes to math."

You might think of the *sweeping generalization* as the reverse of the hasty variety. Here you are applying a fair and reasonably true generalization to an atypical case whose peculiarities you ignore. If the hasty generalization misuses particular cases to arrive at a conclusion, the sweeping generalization misapplies otherwise reasonable conclusions to particular cases; for example, "Literature courses have improved my reading skills; perhaps majoring in English would help Richard with his dyslexia." Although the generalization may be true, its application to Richard's case might not lead to improved skills.

The twin problems of hasty and sweeping generalizations can help you become more aware of related concerns. Because hasty generalizations try to determine rules based on just a few cases, they can alert you to dangers in *statistical evidence*. Be sure to ask how large the sample is and to what extent the sampled group is representative of the larger population. Opinions from a few friends in your dorm, for example, will not permit you to advance claims about student opinion on your whole campus. The hasty generalization also underscores the limitations of *personal or anecdotal evidence*. Although it is helpful to write from your own experience, be cautious about the general claims you advance based on your own case.

Because sweeping generalizations apply rules to specific cases, they can alert you to problems regarding similitude. Most of our thinking is, at heart, analogous; reasoning can break down, however, when we don't recognize pertinent differences among cases and thus pursue *false analogies*. The cry "No more Vietnams," for example, should ask us to pause and examine whether new situations are all that similar to our experience in Southeast Asia. Consider as well the use of *precedent*, which involves the application of generalizations from one case to another, or the *error of extension*, where the characterization of one case is extended to the point of distortion. That one circumstance may lead to similar and perhaps even more unfortunate ones is another form of sweeping generalization. This *slippery slope* or domino reasoning was often voiced during the Vietnam War; the claim was that if Vietnam were to fall to communism, so would all of Southeast Asia.

Hasty and sweeping generalizations can distort the shape you give to your paper. By overlooking pertinent examples or the particulars of a case, you can draw misleading or erroneous links between the reasons that project your paper's organization and the thesis those reasons are meant to justify. Both hasty and sweeping generalizations are fallacies of presumption; you presume relationships between the general rule and the particular case that do not apply. Only by adopting a skeptical attitude are you likely to question such presumptions and the conceptual shape they lend to your paper.

Distractions from the Question at Issue

Revising by argument also asks you to keep an eye on the question at issue that has occasioned your writing and engaged the interest of your readers. As your initial point of reference, the question at issue determines the relevance of the discussion that follows. If you lose sight of your occasion or if you characterize it inappropriately, the remainder of your paper will suffer. Although many distractions and distortions are possible, the following problems should be uppermost in your mind as you revise by argument.

False Dilemma

If your occasion lays out a problem that presents the reader with just two alternatives, you may be engaging in *either/or thinking*. Binary reasoning that proceeds with only black and white dichotomies in mind often distorts both the situation to which you are responding and the available options by which you can respond.

A favorite of politicians and busy bureaucrats, the false dilemma orients the discussion in a way that forces readers to accept your position; for example, "Either we build more nuclear bombs or we must submit to nuclear blackmail;" or "Either we institute a national high-school graduation exam, or we acquiesce to low educational standards." Each example bifurcates the options by excluding any middle ground or a possible third option. Many questions deserve more than a yes-or-no answer.

As you frame your analysis or argument, you will, of course, find some instances where you must make hard choices. In an election, you can vote only yes or no on a ballot proposition. Decisions to approve or disapprove, to convict or acquit, to hire or not hire, all come down to either/or propositions. Unless the situation presents such a dilemma, however, avoid it if you can.

Occasions that frame the question in black-or-white terms tend to oversimplify complex situations. Revising by argument encourages you to recognize gray areas and options you may not have considered. If you have presented a false dilemma, revise your occasion to characterize the question at issue in a more nuanced, realistic manner. Consider whether you might qualify your thesis in ways that respect the complexities of the question. If you adopt the realism that attends conditional thinking, you'll be willing to say, "Yes, if . . ." or "No, to the extent that. . . ." Also bear in mind that false dilemmas tend to distort the views held by skeptical readers, creating antagonistic opponents where none need exist. The dilemma you present in your occasion can determine the kinds of dilemmas you will face when responding to that occasion in the rest of the paper. The question you ask helps shape the answer you write. False dilemmas have a way of inviting further faulty thinking.

Ignoring the Issue

Occasions are useful only to the extent that you observe and use them to shape the discussion that follows. If you ignore or stray from the issue, you do more than lose a valuable point of reference; you make your thesis irrelevant and your reasons inconsequential. Some ignored issues are easy to spot; for example, "Even if I didn't submit any work, shouldn't attendance allow me to pass the course?" Other instances are harder to detect, especially if they occur in a complicated analysis or argument. For example, the question of whether universities should invest in companies that pollute the environment easily can stray into side issues, such as who should have a say in shaping the university's investment portfolio. Likewise, debates about discrimination in housing often ignore the issue of legal rights as talk turns to property values and the character of the neighborhood.

If you ignore the issue, your paper becomes one large non sequitur. Nothing follows. Your reader will have a difficult time following your reasoning or discerning your conclusion, for if you stray from the question, you'll rarely answer it. Along with shaping the discussion, the issue also lends it relevance and significance. If you ignore or stray from the issue, you will have difficulty answering what is perhaps the ultimate question, "Why bother?"

Introducing Irrelevancies

One consequence of ignoring the question under discussion is that you will entertain other issues. Many of them may be irrelevant and nearly all will obscure the one issue to which you accord importance.

Irrelevancies are often referred to as *red herrings*. Some irrelevancies are unintentional; others may be intentional efforts to distract or deceive. The term has its origins in hunting; dragging an irrelevant concern across a line of thinking is like dragging a herring across the trail of an animal pursued by hounds. Just as hounds are apt to lose the scent they are pursuing, so too are your readers apt to lose sight of the direction and purpose behind your line of thinking. For example, a student paper attacking President Clinton's relations with the press corps becomes distracted by an issue whose relevance was unclear, the supposed liberal bias of the press. A red herring represents a step to the side, a moment of *lateral thinking*. If the step is small, your reader will note the discontinuity but will still manage to follow your line of thinking. If the step becomes a long tangent, both you and your reader are off on a new trail, one that seldom returns to your original course.

Early drafts of your paper can help you sort out what is and is not relevant. A moment of lateral thinking in a preliminary draft may uncover an important issue that you might otherwise miss, one that may become central to your next draft. But as you revise what is nearly your final version, lateral shifts caused by red herrings no longer have a place in your writing. Revising by argument can help you identify and straighten the line of your thinking precisely because it focuses on relationships that lend integrity to your case.

Appeals and Dodges:
Addressing Audience and Opposition

As you revise by argument, pay close attention to how words on the page reflect and shape your relationship with audience and opposition. That relationship does as much to shape your paper as the conceptual architecture you design. Inappropriate appeals and dodges can undermine your relationship with your audience and with those who may question your case. Moreover, those appeals and dodges can make the task of lending shape all the more difficult. Your readers' concerns and questions have, from the very start, helped you generate form. If you ignore them or use them inappropriately, you'll be less able to shape a reasoned dialogue with your readers.

Because revising by argument anticipates and even enacts the dialogue between writer and skeptical reader, you are in a position to recognize the influence that appeals and dodges can exert and to revise accordingly. Let's start with appeals to your audience, and then turn to some dodges. As you revise by argument, beware of the following problems.

Emotional Appeals

To engage your readers, you must appeal to them both intellectually and emotionally. If you neglect either aspect, your writing loses impact and reader interest. When carried to an extreme, however, emotional appeals can overshadow or even obscure the reasoning that shapes your case.

The types of appeal vary, as do emotions themselves. An *appeal to pity* ("Do not execute the convicted murderer because of the family he would leave behind") tends to ignore the question at issue and reasoned debate, as does the *appeal to fear* ("If you do not send this rapist to jail, you may be his next victim"). The *appeal to authority* is also, in the end, an emotional appeal, for it plays on the reluctance of readers to question the authority of famous people, tradition, or widely held beliefs.

As you revise by argument, bear in mind that we all experience emotions. The case that does not recognize and use emotion would not be worth writing or reading. Yet emotion alone can obscure vision. Taken to an extreme and used in place of reasoning, emotional appeals can distort the shape and coherence of your case. The skeptical attitude you adopt when you revise by argument can help you determine if emotion replaces rather than reinforces reasoned debate.

Individual and Group

Your relationship with your audience often hinges on the alliances and divisions that you create or to which you must respond. As you appeal to your audience, you can easily become caught up in questions about individual and group ("Whose side are you on? To which group do you belong?").

Problems that you encounter when relating individual and group are not unlike those you encounter when you offer hasty or sweeping generalizations. *False composition* presumes what is true of each member is true of the group

("Each member of the fraternity is a swell guy; why would you think the party might become rowdy?"), while *false division* presumes that the group characterizes each individual ("She's sure to be talkative; she comes from New York City").

When you misrepresent the relation between individual and group, you run the risk of obscuring real issues and cogent reasoning. Consider how the following fallacies concern the individuals or groups to whom or about whom you write.

- *guilt by association* ("He must be a liberal; he voted for national health insurance")
- the *bandwagon* appeal ("Everybody's doing it")
- appeals *ad populum* or to the prejudices of your audience ("Those union members are a bunch of waterfront thugs").

Bear in mind that the role you lend to your audience and opposition can influence how you shape your argument and how you present yourself.

Personal Attack

When you address the person, not the issue, you divert attention from the otherwise cogent reasoning that you may develop for your case. One slip can discredit your entire argument. Personal attack can take several forms, some more subtle than you might think.

- The most abusive and obvious attacks focus on the character rather than the position of your opponent ("How could you think to listen to his views on child care? He's an avowed homosexual").
- Other attacks assume the influence of vested interests ("Of course she voted against the property tax increase; she owns her own home, doesn't she?").
- Another angle of attack seeks to reveal that words may not accord with actions ("Why should I heed his advice about requirements in my major; he's fallen behind on the progress of his own degree").
- Other personal attacks question credibility ("The witness lied before; why believe her now?") or the background or origin of a position or statement ("How could 'Kubla Khan' make sense? Wasn't Coleridge on drugs?").

At times, of course, you should take into consideration matters of character, vested interests, credibility, and origin. Motives always play a role in determining what positions are advanced and why they gain a hearing. By confusing person with issue, however, you run the risk of distorting the shape of your case and undermining your own credibility.

Dodging Opposition

An unwillingness to recognize or treat opposing views can also distract readers from issues that deserve debate. Moreover, by turning a deaf ear to contrary evidence and competing claims, you slight if not insult the very readers whose goodwill and reasoned support you seek. But dodges can do even more damage. Should you dodge opposition, you are left without the essential tools for shaping your own prose, your readers' questions and concerns. They should shape your writing every bit as much as the ideas and points you yourself may want to express.

Among the many possible dodges you may commit or encounter, pay special attention to four.

Shifting the burden of proof   This dodge is essentially a ploy to escape responsibility for justifying your own position ("Technical exercises such as scales eliminate any creativity in piano playing. Anyone who disagrees has never endured boring piano lessons.") The dodge says, in effect, "If I'm wrong, it's up to you to prove it." Another form of this dodge is to use your opponent's inability to disprove you as sufficient proof for the validity of your own position. ("I'm sure eliminating required courses will improve student morale. Nobody's said it wouldn't.") If you shift the burden of proof, you misjudge both your responsibility and the legitimate demands of your audience.

Treating a competing claim as a straw man   A straw man is an opponent who may not actually exist or hold the view that you attribute to him but one that you create so that you will have a presumed opponent that you can easily destroy. Writers may be tempted to turn flesh-and-blood opposition into straw by characterizing the positions of their opponents in a weak or absurd fashion. By doing so, you dispute a view similar to, but not the same as, that held by your audience ("Women who complain of sexual harassment in the workplace simply want to emasculate men and take away all good-natured fun from the office"). The straw man fallacy turns, in the end, on questions of fairness and objectivity. Try to present objections and opposing views in a manner that would lead skeptical readers to comment that you have heard and understood their side.

Selective treatment of objections and opposing views   A version of the straw man fallacy, selective treatment is a dodge whereby you dwell on objections that can be handled easily. Instead of distorting or reducing objections to straw, you single out ones that may be insubstantial or inconsequential ("How could you support mandatory helmet laws for motorcyclists? Don't you realize that helmets can be uncomfortable?"). By addressing only weak or inconsequential points, you leave the most important objections to your own case unaddressed. The dodge invites charges that you have failed to account for the most obvious issues. Selective treatment can make you appear short-sighted and willfully obtuse.

Stacking the deck   The ultimate dodge is to stack the deck and give yourself the best cards. Deck stacking amounts to riding your thesis while giving little or no attention to contrary evidence or competing claims. The most obvious examples are those papers that stubbornly refuse to mention any questions, objections, or contrary evidence. The most troubling examples, however, are those papers that mention inconvenient evidence in passing without describing or exploring the merits of that evidence. Halfhearted treatment of counterarguments is little better than none at all. A one-sided presentation that suppresses evidence and other views amounts to turning your back on the audience. Far from making your case appear strong, deck stacking weakens your credibility and undermines your point.

The various problems you face when revising by argument may seem daunting. Confused conceptual relationships, once they become apparent, are as hard to untangle as a complicated knot. Hidden assumptions lurk undetected. Links between assertion and support mislead where you think they guide. If you haven't ignored the question at issue, you've managed only to confuse it by posing new questions at every turn. And even where you intend to talk straight, inappropriate appeals and dodges may sour your relationship with audience and opposition.

Yet for all these challenges, honest, persistent arguing can help you address and revise the conceptual difficulties that weaken your case. Revising by argument permits you to do what your most discerning readers surely will: ponder, question, debate. It lends focus and method to substantive revision because it attends to relationships that generate your thinking and shape your prose.

To revise by argument, however, you must be willing to adopt the reader's stance. For this reason, dodging opposition remains perhaps the most pernicious of fallacies. Impediments to revising by argument, like those to critical thinking itself, lie in presumed certainty and self-absorption. The urge to oversimplify, the need to persevere in our beliefs, the unconscious desire to confirm our biases— these are the chief obstacles to revision. When you are game enough to look at your work through different eyes—the eyes of your readers—you open up for yourself new vistas, new strategies, new possibilities for deepening and broadening your thought.

Shaping Ideas with Style

8

This chapter connects the shape of ideas to the craft of style. Not only do principles for shaping ideas extend to style; in many ways they *depend* on style. This chapter explains how critical thinking can sharpen your style, and why a clear, graceful style can hone your mental edge.

We fail to draw a connection between ideas and style, or draw it only loosely, if we view the two as coming in sequence; first the thought, then the language that dresses it. We cannot separate ideas and their expression, for language does more than express ideas: it makes ideas happen. Until a thought is expressed in just the right language, some say it cannot exist. In seeking the right words for an idea, we are in some sense seeking the idea itself—its perfect expression, and hence its perfect reality. The relationships we forge among ideas also require clear and graceful expression. And for those relationships to matter, we must engage an audience—its mind, ear, and heart. A clear and forceful style helps us shape ideas even as it shapes our reader's attention and interest.

If we think of style as flourish and flair, as an expression of our personality, as ornament for ideas, it then becomes an afterthought. We will attend to it when we've gotten everything else squared away; thus we attend to it rarely, if at all. Style will be for later—or for the next paper. As a result, it becomes a matter of etiquette, a dress code for words. We look at it in the same way that we glance in a mirror on our way out the door.

The usual injunctions about style amount to moral imperatives: be clear, be brief, be sincere. If we fail to heed these injunctions, we fear that we will be deemed lesser writers, perhaps even lesser people. Yet these injunctions, though widely repeated, fail to provide any real help for the writer in distress. For help, the writer is referred to rules, hundreds of them—do's and don'ts, listed and cross-indexed. For the faint of heart, these rules are enough to render style an impenetrable jungle, and papers little more than the making and marking of errors.

But lists of rules need not be your only relief. The same principles that allow you to shape ideas can help you to create a style. In this chapter we'll look at two aspects of style that most concern college writers: finding a suitable voice and crafting sentences. In each case, the chapter looks beyond rules to uncover their essential rationale. We'll discover how the shape and shaping of ideas establish both a context for style and a method for achieving one.

Voice and Persona

Because writers are not physically present on the page, they are, to the reader, nothing but their words. Those words create tone, a mood or attitude that we detect. They also shape our image of the writer as a person. If an essay speaks to us, the author has used words to project a voice, and through that voice, to forge a relationship to an audience, a subject, even the writer's own self.

We always hear voices on the page. That's one of the pleasures of reading and of writing. Even when those voices are not eloquent or compelling, they influence our relationship to author and idea. If the voice is belligerent, we may withhold belief. If it hides behind bureaucratic anonymity, we may search for the personality—and often for the meaning—that the author seems to withhold. Every essay projects a tone of voice, but not every author adopts a tone appropriate to the essay's purpose and audience. Voice follows from stylistic choices. In making these choices, you find and refine your voice. That voice, in turn, forges the relationship between writer and reader. It determines in part whether your readers trust you, believe what you say, and accept your conclusions.

A Range of Possible Selves

When Eric wrote his essay "Summer Vacation: A Parent's Primer," he wanted his readers to accept his conclusion that a rigid schedule of summer "fun" can often have negative effects on children. To do so, he had to shape ideas, and with those ideas, his voice. Here's how he starts.

> I remember the certainties of the first day of elementary school each year: I had new shoes, new clothes, fresh supplies, a new teacher and classroom, and the essay. The same, old essay: "How I Spent My Summer Vacation." It has been a long time since I've had to eulogize the best and shortest three months of the year, but I've spent the last ten summers trying to give a few children something to write about. Working for the city's Playground Program, an eight-week recreation program for children ages five to twelve, I've had a chance to see a lot of children and to observe how they spend their summers. And I can't help thinking that for a growing number of children, that first-day essay has become more an extensive catalogue than an expository paragraph.
>
> More and more children are finding themselves with less and less free time during the summer. Many parents sign their children up for numerous

activities that run throughout summer vacation: pottery, computers, dance, golf. The children move from one class to the next, often with little or no free time during the day. Such a rigid schedule can have negative effects on the children. Having so much to do during the "vacation" can place undue stress on the children and can lead to burnout. More importantly, it robs them of the opportunity to be kids.

Whose voice do we hear in these words? Eric's, to be sure. It is, however, a special voice, one that Eric has chosen to present to us, not necessarily the voice of the "real" Eric, whose personality may remain a mystery even to himself. Eric's personality, like our own, contains a range of possible selves. What we see behind Eric's words is not necessarily the real person, but our image of him—a self born of the words he writes.

This image is the writer's *persona*, from the Latin word meaning "an actor's mask." True to the theatrical origins of the word, the persona that a writer creates is a verbal dramatization of self. Just as an actor can play many roles on stage, so too can the writer present various personas to readers. Writers can seem to be many different people, depending on the circumstances in which they write, their audience, and their purpose. For example, if Eric were writing a report to the administrators of the Playground Program or presenting a paper before a group of child psychologists, he would no doubt present himself more formally. If he were writing a letter to a friend or talking to the children themselves, he would surely project a more informal, familiar persona. Each of these audiences, in turn, would construct its own image of Eric.

Because Eric is addressing parents, he adjusts his persona accordingly. In doing so, is Eric dishonest or insincere? Hardly. To be personal, his style doesn't need to be a true confession of his real identity. (Do any of us know who we really are?) If Eric were to "spill his guts" on the page, it might make for good therapy, but it would hardly impress the parents. His style follows from how he wishes to present himself as he engages this particular audience. Sincerity, then, is not enough. Eric must suit his voice to the occasion. In this sense, style is always a means for social interaction. Although we should be willing to plumb the depths of our hearts, we mature stylistically by developing a repertoire or range of voices that can speak effectively in different rhetorical contexts. Sincerity remains an admirable virtue, adaptability a rhetorical necessity.

A Matter of Rhetorical Craft

As we take a closer look at Eric's opening paragraphs, we notice that his voice results from stylistic decisions that he makes as he shapes ideas. Eric could have opened his essay in many ways, but he chose to recall the first day of school. Why? He wanted to address parents not as adults but as grown-up kids. For parents to hear his message, they need to adopt a child's frame of mind. Eric establishes that frame of mind by making stylistic decisions that lend voice to his ideas. He "remembers" and "eulogizes," and thereby appeals to emotions and perspectives that busy parents might not otherwise have uppermost in their minds and hearts. He recalls the inevitable first day of school so that parents themselves might recall their own "best and shortest months." He invokes that first-day assignment so that he might offer his own essay.

But childhood memories are far from enough. Eric must also establish his authority. He does so by moving from the "same old essay" about summer vacation to his own summer work, from the simple expository paragraph to the extensive catalog of activities that many kids now must pursue. His experience with the Playground Program enables him to speak persuasively, to find a voice that mixes an adult's authority with sympathy for the child's perspective.

Eric thus balances different facets of his voice. He must address parents seriously, yet convince them that they and their children ought not be so serious themselves. For this reason, the essay's style blends the formal and informal. Eric maintains some distance and reserve even as he strikes a note of intimacy. He establishes the occasion, thesis, and reasons for his case without being unduly academic or heavy-handed. He argues even as he confides. He is ready to reason, but with a leisurely pace that befits his topic and plays to his purpose.

Far from being a psychological inevitability, Eric's voice is a matter of rhetorical craft. Voice follows from purpose, from an engagement with a particular issue and audience. For Eric, finding that voice is not a matter of choosing "right" words and avoiding "wrong" ones. He has a broader context for his stylistic decisions. By shaping his ideas he is shaping a self, a persona. We hear the Eric that Eric persuades us to imagine.

By the essay's end Eric has brought himself and his audience closer together—by reason and by voice.

> Children need to be given the chance to be little boys and little girls. They need time just to play and to be themselves. Let them chase guppies in a stream, or get lost in a marigold. The first day of school and that essay will be upon them soon enough.

Voice can be a persuasive tool because a particular tone can imply particular conclusions. Readers are often convinced as much by the voice in which an author reasons as they are by the reasons to which an author lends voice.

For that voice to emerge, you must present a self that knows what it wants to say. Like Eric, you must make stylistic decisions with analytic and argumentative ends in mind. If you don't draw clear relationships among ideas or if you fill in conventional forms in a mechanical fashion, you won't have the confidence or the conviction with which to craft your style or find your voice.

Persona in Academic Prose

Eric has a good deal of latitude in crafting his voice, as do most writers when addressing a controversial subject. It's clear you can put part of your own personality into the discussion. But a close reading of a James Joyce short story—now that might seem to be a different matter. To the student writing academic prose, especially textual analysis, such a task appears to leave little room for expressing a distinctive persona. After all, the writer is now responsible to a text and other bodies of data. And because readers expect detailed, persuasive support for an analytic point, there's precious little latitude for personal manipulations of style. If there's a persona in your writing, it wears but a faceless mask.

Before you content yourself with anonymity, consider that textual analysis should be anything but impersonal. In fact, text-based writing becomes persuasive only insofar as you imprint your own intellect and sensibilities on the material. Probing analysis becomes, then, its own stylistic resource. To help you understand how you can call on those resources, let's consider Peg Fisk's discussion of Joyce's well-known story "Araby." (We'll continue to follow her essay as we touch on other aspects of voice.) Here's how Peg begins.

> When the protagonist in James Joyce's "Araby" travels through the streets of Dublin, he carries his dream of Mangan's sister above the madding crowd: "Even in places hostile to romance . . . I bore my chalice safely through a throng of foes." But when he takes that "chalice" to the place he deems worthy of his quest—to the exotic fair called Araby—he is dismayed and unfulfilled, for the "place of enchantment" is nothing more than a microcosm of the very world that the narrator has tried to transcend. The people he meets and the darkness he sees are in effect the same as those in the Dublin markets.

Unremarkable, you say. Personality doesn't leap out of this paragraph of third-person prose. Yet Peg's persona is as distinctive and nuanced as her observations. As with Eric's writing, her voice and persona emerge from a self that has something to say. Voice does not precede ideas, it follows from them. Her thesis that the exotic bazaar called Araby is a microcosm of the very Dublin markets the protagonist wishes to transcend shows us a mind engaged with Joyce's text. Her syntax reveals to us her own literary sensibility—one that spots contradiction and counterpoint, one that appreciates how the cadence of a sentence can emphasize its point.

Peg doesn't craft a persona in the hope that it will then present a few ideas about the story. She finds her persona in and through her ideas. Distinctive ideas can lend your academic writing an equally distinctive voice. George Bernard Shaw put it well: "He who has nothing to assert has no style and can have none." With ideas and insight come the opportunity—if not the obligation—to refine and communicate them with style.

With not one but many voices at your disposal, you need strategies to help you make informed choices. We'll now consider three aspects of voice in which the shape and shaping of ideas can guide your stylistic decisions.

Finding Voice Through Diction

What makes the words you choose "right" or "wrong"? The answer is simple: a mismatch with the meaning you intend or the context in which you communicate. Words are not right or wrong in themselves but only in the use to which you put them.

Shades of Meaning

The use to which you put a word depends on more than its literal or dictionary definition, its *denotation*. You must also take into account its *connotation*, the subtle implications and shades of meaning that it develops over time as it rubs shoulders with other words. Connotations arise from the contexts in which you find words and from the habitual use you make of them. Thus, your choice of words not only imparts meaning; it also conveys an attitude.

Consider the distinction between the words *naked* and *nude*. Both refer to a body that is not clothed. Yet what a difference! If you were to write "A naked model appeared before our art class," you would imply a model deprived of clothes, and perhaps the embarrassment that both the model and the class might feel. Substitute *nude* for *naked*, and you project a rather different attitude; not embarrassment, but confidence, not the absence of clothes so much as the presence of natural proportion and beauty.

Which is the right word? It all depends on what you intend to say—and on looking more closely at what you really mean. Was the nightclub you visited *exotic* or *bizarre*? Was your physics lab a *fiasco* or a *failure*? Was your friend *intransigent* or *uncompromising*? Such questions about diction ask you to clarify meaning. They also ask you to represent yourself and your point fairly before your audience. The words you choose may tempt you to slant your case, to suggest conclusions that you cannot otherwise establish. To analyze or argue responsibly, you must not let your diction outstrip your ideas or your evidence. The search to find the appropriate word should send you back to explore your subject and refine your ideas.

The Search for Words

Diction asks more of us than serviceable words; it calls on us to find the telling word true to our ideas, and often the ideas themselves. As I was writing this book a colleague of mine was hard at work down the hall on a historical novel set in the Middle Ages. As he revised his manuscript, he would pause at every sentence to consider the imaginative life his words would lead. Could he say "The town gossip electrified the villagers with her story"? Hardly, unless the gossip were centuries ahead of her time. The continual search for words led him to consider their origins, history, and connotations even as it helped him explore the nuances of his subject.

That exploration is nowhere more crucial than in text-based writing. Close, sustained inquiry into the text on which you are writing allows you to be just as resourceful with your diction as you are when addressing controversial social issues. Textual analysis may seem to limit your word choice, for you must measure your words against those of your text. Yet that measure can enrich your own style. That's what Peg found as she continued her essay on Joyce's "Araby." In her second paragraph, she portrays the Dublin life the protagonist wishes to transcend, for her essay turns, in the end, on the disappointing similarities between his mundane world and the exotic fair. Her own diction capitalizes on her close reading of Joyce's language.

> He bears his "chalice" of romance through the marketplace because he believes that it is finer and more precious than the stuff of which his life and neighborhood are made. He looks askance at the bourgeoisie—his friends, his uncle, the garrulous Mrs. Mercer: they know not the finer things of life. His "confused adoration" can only be expressed inwardly because there is no one to share his passionate thoughts. He tries to make it clear to his uncle that it is important he go to the fair, but the uncle comes home late and drunk, indifferent to his quest. He is distracted by the talkative Mrs. Mercer who speaks of unimportant things, and in the marketplace he is jostled by "drunken men and bargaining women." The boy travels through dark Dublin streets, dim rainy evenings, and short winter days, returning to a dismal house on a "blind" street.

Peg's careful choice of words shows respect for Joyce's equally careful choice. Moreover, her diction is essential to her case. It lays the foundation for her upcoming analysis of Araby as an unexpected microcosm of the very Dublin markets from which the boy would like to escape. Textual analysis need not limit the range of your style. To the contrary, many writers have found that close reading extends their stylistic range, introducing them to the rich resources of our language.

Words and Audience

The words you choose also establish a relationship with your audience. That relationship can be ceremonial, formal, familiar, or even coarse, depending on the *social style* or *register* that your words imply. Who was it that pulled you over for speeding—*law-enforcement officers, police, cops,* or *pigs*? Each of these words carries not only connotations but also a level of style. We choose among levels of style depending on the situation in which we write and the expectations of our audience. Although some college assignments, such as the personal essay, may ask you to adopt an informal, even colloquial style, analytic and argumentative essays tend to demand a somewhat more formal tone.

Yet many college writers overdo the formal style. They are so intent on sounding knowledgeable that they come off as pompous and pedantic. Excessive formality turns ideas into abstractions and an otherwise engaging personality into a stuffed shirt. The best advice is to write honestly and directly about ideas that matter to you and your audience. College writing does demand that you think carefully and express yourself precisely. But don't posture or put on airs. And don't rob yourself of the natural vigor and freshness that can only come from speaking your mind. Lively diction feeds on lively ideas. Matthew Arnold put it best: "Have something to say, and say it as clearly as you can. That is the only secret of style."

As you consider words in terms of audience, you'll quickly find that some words lead special lives among certain groups of people. *Jargon* enables specialists in a particular field to communicate with each other using very precise terms. People outside of the field may use these terms much more loosely, or may not even recognize them at all. Jargon can facilitate communication when you speak to members of your own club or, to use the jargon of my own field, your own "discourse community." Yet the abuse of jargon is everywhere apparent. You abuse jargon if you exclude people, as you can do if you overwork jargon when writing to a general audience unfamiliar with the mysteries of your discipline. You abuse jargon if you seek to impress others with mysterious-sounding terms when a lucid, straightforward style would serve just as well. You abuse jargon when you spurn ordinary words that mean the same thing.

Sexist language shares with jargon a tendency to exclude. Yet unlike jargon it has no legitimate defense. By learning to choose words carefully, you can make your language more gender-inclusive. Instead of *mailman*, opt for *mail carrier*. Revise singular pronouns to the plural: *The author should engage his audience* thus becomes *Authors should engage their audience*. Or recast a sentence entirely to avoid a problem. But even as you strive to eliminate bias, be sure not to banish a graceful, readable style. The doubling *his or her*, when used to excess, may become clumsy, and the coupling *he/she* or *s/he* makes for prose that only a bureaucrat could love and that no one can read aloud. Consider choosing a generic *he*, a generic *she*, or even alternating between the two. Keep your language inclusive even as you keep its style natural. Biased language that excludes others narrows your audience. It has no place in argument and analysis, whose point, after all, is shared inquiry.

Style as Inquiry

The search for style is itself, then, a form of inquiry. To find appropriate terms, we must refine our thinking. To choose our words, we must search for more precise, more cogent ideas. As you begin to control your diction, you may be surprised that the thinking behind the otherwise orderly words on the page remains unclear. Problems in diction may creep into your writing as you explore new words or refine as yet hazy ideas. But as you learn to make conscious stylistic decisions, your thinking will also improve. The shape you lend to your ideas becomes, in turn, a stylistic resource. Were it not for your responsibility to engage an issue, articulate a point, or justify your position, you would have little need to refine words. Yet words are all that you have to relate to your audience, lend point to your ideas, and persuade others to accept your evidence. For these reasons, you must choose words wisely. Your ideas convince only when you find words equal to them; you find those words only by reasoning more closely.

Crafting a Credible Voice

When readers construct their image of you as writer, they are also making judgments about your character. Those judgments can be every bit as influential as the actual reasoning you present. By establishing a credible voice you do far more than add a touch of stylistic refinement; you make your case persuasive.

For readers to grant your point, they must be willing to trust you and trust what you say. Without that goodwill, the sharpest reasoning, the subtlest turns in logic, will do you little good. Thus, experienced writers try to reinforce their reasoning by projecting an appealing and trustworthy persona. They seek to convince others by who they are. When you present your character in a positive light—as sincere, upright, sensible—readers are all the more willing to grant what you have to say. The faith that readers have in you thus becomes as important as the case you present. Only by convincing readers that they are in good hands can you persuade them of the ideas in your head.

The Appeal to Character

We all form judgments based on who is writing or speaking. If authors are well known—famous or infamous—their reputation precedes the text. A byline by a commentator you respect will make you receptive toward what he or she has to say even before you start reading. In turn, opinions voiced by commentators you distrust will rarely convince you, no matter how eloquent or rational they may be. The unethical side of ethical appeals often becomes apparent in modern advertising, which trades on character, fame, and recognition every chance it gets. A television ad in which a star NFL quarterback tries to sell you a car makes its argument in part upon character; if you trust the quarterback with third down and long to go, how could he steer you wrong concerning the dealership he endorses?

Few of us know fame's burden, or its benefit. Reputation does not precede us; we have yet to win it. All the more reason, then, to look closely at the character you project. Only through the words you place on the page can you convince readers that you are worthy of their trust.

Establishing that trust was Paul's concern as he set out to write an essay on the legal responsibilities that bartenders have toward their customers. He knew that rational arguments would not be enough to sway readers on this volatile issue. To win his argument he first had to win their trust. The persona he presents as he opens his essay does as much to persuade us as the substance of his case.

(1) I support my family and pay my way through college by dispensing one of the most dangerous drugs in our society; I am a bartender. (2) My partner and I work a medium size bar that is usually very crowded. (3) Our wait staff of about eight to twelve people handles an average of fifty people an hour and serves as many as 150 to 200 drinks in that period. (4) We must also take and serve food orders, keep the bar clean, and wash glasses. (5) To work at my place you must greet new customers within thirty seconds of their arrival, and the drinks should be on the table three minutes after they are ordered. (6) Any good assembly line person who can remember 600 or more drink recipes and run in circles while doing several tasks at once can bartend. (7) The hard part comes in the seconds right after a bartender greets a patron. (8) It is in these moments—when a customer places an order and the bartender decides to fill it—that the law makes a bartender responsible for the customers' actions and for their

lives. (9) There are, to be sure, reasonable responsibilities that I must bear, but the present laws are forcing bartenders to make judgments that exceed reasonable limits. (10) Two areas of responsibility that challenge even the most conscientious bartender are checking ID's and determining the customers' state of inebriation upon their arrival at the bar.

By shaping his essay, Paul has tools in hand that help him shape a credible persona. Clearly stated in sentence 9, Paul's thesis turns on the question of responsibility and sound judgment. Are the demands we place on bartenders reasonable or excessive? To justify his position, Paul must do more than consider IDs and customers' inebriation; he must establish a persona whose responsibility and sound judgment are themselves beyond reproach.

The occasion for his essay provides that opportunity. Paul opens boldly by acknowledging that alcohol is a dangerous drug. He knows full well that the readers he wishes to convince come to the topic in a skeptical frame of mind. By admitting alcohol's dangers, he disarms them with his honesty. He thereby wins a hearing even from readers who believe that bartenders should bear considerable legal responsibility. The acknowledgment shows the writer to be candid and forthright, someone we can trust. References to family and college likewise present the writer as sincere, hardworking, and upright, thus dispelling some of the negative associations readers may have about bartenders. The character he projects on the page thus persuades us as much as his actual reasons.

Paul's job experience persuades us as well. His references to the bar and its operation set the scene for the essay and supply useful background information. He is already laying the foundation for his proofs about checking IDs and determining inebriation. But those references also convince us that the writer knows his subject and that he is working from firsthand experience rather than a stack of library books. The source of the argument—who Paul is, what he knows, what motives he has for writing—becomes itself a part of the argument. By showing himself to be knowledgeable and conscientious, Paul helps convince us that the responsibilities he bears exceed reasonable limits.

If you wish to establish your credibility, consider how you might craft your own character. You can do so throughout your essay, but the opening paragraphs provide an important opportunity to set the right tone, to find the appropriate voice. Because your occasion articulates the question at issue, it clarifies who you are, who your readers might be, and what concerns divide and unite you. Occasions link writers with readers. As such, the occasion becomes a natural place to establish the appropriate character or persona.

Yet your occasion is more than the proper place; it's also, along with your thesis and reasons, a ready tool. Because your occasion helps you define the issue and set up your thesis, it provides you with a rationale for crafting a particular persona. The choice is by no means purely stylistic. Only by shaping ideas do you have a context in which to make stylistic decisions. Those decisions, in turn, can lend to your ideas the force of your character. How you present yourself on the page influences the case you present; the shape of that case influences, in turn, the character you dramatize on the page.

Character, Credibility, and Third-Person Prose

But what of text-based academic writing—writing that often turns to third-person objectivity? How can Peg make her voice credible in an essay on James Joyce that leaves little room for appeals to character or personal experience? Readers would hardly expect her to relate the narrator's disappointment with the Araby bazaar to her own shopping experience, nor would they find such a connection persuasive. To make her voice credible, Peg must rely on the credibility of her ideas and the detailed observations by which she justifies her interpretation.

The third paragraph of her essay, building on the second, drives home her point, and with it her own credibility and authority. Marshalling detailed evidence from the text, she uncovers the disappointing similarity between the exotic Araby bazaar and the Dublin markets.

> So when the narrator goes to the bazaar, he is searching not only for a gift for Mangan's sister but also for a place that is not "hostile to romance." Araby: a place of "enchantment," a place with a "magical name," a place whose evocation makes all the young man's intervening days "tedious." And when he gets to Araby, what does he find? A world smaller but essentially the same as the world he left behind. The man who takes his ticket is, like his uncle, indifferent. And the counting of the coins in the background makes it clear that this is not a magical place but a material one. As the boy lingers around the young lady's stall "to make my interest in her wares seem more real," we are reminded of his dutiful visit to the gossipy Mrs. Mercer. That the lady is English reminds us also of "the troubles" sung about in the Dublin markets. And as the purveyor of tea pots and porcelain vases, she is similar to the bargaining women who jostle him on shopping trips with his aunt. The poetic words he evoked as a paean to romantic ideals—"O love! O love!"—deteriorate to banal prattle at the bazaar: "O, I never said such a thing!" "O, but you did!" "O, but I didn't!" The similarities to the Dublin he had hoped to leave behind do not end there, because Araby itself is veiled in darkness. As the young narrator confusedly lingers, knowing that his stay is useless, the last light in the upper hall goes out, returning him to the unwelcome though familiar darkness.

Peg's close analysis reminds us that we cannot contrive a credible voice. We must earn it. In text-based academic writing, we earn it by looking closely at the text, advancing an interpretation that sheds new light on it, and justifying that reading with textual evidence and cogent reasoning.

Because good academic writing communicates a probing yet authoritative voice, many students try to imitate it without expending the effort it requires. They're tempted to assume the mantle of authority before they have earned it. As a result, their writing often comes off as stiff and contrived, with all the mannerisms and jargon of academic prose without the precision and imaginative insight that it requires. To avoid this pretense, win your credible voice by attending first to your ideas. Look closely and reason clearly. Care enough about your ideas to make them credible. In that commitment to shared inquiry you'll find a voice equal to your ideas.

Voicing Emotional Appeals

You control your diction as you speak of your subject, and establish credibility as you speak of yourself, for one reason: to move your audience. You speak so that others may hear and, in turn, act. You appeal to your readers because you want them to care—intellectually and emotionally—about your ideas.

Appeals to audience turn on your ability to influence the emotions, values, and desires of your readers. Shared inquiry helps you know your own mind, to make more rational decisions and judgments. Yet your ability to inquire—to think more carefully and deeply—must depend on some passionate commitment. Thus, your rational appeal to an audience must also have its roots in emotion, in shared values and desires.

Because writers and speakers can abuse appeals to emotion by pushing them far beyond what the evidence warrants, it's particularly important for you to base this aspect of voice on the shape of your ideas. If you don't, the appeal may be insincere or overdone. Or, as demonstrated by Adolf Hitler in his highly charged speeches, emotional appeals can undermine and distort the very judgment of an audience. The emotions, values, and desires that you invoke in your readers should reinforce—but not outstrip—the reasoning you provide and the empirical evidence you muster. For this reason, you should choose responsibly the means by which you appeal to emotion.

Most appeals occur as you conclude your essay. In those final lines you hope to encourage readers to adopt certain attitudes or take specific actions. Yet if your final rousing appeal is going to persuade, you must work throughout the essay to evoke specific attitudes and values. Even your opening paragraphs can lay the foundation for your final appeal, for the occasion you announce should lend significance to your closing words.

One important means at your disposal are vivid yet accurate examples. You encourage your audience to respond emotionally when you show, not merely tell. Poignant illustrations can drive your point home. They also provide you with an opportunity to adopt a tone and a style that implicitly communicate the values and concerns that lie behind your examples. Yet clearly the examples you choose are only as effective as the reasoning they are meant to support. If you have confused the question at issue, waffled on your thesis, or drawn an ever-so-slack link between assertion and support, even the most poignant illustrations will not work to your advantage. Only by shaping ideas can you find your voice and use it to make an appropriate appeal.

The Appeal to Values

In her essay on intensive animal husbandry, Genni struggled to find that voice. She was ready to criticize modern agribusiness, and its intensive cultivation of animals, as having divorced itself from the ideals of the family farm. For support she drew on conditions in the veal and poultry industries—industries that she felt were cruel to animals and dangerous to consumers. She had several tear-jerking horror stories at the ready.

Yet she knew that for her audience to accept her thesis, criticism alone would not be enough. Diatribe would only depress her readers. She had to move them to embrace the ideals of the family farm. By appealing to the values that lay behind her own concern for the issue, she hoped her readers would themselves be inclined to scrutinize intensive animal husbandry. With the shape of ideas now in her grasp, she developed an occasion that would reenforce her appeal.

(1) When I was little we had a calf that had been rejected by her mother. (2) Her name was Patience, and I bottle-fed her in the chicken yard. (3) She would lick my arms and my face and lay her head in my lap, her eyes would droop and finally close, and she would sleep. (4) Her slow, rhythmic breathing would soon lull me to sleep, too—a girl and her cow, asleep amid scratching chickens on an early summer afternoon.

(5) Growing up on a farm I saw chickens and cows and pigs and sheep in every stage of their lives. (6) I saw the pain in birth and in death. (7) And I saw that, regardless of their "rationality," these animals are capable of affection, love, and suffering. (8) On traditional farms there exists an inherent respect and understanding of an animal's life . . . and death. (9) But "intensive animal husbandry" has divorced itself from the ideals of the family farm. (10) From birth to the table, it disregards even the most basic needs of the animals raised for slaughter, and the consequences to the public that

follow from such treatment. (11) Modern agribusiness techniques are cruel and inhumane to animals and misleading and dangerous to consumers.

Genni's opening paragraphs do communicate the ideals of the family farm. And it's those ideals that move her—and, she hopes, her readers—to question modern agribusiness. With her thesis clearly stated in sentence 9 and elaborated upon in sentence 10, Genni is ready to support her case. As she does, the ideals she establishes in her opening provide a constant point of reference throughout the essay. What's more, the very scene she sets—bottle-feeding her calf in the chicken yard—anticipates her close look at the "modern" treatment of calves and laying hens and the potential danger of that treatment to consumers.

Genni's ability to recognize and influence the emotional set of her audience early on pays off as she concludes. Her final appeal is not a last-minute emotional plea, but the culmination of conscious stylistic decisions throughout her essay.

(1) Although the danger to consumers who eat factory farmed meat and the agony that the animals raised for consumption must endure are great, they could be diminished if modern agribusiness techniques were changed. (2) If we were to raise animals with regard to the *quality* of their existence, we would help stop the torture of the veal calf and laying hen and all other animals raised for food. (3) No longer would these sentient creatures be forced simply to "exist" in unnatural environments, unable to scratch, graze, roll, run, or play. (4) No longer would they be fed unnatural food and pumped full of chemicals, their welfare and health ignored by their guardians. (5) And no longer would consumers be exposed to the risk of disease from the flesh of an abused and exploited animal. (6) To return to the ideals of the family farm, where little girls can bottle-feed calves in the warm summer sun, is to return to a more humane, healthful life.

Her appeal rises in a crescendo with "no longer" thrice repeated. She can sustain this emotion because she has built her appeal on her ideas from the very start.

Disarming Emotional Objections

Readers seldom come to your ideas, however, without a few of their own, or respond to your appeals without setting into play their own emotions. Their set of emotions, values, and desires can run counter to yours. Unless you recognize and respond to the emotions your readers bring to your essay, you may never get them to read past your opening lines. Thus, your appeal to an audience often turns on your ability to disarm emotional objections.

Susan anticipated this problem as she was writing her analytic paper about hemp as an environmentally sound, renewable resource. The very readers she wanted to convince would be those who would dismiss any mention of marijuana as unpatriotic, the obsession of some radical fringe group. Her challenge was to appeal to reason even as she disarmed and transformed hostile emotion. Like Genni, Susan had to find a voice that would use ideas to make her appeal.

(1) Before 1937, the hemp plant, otherwise known as *Cannabis Sativa L.* or marijuana, was present in people's everyday lives in materials such as rope, cloth, canvas, and even protein-rich foods. (2) In fact, Betsy Ross made the first American flag out of hemp cloth, and our forefathers wrote the Constitution on hemp-based paper. (3) That does not necessarily mean that our forefathers were smoking the plant; they were merely using the plant as a resource. (4) The prohibition of hemp was due in large part to the corporate arm twisting that occurred in the 1930s when companies discovered that the hemp plant could interfere with their petrochemical products. (5) Sixty years later it is apparent that the United States is overlooking an environmentally sound, renewable resource. (6) Our nation could produce a significant amount of its fuel by utilizing hemp's oils. (7) Producing hemp-based paper would create less dioxin pollution than wood-based paper and reduce the depletion of trees now used for paper. (8) Hemp is, finally, an ideal base for ecologically unsound products such as plastics, paints, and varnishes derived from petroleum.

The references that Susan makes to Betsy Ross and the Constitution do more than give examples of hemp's many uses. They appeal to and transform the emotional set of her most skeptical and conservative readers. Our flag and our Constitution, far from belonging to one political camp, thus become points of mutual interest. Although Susan herself does not appeal to emotion, she implicitly makes an appeal that disarms what would otherwise be a negative emotional response to hemp. She is able to make that appeal because she understands how it relates to the shape of her ideas. By thinking carefully about her occasion, she knows how her question at issue may divide her from some of her readers. She knows, moreover, that for her readers to consider her thesis and her support, she must transform their emotions. She therefore appeals not to narrow political interests but to a shared sense of history and patriotism.

Emotional Appeals in Academic Prose

The emotional appeals of text-based academic writing may seem tame compared to Genni's plea for the values of the family farm or Susan's savvy treatment of a potentially hostile audience. Yet text-based writing also depends on shared emotional response. Peg's fourth and concluding paragraph uses the disappointment of Joyce's narrator at the Araby bazaar to explain and confirm the visceral reaction of many readers to the story. She begins that final paragraph by probing the narrator's response, and ends by acknowledging and enriching ours.

> But if the narrator has been able to carry the "chalice" of his love through those bourgeois market streets in Dublin, high above the "throng of foes," why can't he continue that uplifting mission in the marketplace called Araby? Because he had hoped that this place would be sacred, not "hostile to romance." Mangan's sister gave him that expectation when she said that it would be a "splendid bazaar and that she would love to go." This hope sustained him through the discouraging darkness and the philistines of Dublin. When these hopes were not realized, the boy recognized the futility of trying to transcend his drab, dark world. This realization accounts for the fatalistic mood at the story's close: Joyce's protagonist cannot escape.

We write about texts to understand and explain our responses to them. Peg closes her essay with an appeal to shared emotional response. Her final lines, especially that last phrase, re-create the narrator's fatalistic recognition. Yet her appeal is more than just emotional, her purpose more than an evocation of mood. She analyzes the textual basis of that emotional response. To do so, she rests her appeal on her interpretation and on the care with which she explores and justifies it before discerning readers. Like Peg, you'll find that interacting with the ideas and textures of a text—its nuances, its hidden structure, its uncertainties—becomes a way to interact with your audience. For emotional appeals to persuade, your readers must also believe your ideas.

As with your diction and your credibility, your emotional appeals must rest on clear thinking. Unless you know how you are shaping your ideas, you have little basis for making decisions about "right" and "wrong" words, the credibility of your persona, and the emotional response you wish to invoke. In turn, as you discover the stylistic resources available to you, you will be able to press your thinking even further.

Making Sense of Sentences

Only by setting ideas in relationship can you shape an essay. The same holds true of sentences but on a smaller scale. Sentences draw relationships among ideas. You choose words and arrange them to make a point. Sentences, like essays, lose their shape when you fail to connect ideas.

How should you craft your sentences to make your ideas meaningful, even memorable? You'll find it hard to decide unless you have at least some preliminary notions about the central purpose of your essay, the issue that launches it, and the reasons that justify your thinking. You may write your essay sentence by sentence, but you can only craft sentences that make sense for your essay if you keep in mind the analytic or argumentative purpose they are meant to serve.

In this section we'll draw on principles for shaping an essay to help you make sense of sentences. The connection between shaping ideas in an essay and crafting sentences is vital. Miss it, and your sentences, though grammatically correct, may not lend clarity to your point or help you pursue your larger purpose. Miss that connection, and you lose a common framework for understanding individual rules. Sentences need not be hit-or-miss affairs, nor should you feel bewildered by those red penciled "awks" in the margin that announce each error. The key to crafting sentences—and essays—lies in recognizing the link between shape and meaning.

We'll begin where readers begin—by looking for meaningful patterns among words. Among those patterns the most important is the core element of each sentence. You can lend meaning and force to your statements by expressing your main point at the core. We'll help you recognize that core element and use it to clarify your thinking. In the process, you'll discover the common rationale behind commonplace rules.

Establishing the Core Statement

When you encounter a sentence, you read not so much words as the patterns into which those words fall. For example, only by setting the following words into relationship are you able to create meaning.

> Sentences without even short overwhelm literally you would patterns.

Set into their proper relations, the words look as follows.

> Without patterns, even short sentences would literally overwhelm you.

The point of this sentence becomes clear only when you place key words in emphatic positions. If you accord equal weight to every word without setting them into patterns, reading would be more than slow and tedious; it would result in nothing but a cognitive blur. Readers perceive meaning by highlighting some elements while treating others as minor or subordinate.

The same holds true for the essay as a whole. As you'll recall, we opened this book by considering the questions that readers ask of virtually any document:

What is the question at issue? What is the author's point? And do the author's reasons elicit belief? These questions—and the answers that writers provide—help readers distinguish the meaningful shape of an essay. Otherwise, strings of sentences, each with bits of information, would simply overwhelm us.

Strong sentences thus adhere to the same principles that make for strong essays. Both require a point, a leading idea. And both communicate that point by placing the leading idea emphatically while giving other elements a supporting or subordinate role.

The most important pattern in a sentence is its *core*, or as it is sometimes called, its *kernel*. You can recognize the core of a sentence by finding the part that can stand alone and still make sense by itself. Some sentences will have more than one core statement, but each will have at least one. At the core of a sentence lies the basic statement it makes or the question it asks. The core carries its essential message.

Core statements seem simple by themselves; rarely do they consist of more than several words.

> A bunch of us drifted away.
>
> I watched the field.
>
> The river seems real.

We make sense of sentences because, at their core, they name a subject and say something about it. Core statements thus draw relationships among the strongest grammatical elements in a sentence—the subject and the verb, and perhaps a direct object or complement. The core is that part of the sentence at center stage; it names your actors and specifies the action. To these core statements writers can add others words, phrases, and clauses to produce richly nuanced sentences.

> After the lions had returned to their cages, creeping angrily through the chutes, *a* little *bunch of us drifted away* and into an open doorway nearby, where we stood for a while in semidarkness, watching a big brown circus horse go harumphing around the practice ring.
>
> —*E. B. White*, "The Ring of Time"

> Each year *I watched the field* across from the Store turn caterpillar green, then gradually frosty white.
>
> —*Maya Angelou*, "Picking Cotton"

> Like any out-of-the-way place, *the* Napo *River* in the Ecuadorian jungle *seems real* enough when you are there, even central.
>
> —*Annie Dillard*, "In the Jungle"

If you wish your readers to grasp your idea, make your sentence readily understandable on a first reading. The core helps you do so in that it contains the most grammatically important words—the subject and verb. Your job is to align your meaning with those words. If your key ideas wander off into the nooks and crannies of a sentence, the core statement remains underpowered—and your meaning hard to decipher.

Try your hand at this grammatically correct but vagabond sentence.

> The timely arrival of the flight from Chicago is thought to be necessarily conditional on the state of the weather.

The core statement—"the arrival is thought"—provides only scanty information. We are left to ferret out the meaning by looking elsewhere. The point is that bad weather, now only implied and tucked away in two prepositional phrases, may affect the flight from Chicago. Now all we need do is straighten out the roundabout expressions: "The timely arrival . . . is thought to be necessarily conditional on" thus becomes "may delay." The revised sentence places essential information in key positions. Bad weather may delay the flight from Chicago.

With some effort, most readers can grasp the point of the original sentence, and more than a few can revise it. But they shouldn't have to. Readers struggle when you don't put your meaning in the grammatically important words. Even a few vagabond sentences will discourage them from staying with you. To keep readers with you sentence after sentence, heed Jonathan Swift's advice about style: put the proper words in proper places.

As you learn to recognize the core statement in your sentences, you'll have profited from more than a grammar lesson. When you put key ideas at the core, you clarify your point. The core thus helps you craft sentences to pursue specific purposes. Even when two sentences contain virtually identical words, what you put in the core makes all the difference.

> Although the date had its embarrassing moments, we kissed goodnight.
>
> Although we kissed goodnight, the date had its embarrassing moments.

Both sentences make sense, but that sense differs. By reversing the clauses, you shift the emphasis, and with it your point. You establish that point—either the redemptive kiss or unredeemed moments of embarrassment—by setting words in relationships to highlight one idea while subordinating the other. Relationships among words, not just the words themselves, allow you to compose or revise sentences with specific purposes in mind. As with essays, you shape sentences by forging relationships.

Using the Core to Clarify your Thinking

Because the core of a sentence carries its essential message, you can use it to check what you are saying and, in turn, to discover what you mean. Far from a grammatical straightjacket, the core serves as a critical-thinking tool. We'll consider five instances in which attention to the core can clarify your ideas. In each you'll recognize a commonplace rule that admonishes you not to commit an error. I prefer to keep in mind their common and far more positive rationale—that by forging relationships we shape ideas.

Garbles

A garbled sentence is one so tangled that it doesn't make sense. We might recognize the individual phrases that are strung together, but we lose the relationships among them—and thus the very point of the sentence.

> Limit the size of the administration and cutting the salary of the college president is an idea for reducing by student leaders.

The author probably wanted to say something like this.

> Student leaders proposed two ideas for reducing the college's budget deficit: limiting the size of the administration and cutting the salary of its president.

Our attention may go to the immediate problems in the sentence—faulty parallelism (*limit/cutting*), subject/verb agreement (*limit and cutting is*), and missing words. But a common problem lies behind them. The writer hasn't shaped the core statement, and with it his or her own thoughts.

Garbles occur when you dash off sentences without actually crafting them. Because thinking or even speaking outpaces the far more deliberate act of writing, it's easy for such sentences to go vagabond. You may know generally what you want to say, but you haven't shaped a core statement or kept it firmly in mind. The phrase or two you have on your tongue tempts you to launch the sentence. But once you're under way, you may forget how you began or where you are going.

You can clear up garbles once they occur by checking your core statement. You can prevent them by using the sentence core to shape your ideas. Sit back and take a deep breath. Form the core statement in your mind, and only then commit it to the page. Once you grasp your main idea, you can add phrases and clauses to develop your thought more fully.

False Predication

Predication—saying something about a grammatical subject—lies at the heart of virtually every statement you make. Predication establishes a connection between the subject and the elements that make up the predicate, namely the verb along with perhaps a direct object or complement. False predication occurs when you try to link elements whose meanings are mismatched. The result can be a sentence that seems to make sense but actually yields nonsense.

Three types of mismatches are common. One involves the subject and an active verb, whereby you name an action that the subject could not possibly perform:

> The rules in my uncle's house expect guests to be well behaved.

> The standards of most elected officials function on a high ethical level.

Once you look closely at each core, you'll realize that rules can't expect anything (though your uncle can) and that standards can't function (though we hope our elected officials do). To revise, we must match subject and action.

> My uncle expects guests to be well behaved.

> Most elected officials have high ethical standards.

As these examples suggest, faulty predication often comes from treating abstractions as if they could perform an action.

A second type of faulty predication uses the verb *to be* to mismatch a subject and complement.

> A characteristic that I frown upon is a person who is greedy.

> Bulimia is where people have an abnormal and constant craving for food.

> The fairness of SAT exams is a controversy that cannot be easily resolved.

Only by examining the core statement can you identify faulty relationships and thereby clarify your thinking. A characteristic is not a person, nor is bulimia a place. And when has fairness ever been a controversy? Hence the revisions:

> I frown upon people who are greedy.

> Bulimia is an abnormal and constant craving for food.

> SAT exams have become controversial because their fairness cannot be easily determined.

Writers frequently invite this sort of faulty predication when they use formulaic expressions out of habit, among them "[X] is when," "[X] is where," and "The reason . . . is because."

Yet another faulty predication finds you mismatching the object with a subject and verb.

> The local steel mill fired twenty positions that they had only recently filled.

By now you've developed both an eye for faulty predication and some skill in revising your way to clearer thinking.

> The local steel mill fired twenty employees they had only recently hired.

More importantly, you're aware that sentences, like essays, draw relationships among ideas. By revising the ill-cast sentence, you are doing more than correcting an error; you are refining your thinking by consciously shaping your ideas.

Faulty Modifiers

Modifiers are single words, phrases, or clauses that limit or describe another sentence element. Modifiers become faulty when the relationships that they draw become unclear or express a meaning you don't intend. Once again, the shape of your sentences bears on the shape of your ideas.

Even a single word can draw different relationships when positioned differently in a sentence.

> *Only* off-campus students feel isolated at our college. [No one but off-campus students feels isolated.]

> Off-campus students feel *only* isolated at our college. [Apparently, they don't feel anything else.]

> Off-campus students feel isolated *only* at our college. [And presumably, nowhere else.]

To understand the very different points made by these sentences, you must recognize the core statement and then consider how a modifier limits or describes a particular sentence element.

The same principles apply to phrases and clauses. Unless you clarify how phrases relate to the core, you risk confusing your reader. Modifiers become misplaced when they draw links to the wrong sentence elements or even draw two links at once:

> I pointed out the impressive paintings to friends mounted on the museum walls. [Were friends or paintings mounted on walls?]

> Hidden away in the attic for twenty years, my grandfather stumbled across his old violin. [Was your grandfather gathering dust, or was his violin?]

> Football coaches were asked to attend a seminar on sexism at our college. [Did the seminar take place at the college, or did it concern the sexism that takes place at that college?]

You can revise these sentences by keeping modifiers close to what they modify. This will help readers know at a glance what relationships are involved.

> I pointed out to friends the impressive paintings mounted on the museum walls.

> My grandfather stumbled across his old violin, hidden away in the attic for twenty years.

> Football coaches were asked to attend a seminar on sexism held at our college.

Although some misplaced modifiers amuse more than they confuse, others can be thoroughly ambiguous, as with the seminar on sexism. Unless you clarify relationships among ideas in each sentence, readers won't have a clear idea what you mean.

A dangling modifier tries to draw a link to something that isn't stated explicitly.

> Upon seeing the pothole, my bike skidded out of control. [Can a bike see?]

> Anticipating student objections, the exam was graded on a curve. [Can an exam anticipate?]

> To win an Oscar, a filmmaker's supporters must launch a media campaign. [Can supporters win an Oscar?]

In each case, the subject implied by the modifier differs from the actual subject named in the following clause. In other words, we dangle modifiers when we draw relationships incompletely, or not at all. To undangle a dangling modifier, name in your main clause the actor implied by the modifier or revise the introductory clause so that it includes the actor:

> Upon seeing the pothole, I lost control of my bike. Or: When I saw the pothole, my bike skidded out of control.

> Anticipating student objections, the professor graded the exam on a curve. Or: Because the professor anticipated student objections, she graded the exam on a curve.

> To win an Oscar, a filmmaker must have supporters willing to launch a media campaign. Or: For a filmmaker to win an Oscar, supporters must launch a media campaign.

Unless we have a clear sense of the core statement and the relationships we draw to it, we loosen the very ties that hold sentences—and ideas—together.

Digressions

By looking for the core statement, you can find your point. And as you do, you'll notice sentence elements that have little or no connection to your main idea. Such digressions weaken the point you make, and may even distract or confuse readers.

> John F. Kennedy, whose assassination still fascinates the public and puzzles even expert investigators, launched our space program with his promise to land a man on the moon by the end of the 1960s.

At the core of this sentence lies its main point: Kennedy launched our space program. Yet the point is muddled by comments on Kennedy's assassination that bear no relation to the space program. The sentence asks its readers to pursue two different lines of thought, and thus provides little direction of its own. You can direct attention to your point by cutting digressions. If a digression does bear on your main statement, you'll need to show how, either in that sentence or in the paper.

Digressions are common in early drafts. Overwhelmed by the information at your disposal, you may still be sorting out what is useful and what is not. Perhaps you want to impress others with the information at your disposal, or perhaps you cannot bear the thought of leaving out interesting points. Such digressions usually mean that you are still unsure of your way. Writers find their way by using these digressions to reconsider their ideas. What exactly is your point, and how do other ideas support or modify it? As you clarify your leading idea, you'll be able to spot digressions for what they are. Loosely related ideas lose your readers. Only by cutting digressions can your sentences, like your essay, pursue a point.

Empty or Weak Statements

When you attend to the core, you'll often find that there's less there than you thought. Use that opportunity to do some fresh thinking. We sap energy from our statements when we use empty subjects and weak verbs.

> The thing the columnist seems to say is that all sorts of people are lacking what is needed in the way of actual effort and achievement to have the self-esteem they would like.

This whole sentence rests on a core statement that says virtually nothing: "the thing is." To shape a sentence that says more, you must locate key ideas and relate them at the sentence core.

> Self-esteem, according to the columnist, has replaced the actual effort and achievement on which it depends.

Now the key elements of the sentence—its subject, verb, and direct object— carry the burden of your point.

Some sentences appear weak when our expectations of them far outstrip what they actually say. That's often the case with thesis statements. We look to these statements for the essay's point. We dull that point if their shape fails to do justice to our thinking. When the task at hand requires analysis or argument, a thesis statement shaped to describe will not be equal to the job.

Consider this thesis offered by an aerospace student interested in analyzing NASA's space communications systems.

> Despite its technological complexity, NASA's Deep Space Network is not being expanded to a capability that is necessary for future space missions.

At the core of this sentence we find only a fact: the network is not being expanded. Given its descriptive focus, the thesis will frustrate attempts to generate an analytic paper. Far more interesting material for analysis lies in the sentence's nooks and crannies. What of the opening phrase? Subordinated to the descriptive core, the comment about technological complexity remains puzzling. We don't hear about the relationship between technological complexity and network expansion. Yet that relationship carries far more analytic potential than does the descriptive core. And what of the phrases that follow the core? They too raise questions for analysis while the core remains mute. We can only guess how network expansion might bear on the success of future space missions.

Revision can sharpen the point of this thesis statement, and with it the point of the essay. By placing key ideas at the core, you'll draw tighter, more interesting relationships. Here's one possible revision.

> Without significant expansion, the Deep Space Network will compromise the future missions that NASA has planned.

As you refer back to Chapter Five for tips on troubleshooting your thesis, you'll find that many of the strategies use sentence-level revision to help you reconsider the thrust of your entire essay. To pursue this kind of revision, you can't rely on vague notions in your head, or plead "I know what I'm trying to say." Only by looking at sentences—not through them—can you consider how the words you put together shape your meaning. Sentences, like the essays we build from them, set ideas in action by drawing relationships among them. You can shape—even discover—those ideas by making fresh sense of sentences.

Trimming Fat

By looking at the shape of your sentences to make sense of your ideas, you'll quickly discover that many of those sentences are out of shape. They're bloated, overstuffed with words. If those words outweigh your ideas, readers will grow impatient or leave you altogether. At the very least, wordiness can muddle a clear idea and blunt an otherwise forceful point. To be vigorous, writing must be efficient. Use only enough words to convey your message. Trim the remaining fat. A lean style highlights ideas and, in turn, enlivens your thinking.

Sentences can put on weight when you try to impress others with weighty ideas. Reluctant to let ideas speak for themselves, you may try to pump them up. After all, who doesn't want to sound knowledgeable, respectable, or official? Why say "We must read closely to understand this essay," when you can sound far more academic and profound by intoning "The possibilities of cognition will maximally increase if we consider this discourse proximally"?

What drives this pumped-up prose? Fear. We strain for effects because we fear being natural. We try to impress because we lack confidence in our own ideas. We keep readers at arm's length because we worry they might look closely. We complicate matters lest we become responsible for what we say or do. Bloated by insecurities as much as extra words, our sentences soon become unreadable. They may win praise from faceless bureaucrats or readers cowed by their own fears. But for anyone actually interested in understanding what you have to say, inflated sentences invite the pin prick of common sense. Once deflated, they may express little more than hot air.

A second reason leads us to burden our sentences with empty weight. Habit. We add words in much the same way we add pounds—without thinking twice. We're conditioned to fill up the page, not whittle down ideas to a sharp point. We're accustomed to stretching phrases, lest we come up short on ideas. An abundance of ready-made expressions adds to our temptation. They sound elegant and keep words flowing without our having to invest much effort or thought. Phrases like "In reference to the essay by" or "At this point in time" put writing on automatic pilot. Yet they also put brains in neutral and readers to sleep. As with any other habit, stock expressions dull our senses. With phrases at the ready, why look at words or how we shape them? For that matter, why look at ideas, if we can begin to write without them? Here, as with most habits, indulgence leads to regret. When we lose our respect for language, for the precise word or the carefully crafted sentence, we lose with it our ability to think.

A strict diet seems in order, a shape-up routine for shapeless sentences. But the regimen need not be grim. When you take pains to craft your sentences, you'll enjoy the pleasure of putting words to work for you. Because part of their work is to push your thinking, a vigorous style helps you discover ideas.

Find Vigor in Verbs

To work off the fat and get your sentences into racing trim, you'll need to do more than reduce their word count. Empty words, like empty calories, should be your focus. The measure of brevity is not mere length but your ability to convey your point concisely. You can meet that measure by applying the principle that runs throughout this book; we shape—and shape up—our writing by drawing clear, forceful relationships among ideas.

You can implement this principle by following one central strategy.

Let a vigorous verb help you reshape the core of your sentence.

Verbs establish relationships; they let the actors of your sentence act. The linchpins of your core statements, verbs hold together your ideas and call them into action.

Sentences bloat when verbs become lethargic. They may not lose their meaning entirely, but they do become indirect, vague.

There were one hundred students in attendance at the lecture.

A vigorous verb shapes up this sentence and sharpens its meaning.

> One hundred students attended the lecture.

We all but lose meaning when lethargic verbs permit sentences to add layer upon layer of empty words to an already weak core. Just listen to this out-of-shape sentence huff and puff its way through twenty-eight words.

> Central to our understanding of administrative personnel on this campus is the use that is made of public relations in creating favorable or unfavorable perceptions of the institution.

Nouns and prepositional phrases balloon until we no longer recognize what the sentence asserts. Why? The core statement ("central is the use") means next to nothing. Any remaining verbal force is scattered throughout the sentence and thus lost. For the verb we make do with "is"—a lethargic verb if ever there was one. The sentence doesn't assert; it just sits. Without a strong verb to draw taut connections among ideas, the sentence becomes little more than a duffle bag for words.

To shape up this sentence and others like it you need to place the real action of the sentence at its core. Right now the verb "is" hardly helps to set ideas in action. Readers must sort through verbiage to find what remains of the sentence's verbal force. You can spare them the trouble by reconstructing the core statement, and with it the entire sentence. First, locate the individual key words or ideas in the sentence. Then clarify relationships by identifying actors and action. Here the key ideas concern "administrative practice" and "public relations." Where's the action? Hidden in the nouns "understanding" and "use." What about the actors who are "understanding" and "using"? Implied, but never stated, are "we" and "administrators." By identifying hidden actors and actions, you can now reconstruct a meaningful sentence around a new core statement.

> We can understand our administrators by examining how they use public relations.

Vigorous verbs tighten relationships among key ideas. The shape-up routine has trimmed this sentence from a bloated twenty-eight words down to a sleek twelve. More than merely shortening sentence length, tighter form has clarified its meaning.

Writing acquires shape as you relate ideas. Once you understand this principle and the shape-up strategy that follows from it, you'll recognize the common rationale behind commonplace rules. You've met many of these rules before; now you can make better sense of them.

Avoid Habitual Use of the Verb *To Be*

State-of-being verbs (also called weak linking verbs) include forms of the verb *to be*, among them *is, am, was, were, been,* and so on. State-of-being verbs may do a fine job of defining one term by another (a rose is a prickly shrub with a beautiful flower), expressing a similarity (my love is like a red, red rose), or describing a condition (the rose is blooming). But these verbs can't act. If you use *to be* in a sentence that involves actors and actions, you'll only succeed in hiding the action elsewhere in the sentence.

> Weak: Vigorous relationships are a requirement for good writing.
> Better: Good writing requires vigorous relationships.

Don't fret about using *to be* verbs occasionally. Our language couldn't do without them. But if you find yourself droning on sentence after sentence with *to be*, realize that literally nothing is happening in your writing.

Favor the Active Voice

In active constructions, the subject of the sentence acts, as in this example.

> The FBI wiretapped his phone.

In passive constructions, the subject of the sentence is acted upon. We may only know the agent of the action if the information is included in a prepositional phrase.

> His phone was wiretapped [by the FBI].

Note that this sentence highlights the phone, the "patient" rather than the "agent" of the sentence. Unless the immediate focus in the paragraph is the phone itself, not the FBI, the sentence highlights the wrong information. What's more, passive constructions can stuff sentences with extra words. Worse, they often don't reveal the agents involved in the action. They supply more words but less information. That may be harmless enough in a short sentence, but it's a dangerous combination when you're pursuing a complex point.

The passive voice can also prove dangerous because it often doesn't assign responsibility. Who did the wiretapping? We aren't told. The agent literally remains secret. The passive voice passes the buck—or perhaps I should say, in constructions that use the passive voice we find that the buck is passed. Impersonal constructions—"It was decided to wiretap the phone"—only further evade responsibility. They make the wiretap sound like the frightening work of Big Brother, or some careless computer error.

An abundance of passives makes your writing vague. They throw up a smoke screen in front of ideas when your real job is to clear the air. But don't be too hasty to banish the passive voice altogether. It's often appropriate when you want to emphasize the result of an action, when you don't know the agent involved, or when mentioning the agent doesn't bear on your point. Scientific writing, for example, often favors the passive voice because its focus lies on the procedure or result, not on the individual conducting the work. Because you may have good reason to use the passive voice, use it with a reason in mind. Otherwise, favor an active voice that clarifies relationships among ideas.

Cut Prepositional Phrases

Sentences become bloated when your words—chiefly your nouns—begin to suffocate the verbs that give them life. When you string together prepositional phrases, nouns can overwhelm a sentence and obscure your point.

> The novelist sees the primary function of art as a revelation of the realm of imagination.

The sentence tags on various ideas without actually connecting them. The all-purpose verb "sees" hardly gives us a clear vision of what all those nouns mean. What's more, the prepositional phrases and the polysyllabic nouns make for hard reading. By cutting these prepositional phrases and transforming one or more of the nouns into verbs, you can liberate the sentence's real action from under the deadweight of its nouns. That action deserves a place at the sentence's core.

> Art, says the novelist, reveals the imagination.

Now the shape of the sentence clarifies its meaning. When you place key words at the core, the real action of the sentence, once muffled by abstract nouns, can speak for itself.

Replace Clauses with Phrases and Phrases with Words _____

Sentences communicate most efficiently when readers can easily recognize the core statement. Other clauses and phrases can stand needlessly in the way. You can clear out the verbal underbrush by turning long clauses into snappy phrases.

> Weak: Charlie, who at one time served in the Vietnam War, now writes fiction to exorcise battlefield ghosts.
>
> Better: A Vietnam vet, Charlie now writes fiction to exorcise battlefield ghosts.

You might even turn an entire clause into one or two words.

> Weak: Gabriel García Márquez, who writes in a style known as magical realism, led a resurgence in South American fiction.
>
> Better: The magical realist Gabriel García Márquez led a resurgence in South American fiction.

The same principle applies to phrases. Here we have exchanged two phrases and six words for one telling verb.

> Weak: With some vacillation, Katie stood for a moment at her boyfriend's door.
>
> Better: At her boyfriend's door, Katie vacillated.

Use the simplest, most direct structure you can. Although bloated phrases and clauses may appear in early drafts, careful revision can reduce them to lean essentials. Your sentences thereby gain power, purpose, and speed.

Don't Belabor the Obvious _____

Unnecessary words do more than clutter a sentence; they weaken the words that should convey its meaning. When you write "during the course of" you only sap the energy that "during" could provide. A sentence muddled with "due to the fact that" sacrifices the strength it might otherwise have with a simple "because." When four or five words do the work of one, they all become lethargic. By shaping up your sentences, you release the power of words.

Begin by trimming redundant expressions. You'll find them whenever you needlessly double words ("each and every" or "basic and fundamental"). Modifiers can also be redundant ("advance planning" or "final outcome"). You might also repeat what another word already implies ("during that period of time" or "light in weight"). Redundant expressions only make your prose stutter.

Indirection, in turn, makes your writing wander. Circumlocutions are roundabout expressions. Because they take the long route, not the direct path, they loosen the very relationships you are trying to draw. "In a situation in which students become ill . . ." is a roundabout expression for "When students become ill. . . ." "The house was of a shabby nature" likewise begs for the more direct "The house was shabby." Cumbersome verb phrases are also culprits: "render inoperative" is but a smoke screen for the more direct "destroy." You can easily become indirect when you express statements in the negative. Translate "In the not too distant future" by making a positive statement, "soon."

Roundabout negative expressions can so bloat a sentence that you no longer recognize its meaning.

> Except when students enroll without having fulfilled appropriate prerequisites, admission to the course will not be denied.

Only by translating the negatives can you shape the sentence so that its meaning becomes apparent.

> You will be admitted to the course if you have fulfilled the prerequisites.

Or better yet:

> To take the course, you must have the prerequisites.

You can also belabor the obvious by using adjectives and adverbs as empty intensifiers. Phrases such as "very important," "horrible disaster," and "absolutely disagrees" needlessly pump up your prose without adding meaning. If you're tempted to add an intensifier, look instead for a stronger word. "She was very happy at the news" thus becomes "She was delighted at the news."

Writing and reading become tedious when each word no longer matters. What's more, whole sentences can lose their shape when you belabor the obvious. Here's a statement so diffuse that you may not recognize its point.

> When you compose your thoughts on the page, consider that your audience of readers can only judge the meaning behind what you have written by examining closely the structural relations you create among the words and phrases you use in your sentences to convey that meaning.

Translation:

> Readers know what you mean by looking at how you shape your sentences.

If you belabor the obvious over an entire paragraph, few readers will care to look for the pithy sentence or two that lie behind it.

Avoid Vagabond Openings

You can shape up sentences by tightening how you begin them. Slow starts merely delay your point and displace it from the sentence core.

> There are many reasons to suspect that there is a connection between weak sentence openings and rambling prose.

The delaying formulas "there is . . . that" and "there is" place important words in weak positions, in this case a prepositional phrase. The "connection" is implied but never stated. A swift start clarifies your point.

> A weak opening can make a sentence ramble.

Other delaying formulas include "It is . . . that" and "What . . . is."

> Weak: It is the core statement that should relate key ideas.
> Better: The core statement should relate key ideas.
>
> Weak: What is troublesome to me is her indirectness.
> Better: Her indirectness troubles me.

Writers sometimes use delaying formulas to achieve special effects or to introduce a specific yet unknown referent (as in the sentence "There's a woman in my class who's a linguist"). But unless you have both your meaning and a particular effect in mind, you had best start quickly. As they say in the movie business, cut to the chase.

Delayed openings are common in first drafts because they allow you to get into a sentence without a clear point in mind. In sentences, as in essays, vagabond openings postpone commitment; they put off your point. As a result, you rarely express that point as clearly as you might. Fast starts do more than lend your writing speed and efficiency. They help you arrive at, even discover, your point by prompting you to draw vigorous connections among ideas. Fast starts encourage forceful thinking.

The commonplace rules we've just discussed amount to more than a schoolmarmish list of do's and don'ts. They all share a common rationale: to call ideas into action, you must draw vigorous relationships among them. That rationale helps you shape up sentences even as you sharpen your essay's point.

Building on Ideas

Some writers, unaware of setting ideas in relationship, tend to create shapeless, overstuffed sentences that can leave readers uncertain about their meaning. By trimming fat you can shape up both those sentences and the ideas they express. Other writers, however, hesitate to forge the relationships that would do their ideas justice. They revert to "Dick and Jane" sentences—the short, simple utterances that they've long since learned to control.

> We were newcomers. We had heard about tornadoes. Then we saw the black funnels in the sky. Now we understood their destructive power. They demonstrated that power by reaching down from the sky to the earth. They also showed their power by plucking up farmhouses.

While clear, these sentences don't say much. They are unequal to the ideas that lie scattered in the individual statements. The writing seems choppy because the sentences are short; they needlessly repeat words and follow the same structure. More importantly, the writing's choppy because the ideas remain unconnected. The writer hasn't balanced similar points with each other or subordinated minor ideas to major ones.

To say more, you must build on ideas by connecting them. Notice how a revision links points of equal importance and highlights major points while lending others a supporting role.

> We had heard about tornadoes, newcomers that we were, but as we saw the black funnels reach down from the sky and pluck up farmhouses, we finally grasped their destructive power.

This sentence says more than the other six because it builds on separate ideas to create a richer one. It lends force to that idea by drawing relationships that drive the sentence to its final word and point: "power."

Once you make sense of sentences and trim their fat, you can use core statements to build on and extend your ideas. We did so just now by calling on two strategies: *coordination* and *subordination*. They can help you expand your sentence repertoire and with it your mental horizons. Commonplace rules about coordination and subordination tend to remind you how you might fail. But behind those rules lies a common rationale that can help you use these strategies with confidence.

Coordination

Coordination builds on a single idea by matching it with other equally important ideas. The sentence about tornadoes, for example, uses coordination (here in italics) to bring two main ideas together.

> *We had heard about tornadoes,* newcomers that we were, *but* as we saw the black funnels reach down from the sky and pluck up farmhouses, *we finally grasped their destructive power.*

Within this overall coordinate pattern we also find a smaller one: "reach down" and "pluck up."

Coordination balances one element with another. It draws equal attention to elements closely related in meaning by giving them a parallel structure. Coordination does not rank ideas by having minor ideas serve major ones. Rather, it creates equal emphasis among ideas by making those ideas grammatical equals. Coordination builds on and sharpens your ideas by calling on the virtues of balance and symmetry.

Coordinate patterns signal the relationships they draw. In our example, that signal is "but," one of seven coordinating conjunctions. The other six are *and, or, nor, for, so,* and *yet.* You can use these conjunctions to link ideas that deserve equal emphasis. Commas, colons, and semicolons can also signal parallel relationships. Note the common rationale behind these four rules.

Don't break grammatical parallels among like ideas   To match ideas in coordinate patterns, you must express those ideas in parallel grammatical form. Balance single words with single words, phrases with phrases, clauses with clauses.

> There was nothing left for us to do but *hope* and *wait.*

> She could face humiliation *before her friends in the dorm room* or *in front of her parents in the lobby.*

> He pushed his chair back from the table, *food in his belly, a grin on his face.*

> *Two supervisors run the research program,* but *one is on leave this year.*

> When he left the store with his first tuxedo, he finally had *what he always wanted: proper attire for an elegant, romantic evening.*

> *Al Capone didn't rise through hard work and dedication; he found other means.*

You gain clarity, even power, by placing parallel or antithetical ideas in a coordinate pattern. You lose both, however, should you disrupt the grammatical patterns that link your ideas. The commonplace rule warns you not to break grammatical parallels among like ideas. The hidden rationale is that those grammatical parallels help you relate ideas. The following revisions restore the balance and symmetry that coordination ought to provide.

Weak: Sexual harassment can result in suspension or even being dismissed from your job.

Better: Sexual harassment can result in suspension or even dismissal from your job.

Weak: The football program gives too much thought to a winning record, how much money the team brings in, and pleasing alums.

Better: The football program gives too much thought to winning games, raising money, and pleasing alums.

Weak: Nathan told the company that he has a solid academic record and of his interest in the field.

Better: Nathan told the company of his solid academic record and his interest in the field.

Weak: Now confined to a wheelchair, Laura has become an inspiration to her classmates, the professors, and to her friends.

Better: Now confined to a wheelchair, Laura has become an inspiration to her classmates, professors, and friends.

Clarify coordinate elements   Even when you keep grammatical elements parallel, coordination can muddle your prose when it becomes unclear which ideas are matched. The commonplace rule: don't lose the very connections you want to coordinate. Try keeping those connections straight in this maze of a sentence.

Faculty advisors should remember that their student advisees need help in understanding the bureaucratic workings of the university that they themselves take for granted, workings that puzzle even new faculty members, and that familiarity with policies, not just the academic requirements, helps them exit that bureaucratic maze with a diploma in hand.

To help readers make it through this one sentence without getting lost, clearly signal the coordinate pattern by repeating key words.

> Faculty advisors *should remember* that student advisees . . . and *should also recall* that familiarity with policies. . . .

Better yet, break the sentence in two, with a fresh start at "They should also recall that familiarity with policies. . . ."

Avoid excessive coordination   A third commonplace rule reminds you not to coordinate excessively, lest you highlight minor ideas that deserve to be subordinated.

> Thirty minutes went by, and the professor finally arrived with the exams, but by then well over twenty students had left the room.

Three independent clauses become excessive and confuse which ideas are to be matched. By putting secondary information in a supporting role, you clarify the intended contrast.

> After thirty minutes, the professor finally arrived with the exams, but by then well over twenty students had left the room.

Coordinate for balance and symmetry   The common rationale behind these rules is simply this: to lend ideas shape by linking equally important or parallel points. Balance and symmetry clarify meaning; they also make that meaning memorable. Notice how these famous statements balance ideas like weights on a scale.

> And so my fellow Americans, ask not what your country can do for you; ask what you can do for your country.
>
> *—John F. Kennedy*

> Speak softly and carry a big stick.
>
> *—Theodore Roosevelt*

> Many are called but few are chosen.
>
> *—Matthew 22:14*

> Where there's marriage without love, there will be love without marriage.
>
> *—Benjamin Franklin*

Used judiciously, coordinate patterns can help you expand your sentence repertoire and extend your thinking. Coordination trains your eye and ear to recognize ideas that deserve balance or contrast. And it permits you to highlight those relationships more clearly than you otherwise might. Because coordination often asks you to weigh and balance ideas, one against the other, it can even prompt you to discover ideas. More than a stylistic nicety for expressing thoughts you have, coordinate patterns can extend what you know or contradict what you thought you knew so well. Coordination takes some care, but as Samuel Johnson said (in fine coordinate fashion), "What is written without effort is in general read without pleasure." That pleasure, both stylistic and imaginative, lies in finding and shaping ideas.

Subordination

If coordination builds on an idea by matching it with another, subordination builds on an idea by placing another idea in a secondary or subordinate role. For example, the sentence about tornadoes uses subordination to relate minor points to the two coordinated core statements.

> We had heard about tornadoes, *newcomers that we were*, but *as we saw the black funnels reach down from the sky and pluck up farmhouses*, we finally grasped their destructive power.

The first phrase in italics, "newcomers that we were," renames "we" and thus provides more but nevertheless subordinate information. The other italicized phrase, "as we saw . . . ," is a subordinate clause that tells when we finally grasped their destructive power. Like other subordinate structures, these two elements support or modify core statements expressed in independent clauses.

Subordination creates different levels of significance, and thereby distinguishes major from minor ideas. It makes your core statement more distinct even as it provides further information about it. Subordination builds on and sharpens your ideas by differentiating among them. As you identify your leading idea and relate other ideas to it, you clarify your writing and extend your thinking.

Signal the subordinate relationship you intend   Subordinate patterns often signal the relationships they draw. Subordinating conjunctions such as *when, where, because,* and *although* not only point to the core statement but suggest how the subordinate element relates to it. Punctuation also helps differentiate subordinate from core material, with subordinate elements set off from your main statement by commas.

Subordination helps you evaluate the relative importance of your ideas. Note the ideas in this sentence.

Eric has dyslexia and works hard to improve his writing.

The coordinating conjunction "and" announces that you are placing equal emphasis on both core statements. But are they really equal? If not, what exactly is the relationship between the two ideas?

Perhaps Eric's hard work deserves emphasis. In that case, you would subordinate mention of his dyslexia to highlight hard work.

Because he is dyslexic, Eric works hard to improve his writing.

But the kind of subordinating relationship can vary. Perhaps you mean to say:

Despite his dyslexia, Eric works hard to improve his writing.

In both instances, you are stressing his hard work. Then again, you may wish to highlight Eric's difficulty with dyslexia. In that case, you might say,

Although Eric works hard to improve his writing, he remains dyslexic.

Or even:

In spite of his hard work to improve his writing, Eric remains dyslexic.

As you can see, the meanings of these statements vary considerably as you adjust the relationships among major and minor elements. Subordination helps you define those relationships and, in turn, explore your own thinking.

Don't subordinate your major idea   There are a few commonplace rules to keep in mind about subordination. One such rule warns you not to subordinate major ideas, lest you bury your main point.

I was flying back to college, looking over the wing at the rolling Kentucky hills far below, when I recalled our intimate summer walks.

If you're revising this sentence for your friend to read, you had better place the key idea—memories of intimate summer walks—at the sentence core.

As I was flying back to college, looking over the wing at the rolling Kentucky hills far below, I recalled our intimate summer walks.

Faulty subordination turns emphasis into an afterthought. It may even obscure your thinking altogether.

Avoid excessive subordination   Another commonplace rule reminds you not to subordinate excessively. Two or more dependent clauses can crowd a sentence, and may even crowd out your core idea.

> Our basketball captain, who was an arrogant junior who instructed us as if he had been an NBA veteran and we had been green players signed up in some summer youth league, designed the play during the last seconds of the game which could have won it for us if only he had landed the shot which he gave to himself.

By pruning back dependent clauses, turning some of them into modifying phrases, and breaking the sentence into two more manageable statements, you clarify the thinking and reveal the hidden irony.

> Our basketball captain, an arrogant junior, instructed us like an NBA veteran coaching green players in some summer youth league. He designed the last-second play only to miss the winning shot himself.

You should subordinate minor points, but don't carry the advice so far that readers have trouble finding your leading idea. Remember the common rationale behind the otherwise negative commonplace rules; draw connections among ideas that reveal your essential point.

Distinguish between restrictive and nonrestrictive elements   As you build on your ideas by placing some in supporting roles while giving others center stage, you'll also find that subordination helps you evaluate the core statement itself. Consider the subtle yet important differences between these two statements.

> The summer camp that he remembered fondly had changed over the years.

> The summer camp, which he remembered fondly, had changed over the years.

In the first sentence, the fond memories restrict the meaning of summer camp. Apparently there were other camps that he hated, and they may or may not have changed. Thus, the clause "that he remembered fondly" is a *bound element*, being part of the core statement; it defines the core and thus is *restrictive*. In the second sentence, by contrast, the fond memories do not restrict the meaning of summer camp. They simply describe or modify the camp. The clause is a *free element* in that the core statement wouldn't change if it were left out. It doesn't define the core and thus is *nonrestrictive*.

How can you tell the difference between restrictive and nonrestrictive elements? Experienced writers use *that* to introduce restrictive or bound clauses, while only words like *which* or *who* can introduce nonrestrictive or free clauses. But the far safer distinction resides in your punctuation. You should set off nonrestrictive or free elements by commas. Those commas are clues that the free elements are not part of the core, and thus can be moved around or deleted without radically altering the essential point.

Yet the question remains, why bother? Is the distinction between restrictive and nonrestrictive elements anything more than another commonplace rule enforced by severe schoolmarms? Yes, for unless you know what belongs in your core statement and what that statement actually says, you cannot make sense of sentences. You will only obscure your meaning and confuse your readers. This commonplace rule thus shares with others a common rationale; only by drawing clear relationships among ideas can you shape meaning.

Set some restrictive elements free   The distinction between bound and free elements also pays a handsome stylistic dividend. It helps you shape ideas with a mature and masterful style. You can often improve a sentence that is clogged and clumsy at the core by finding unnecessarily bound or restrictive elements (here in italics) and setting them free.

> Weak: Decisions *about what unrecognized but deserving literary works to teach that are made by professors when they draw up the syllabus for a survey course* may be questioned by parents who want their children to learn the traditional masterpieces.

> Better: *When professors place unrecognized but deserving literary works on the syllabus for a survey course,* parents may object that their children should learn traditional masterpieces.

In the revision, the subordinating conjunction "when" and the comma that follows now signal a clear relationship between the opening subordinate material and the core statement. Note too that by setting bound elements free, you can often revise passive constructions into the active voice and trim wordy phrases.

Once you distinguish between bound and free elements, between what needs to be at the core and what could be subordinate material, you open up endless stylistic and imaginative possibilities. Let's return to that relatively simple sentence about summer camp.

> The summer camp, which he remembered fondly, had changed over the years.

Once you determine that the phrase "which he remembered fondly" is free, not bound as part of the core, you can link it in various ways to create subtle shades of meaning. One option, of course, is to use subordinating conjunctions:

> *Despite his fond memories,* the summer camp had changed over the years.

> *Although he remembered it fondly,* the summer camp had changed over the years.

But you should also look beyond subordinating conjunctions for other options.

Use free modifiers to extend your stylistic range   You can also set restrictive elements free by calling on free modifiers, subordinate constructions that don't require a conjunction. Note how these four constructions let you add free elements swiftly and imaginatively. They can lend a touch of class to your writing.

> He sensed the summer camp had changed, *searching for memories as he looked about.*
>
> [Here we use a **present participle,** an -ing verb form that tells what a noun or pronoun is doing, in this case "he."]

> His old summer camp, *fondly remembered*, had changed over the years.
>
> [Here we use a **past participle,** a verb form in the past tense that describes a noun, in this case "camp."]

> His old summer camp, *now but a fond remembrance*, had changed over the years.
>
> [Here we use an **appositive,** a noun that renames another noun, with "remembrance" renaming "camp."]

He saw that the old summer camp had changed, *his fond memories shattered*.

[Here we use an **absolute,** a phrase that modifies the entire sentence core; it contains a new noun that is itself modified by a participle.]

By compressing action even as it incorporates information, free modifiers speed your pace and lend vigor to your prose. They clear the sentence core of clutter while making taut connections among ideas.

Those connections make your sentences ring and allow your voice to be heard. In those vigorous connections lies the key to style. To forge them, you must look *at* your style, not *through* it to the meaning you *presume* it expresses. Reread your writing, and above all read it aloud. Consider how the structure of each sentence shapes your ideas. Listen to the voice you project, and let it match the ideas to which you lend your voice. In short, use style to explore and refine your own thinking. By shaping ideas with style, you call ideas into action.

Part IV

Acting
on Ideas

Ideas in Assignments 9

College assignments can be so varied that they hardly seem related. This week you may have to write a lab report in your biology class, a memo in introductory finance, a research paper in modern European history, an essay exam in psychology. Little seems to connect these assignments other than the ten-minute walk you take to each class. This chapter helps you relate principles for shaping ideas to the conventional expectations that turn up in class assignments, regardless of discipline.

Legend says that after the Tower of Babel fell, we lost our ability to speak intelligibly to each other. Given the diverse assignments you encounter, you may wonder if we ever could. Each course seems at first to require a separate language, and helpful advice on drawing connections among various course assignments remains scant. All too often you're merely told to keep your style clear and direct and the finished product free of grammatical flaws. You're encouraged to plan each assignment in advance, and admonished to revise before you turn in your work. Thus, despite the scores of writing assignments you've already completed, each new task may present itself as an inscrutable challenge.

It needn't be so. Courses can converge, and the writing you do in them can build on previous experience and prepare you for future tasks. This chapter shows you how to control the melange of written materials you produce and how to make sense of that mix. It applies common principles to particular academic contexts.

What accounts for the melange? Most writing tasks are context-driven. What you write is occasioned by concerns that you share with readers and objectives that you must meet. Moreover, the shape you lend to your writing is in part determined by public expectations. The actual form that each writing task acquires is negotiated not just by writers and readers, but also within and among communities and cultures. Form makes visible the way in which communities think and how their members go about their work.

How might you make sense of your work as you move from one disciplinary community to another? Look for essential concerns that underlie surface variation. Discourse communities are not mutually exclusive. Just as you participate in four or more classes across campus, so too do communities interpenetrate to form a larger academic environment. Although the specific shape you lend to your writing may vary as you move from lab report to memo, from research paper to essay exam, the essential questions that allow you to shape your writing remain surprisingly similar. They are the same questions that intelligent, skeptical readers are likely to pose.

- What question deserves attention or remains at issue?
- What can you reasonably assert in reply to that question?
- What reasons can you present to justify your assertion?

The writing and thinking required of you in college is a continual search for the most reasonable assertion and the best evidence to support it. Although the format you lend to your writing may vary as you move from discipline to discipline, academic writing asks the same form-endowing questions for any analysis or argument. These questions offer a method for drawing relationships among ideas. They also allow you to shape your writing to suit changing contexts.

This chapter presents six variations on a theme. That theme has already been sounded; you call ideas into action by shaping relationships among them. Variations on this theme help you connect what I've found to be six of the most common assignments you face in college. You'll also encounter some of them in your professional life.

- essay exams
- summaries and abstracts
- research papers
- laboratory reports
- business memos
- oral presentations

You can shape ideas in these seemingly unrelated assignments by responding to readers' questions. Those questions challenge you to think and write critically. They also make your education more than the sum of your assignments.

Essay Exams

Fifty minutes, four essay questions. These two constraints—the ticking clock and unknown questions to which you must reply—make the in-class essay exam an unnerving ordeal. Whether a student approaches the exam with panic or stoic endurance, given a choice, few would choose this writing situation. But then choice is usually not what the essay exam is about. Fifty minutes, four questions. Constraints carry the day.

The key to surviving the ordeal lies in understanding these constraints and knowing how you can use them to shape both your preparation for the exam and the written replies you hand in as time runs out. To write well under the pressure of a ticking clock, consider the following five points.

What Purpose Does an Essay Exam Serve?

Essay exams prompt you to write by posing questions. Those questions shift the focus of the exam away from sheer recall of information for its own sake; they emphasize instead your own ability to apply and use course materials intelligently, even creatively. Were information all that mattered, essay questions would hardly be necessary. Professors could simply list topics, and then turn you loose to fill pages with facts. Essay questions call for more. They ask you to place information and ideas in the service of a pointed, well-reasoned response. The notion that essay exams stress sheer recall of facts—a memory dump, if you will—has led students to no end of grief. Only by actively using (not regurgitating) information and ideas can you demonstrate your mastery of course materials and methods.

What's in an Essay Question?

What should you look for in an essay question? In a word, clues. Essay questions not only prompt response but contain indications that can shape and direct your reply. To understand how an essay question can prefigure your reply, bear in mind the two basic functions performed by an exam question.

The question serves as your essay's occasion   What you write must respond to the question that your professor sets at issue. In this sense, the exam question is not something apart from your answer; the question is itself an aspect of your answer, a defining element in the form and substance you lend to your reply. You might say that your essay is already under way before you write word one. The question not only asks you to reply, it also foreshadows the kind of reply you might give.

The question sets both your topic and your task   In so doing, it can prefigure the shape you lend to your essay. The topic is what you write about—be it a Shakespearean play or Civil War history. The task defines how you should write—do you analyze or argue, do you trace historical development or evaluate worth? Many essay questions highlight your task by using obvious commands: "Define *bel canto* and trace its development in Italian opera." "From the data given, evaluate the effect of winter snowpack conditions on yields for different crops." Other types of questions may offer at best implicit tasks. Here's one where the question comes only after you're told something first: "According to the author and playwright Max Frisch, 'Technology [is] the knack of so arranging the world that we don't have to experience it.' What does Frisch mean by this comment? And how would you respond to Frisch?" Look for these kinds of follow-up questions that place a special focus on your main task or broaden its implications. Although indications about topic are generally easy to discern, clues about your task vary from obvious command words to implicit suggestions. Virtually all tasks, however, ask you to advance and support an assertion.

The quality of your essay depends on the care with which you read and respond to questions. Neglect the clues that your professor gives, and your essay will not reply to the occasion that the question has set for you.

How Can the Question Help Shape My Reply?

The task presented in your question can help you plan your response. Let's consider how specific command words offer clues that prefigure the direction—and even the organization—of your essay.

Analyze, evaluate, argue   Each of these tasks calls for an assertion that extends beyond description and narrative. You must make and defend inferences from observations, and support your point with clearly articulated reasons. Those reasons will organize your response. Let's say you're asked, "Analyze Ibsen's *A Doll's House* as a response to the conventions of 19th-century melodrama." To reply analytically, you'll need to do more than pick apart those conventions and describe aspects of the play. You'll have to interpret or make sense of the response, perhaps by asserting that Ibsen, in thwarting melodramatic expectations, rebels against social convention. Or let's say you must use evidence from child language acquisition to evaluate Chomsky's theory that language acquisition is innate. You may wish to describe the theory, give examples from adult speech, or talk about child language, but you can't rest content with that. You must assert whether or not his theory can be supported in light of how children actually acquire language. Tasks that have you argue seem straightforward enough, for you must take sides: "Was imperialism an inevitable consequence of Japan's social conditions in the early 20th century?" But in taking sides, your essay need not be one-sided. You'll also need to engage counterarguments that complicate or even undermine your position.

Trace the development of, trace the process by which   Each of these tasks ask you for more than a narrative that retells a story. You must interpret events in light of their pattern, causal relationship, or significance. Let's say you are tracing the Don Juan legend in your humanities course. It won't be enough to describe various treatments of the legend by de Molina, Molière, Mozart, Byron, and Shaw; you'll need to draw and defend inferences about society's changing view of the libertine. Or let's say your political science professor asks you to trace the process by which legal decisions are appealed. Your response should do more than identify each step; it should clarify what legal protections or consequences follow from appeal procedures.

Compare and contrast   This task should generate more than a list of similarities and differences. Articulate and then support the point to be won by the comparison. When comparing, for example, the different social-contract theories developed by Hobbes, Locke, and Rousseau, you should establish what the various similarities and differences teach us about the freedoms we surrender for society's protection and the responsibilities that government assumes toward its citizens. Likewise, a comparison of mitosis and meiosis should not only distinguish these two types of nuclear division in a cell; it should also tell us why the distinction matters.

Describe, define   If you are asked to describe or define, do more than inventory features; clarify their relationship and significance. Suppose you're asked to describe the artistic technique chiaroscuro. You'll certainly need to present the details of the technique, its particular treatment of light and dark areas without regard to color. But a good reply would do more; it might touch on the advantages of the technique or its significance in art history. Likewise, if you're asked to define the Buffer Model of memory for your psychology exam, you should certainly identify that model in a way that sets it apart from others. But once again a good reply would do more. You might, through your definition, touch on how the Buffer Model addresses problems in both short- and long-term memory and its place in cognitive research.

Discuss, comment on   Don't be seduced by these commonly used words into thinking that any sort of rambling reply will do. Lend shape to what might otherwise be random observations by advancing a point. For example, when discussing the influence that the televised sound bite has had on political campaigns, you should offer more than a series of one- or two-sentence sound bites yourself. Even in a short reply, be sure to sustain your discussion; support your assertion by developing a line of reasoning.

How Should I Prepare for an Essay Exam?

Because the basic design of an essay exam relies on the dynamic of occasion and response, your preparation ought to mimic that structure. Here's how.

Approach course material in terms of tasks   Instead of passively reviewing readings and your own notes, give yourself tasks; set topics into relationship, draw connections, argue and analyze, trace developments, compare and contrast, pose questions and counterarguments. By using tasks to approach topics, you'll improve your active command of the material. Tasks will also help you recall the methods and theoretical approaches emphasized in your course.

Anticipate questions by setting yourself occasions that elicit response   Pose specific questions that ask you to synthesize course materials and then actually sketch out your replies. Instructors often give hints about the kinds of questions the exam will cover; even if they don't, the course itself should tell you what concerns were particularly important. Although your own practice questions may not appear on the exam, you will have gained experience in handling questions and formulating replies.

Turn essay exams into learning experiences by actively preparing for them   Because essay exams ask you to synthesize what you know, they can help you discover new insights. Be ready to apply what you know to specific or even new contexts. By narrowing your preparation to passive memorization and rote response, you limit what you can learn. Moreover, if you don't pull ideas together as you prepare, you and your essay may fall apart as time ticks away during the actual exam.

What Should I Do When I Get the Exam?

With precious seconds already ticking away, you may think that time not spent writing is time wasted. Don't forget that the exam questions are themselves part of your reply. Instead of diving into the first question that meets your eye, take a few moments to do the following.

Peruse the entire exam   This will help you determine the form it takes and where its emphasis lies. The design of the exam will shape the work you do during the next fifty minutes or two hours. Points or time limits allotted to each question can help you gauge where to focus your own attention.

Read each question   In this way you can identify topic and task. Remember that the point and reasoned support of your essay should respond to the occasion already set for you.

Plan your reply   Use the question to prompt a brief key-word outline of your point and supporting reasons. Don't dive in without knowing what you wish to assert and why.

How Should I Write the Actual Essay?

The question you are given can go a long way in shaping your reply. Use it to your advantage. Let's consider an essay question from a humanities course in which you read Greek tragedies.

> Greek tragedy often turns on the relationship between the hero and the gods. How do changes in that relationship suggest ways in which Greek drama developed?

Treat the question as your actual occasion   Don't bother to restate the entire question or funnel in with long-winded background. You needn't justify a question already presented to you. On the other hand, don't start in with an answer that prevents anyone but your professor from reconstructing the question to which you are responding. Use your opening sentence to orient your readers. Note how this first sentence of a reply implies the question or occasion even as it answers it.

> The changing relationship between hero and gods in Greek tragedy signals a growing interest in individual psychological motivation.

Answer the question directly, preferably in your first sentence   Treat the opening of your essay as your thesis statement. By quickly implying the occasion that the essay question presents, you are able to move directly to your main assertion, as we just saw in the snappy reply to the question about Greek tragedy. If you had to answer your question in twenty-five words or less, what would you say? A strong, forthright opening makes a favorable impression on a weary grader, who may otherwise hunt for or even miss your point. Moreover, a strong opening provides you with a point of reference from which you can develop your reply. Should you run short of time, a strong opening will at least convince the grader that you have gone to the heart of matters. Don't use your essay as a chance to brainstorm ideas or to come up with possible answers along the way. If you drift toward a thesis, time may prevent you from arriving at one.

Orient yourself and your reader to the shape you will lend to your essay   You're apt to lose your reader in a labyrinth of loosely associated ideas unless you clarify the relationships you draw and the basic plan by which your essay proceeds. Announce the reasons that justify your thesis. In his reply to the question on Greek tragedy, note how this student follows his thesis with a preview of supporting points.

> The changing relationship between hero and gods in Greek tragedy signals a growing interest in individual psychological motivation. While Aeschylus has the gods determine the fate of heroes, Sophocles sees their fate in terms of heroic faults. Euripides, in turn, often views his characters in less-than-heroic terms, with an eye to their complex psychological motivations.

By announcing your thesis and support at the outset, you help the harried grader understand the point and plan behind your reply.

Remain loyal to both the reply you have announced and the question that has occasioned your thoughts   As you write the full essay, bear in mind your point. With little or no time for revision, you can't afford to wander off on a tangent. To keep yourself on track, and to orient your reader, use your reasons or supporting points to organize your reply. And as you discuss each reason or point, don't forget to provide some detail and support. A steady diet of broad assertions and generalizations won't demonstrate your mastery of course material.

Read your essay answers before you turn in your work   Although you won't be able to revise thoroughly, you can improve the readability and focus of your response with some light editing.

Essay exams surely test your nerve. But they also test more than your passive knowledge of the material. Exam questions are occasions for your own reasoned assertions. Once you recognize the form underlying essay exams, you will be able to formulate cogent replies.

Summaries and Abstracts

A summary is an exercise in the art of the miniature. It's a condensed representation of material appearing elsewhere in fuller form. Just as a doll represents human features on a smaller scale, or an architect's model reduces a large building so that it might rest in the palm of your hand, so too does the summary condense an essay, a report, or a book to a short statement. Scores, even hundreds of pages are often rendered in one or more paragraphs.

In an age when technological miniaturization has become commonplace, writing a summary may at first appear straightforward, if not trivial. If we can place the entire *Encyclopaedia Britannica* on a compact disk, or reduce yards of wire to a circuit the size of a thumbnail, why should rendering the essential thrust of a twenty-page essay in two hundred words remain such a challenge?

Summaries require that you portray the ideas of another piece of writing in a brief text that must itself acquire shape and serve a purpose. Although summaries seem merely descriptive, they challenge even the most accomplished writers because they ask you to comprehend and render the underlying logic of what you summarize. Reduced scale becomes but one of several concerns. You must do more than inventory the author's points; you must represent issues, assertions, and reasons, all of which function in dynamic relation to each other. As words don't shrink the way scale models do, you must discern what is essential to the line of argument, and how individual statements relate to the thrust and function of the whole. Summaries present, then, a double dilemma: you must discern the shape of another piece of writing even as you try to shape your own representation of it.

A General Framework

Principles for shaping ideas can provide a general framework for writing a summary. Because those principles have their origin in the concerns of readers, they provide a useful bridge between reading and writing, source text and the text you now produce. You can apply those principles by thinking of your summary as a "closed" introduction to the text you are summarizing. Let's say you've been asked to write a one-paragraph summary of a much longer essay. Your closed paragraph will have an occasion, thesis, and reasons, but it won't propel author and reader into a full paper, as an opening would otherwise do. Instead of introducing, the paragraph summarizes. It presents a closed statement—independent and coherent in its own terms.

Let's see this framework in action by considering a summary that a student wrote of a challenging source text, Martin Luther King, Jr.'s "Letter from Birmingham Jail."

> Martin Luther King, Jr.'s "Letter from Birmingham Jail," written in 1963 from a jail cell, addresses eight clergymen who have criticized as "unwise and untimely" King's attempts to establish racial equality. King argues that immediate nonviolent direct action is the only viable alternative remaining for American blacks. One by one, King addresses the various questions

raised by those clergy. He states that, though technically an outsider to Birmingham, he has an obligation to fight injustice wherever it may be. He counters the sentiment that recent demonstrations in the city were unfortunate by noting the lamentable conditions that the city's white power structure forces upon blacks. Responding to charges of extremism, King explains that he has prevented violence by directing the anger of an oppressed people through nonviolent protest. He notes that tension is often necessary for social progress and justifies nonviolent direct action even when it entails openly breaking unjust laws. Drawing upon American tradition, Biblical allusions, and church history, King expresses his disappointment with the white church and white moderates in general, who agree with the principle of equal rights but are reluctant to aid the cause. Racial justice, King argues, will come about only by taking nonviolent action now.

This summary captures the essence of King's letter because, like that letter, it draws relationships among key ideas.

Let's take a closer look at the strategies behind this summary. Here's how the very elements of form that lend coherence to your summary can link it to the ideas that shape your source text.

• *Your occasion* for the summary should reflect the *author's occasion* for writing. What's the question at issue? What concern prompts the author to write the essay, article, or book? Be sure to provide some context about your source text; for example, the author's name, the title of the work, and the circumstances of publication. In the summary of King's letter, the student found his occasion by recalling King's own.

• *Your thesis* in the summary should reflect the *author's thesis*. What, exactly, is the point of the essay or book? The conclusion that the author justifies should serve as the central statement in your own summary. Note that the second sentence of the summary clearly articulates King's basic point.

• The *body of your summary* should capture the *author's main reasons* that justify his or her point. How does the author structure and develop the discussion? What methods were employed? Having clarified King's point near the outset of the summary, the student is now able to render the ideas in King's letter that justify his assertion.

• The *concluding point* or sentence in your summary should reflect the significance of the article or essay, as might be the case in the *author's own conclusion*. What contribution does the author make? Why is the problem being addressed important? The student rounds off his summary by relating King's interest in nonviolent action to the cause of racial justice.

This general framework for writing a summary provides you with a method for discerning the shape of the author's ideas even as you shape your own representation of them.

Key Criteria

Because this framework enables you to draw connections between two texts, it can also help you understand and meet the key criteria that a summary ought to fulfill.

A summary must be comprehensive and accurate   By focusing on the shape of ideas in both your summary and your source text, you can check whether you include points essential to the statement and development of the author's thesis.

A summary must be concise   Your summary should be considerably shorter than the source. In many cases it need not be any longer than one paragraph. You are providing an overview, so do not feel compelled to include every detail or supporting point. By recognizing and rendering only those key elements that generate the author's analysis or argument, you are in a position to make your summary concise.

A summary must be coherent   Your summary should make sense in its own right; do not rely on the presence of your source or assume that your reader has already read it. You have a good chance of making your summary coherent if you focus on and represent the key conceptual moves that underlie analysis or argument. Those very same moves lend your source whatever coherence it has.

A summary must be independent   Even as you offer an accurate summary of another author's views, you should maintain your own voice and use your own words. You're writing the summary, after all. Paraphrase, except when you need a brief quote to capture a key phrase or idea. As you paraphrase, however, be sure that you do not misrepresent the author or employ a voice inconsistent with that of the source. Accuracy, however, need not make your summary dull. Try to capture what compels the author to engage the subject.

A summary must meet your reader's needs   Keep in mind the audience and purpose for which you develop the summary. Unless you are writing for a very specific audience, do not assume that your readers have specialized knowledge about the subject.

Specific Applications

Here are some of the very specific formats and purposes to which this general framework lends itself. Be ready to adapt the framework to suit specific applications.

Brief annotation, as in an annotated bibliography   An annotation offers an explanatory note about a work cited in a bibliography. It rarely exceeds several sentences. An annotation focuses on the author's thesis and the general relevance of the work. It may also suggest how an entry relates to the study that provides the annotation or to the purposes to which the bibliography may be put.

Abstract of a published article   An abstract is a specific type of summary. It is more formal and impersonal than many summaries, and often serves as an informative digest of material presented in a technical or research publication. Whether placed at the very beginning of a published article or compiled with other such summaries, an abstract allows potential readers to decide whether the issues or conclusions hold relevance for them. Typically 150 to 250 words long, an abstract previews the article and provides busy readers with essential information in capsule form. When writing an abstract of your own work, you should address the question that motivates your study or research, your results or conclusions, the reasons that justify your point of view, and the implications of your work. Abstracts of technical papers may also indicate what methods or procedures were used in your study. An abstract must be self-contained and comprehensible, for it often stands in for the entire paper when listed in journals or catalogs of abstracts. An abstract can determine how—or even whether—the full article is read.

Executive summary   A close cousin of the abstract, an executive summary offers a nontechnical, action-oriented condensation of a long report to busy managers or executives. Typically no longer than one or two pages, an executive summary highlights the issue or problem to which the report responds, the conclusions drawn, and the recommendations or action items that follow from those conclusions. An executive summary usually places somewhat less emphasis on the detailed reasons or specific methods by which the report arrived at its conclusions. An indispensable tool in the business world, the executive summary influences decision making where it counts, be it in the manager's office or in the corporate boardroom.

Promissory abstract   You can also write summaries for longer works still on the drawing board. Such abstracts can help you think through the issue, point, and plan behind work in progress. When submitted to and accepted by an editor, publisher, or conference organizer, promissory abstracts assume the status of a contract; they commit you to write the full work according to the essential thrust of the summary. Promissory abstracts usually focus on the distinctive features of your work and its relevance to a particular audience. Although they tend to be overtly descriptive, most authors sharpen them with a persuasive edge; there is usually a hidden thesis to the effect that the work (as yet unwritten) should be accepted.

The summary in the context of other writing   Summaries frequently appear where you may not expect them, in the context of other types of writing that pursue their own distinctive purposes. When you offer a *critical review* (or critique) of another author's work, you would do well to summarize before you evaluate. In *argumentative writing*, the positions that you may wish to consider or refute likewise deserve fair-minded presentation. And in the *research paper* or *term paper*, you must frequently characterize the work of authors on whose shoulders you stand. When summary appears in the context of other writing, you need to adapt the general framework presented here to the immediate requirements of your task. Such summaries may be less formal or comprehensive than stand-alone versions and must be oriented to the occasion that has prompted you to summarize. Summaries—of whatever stripe—serve your reader well when you lend them a shape that reflects the key ideas of your source.

Research Papers

By reputation, the research paper looms before you as one of the more difficult and time-consuming writing tasks in college. It's not hard to understand why. The assignment has you wander the labyrinth of library stacks, compile note cards, and figure out bibliographic format. When it comes time to write the paper, shaping ideas all too often becomes a matter of shuffling note cards; you are left to stitch together pieces of information, string together a few quotes, and document the requisite number of sources. If the paper makes for dull reading, you console yourself that turnabout is fair play since the paper was even duller to write.

A preoccupation with clerical tasks—thumbing through library card catalogs to "look things up" and committing to note cards what you find—can easily distort the shape you lend to a research paper and even its very purpose. Those tasks can tempt you to retell the story of your research efforts or describe the information that you have found in the process. They may lead you to shape your paper based on your sources, not on your own ideas. Too much emphasis on research tasks can dull the analytic or argumentative edge that your paper should carry and even obscure the very point of research itself.

In this section, we'll put immediate tasks in context. Instead of focusing on step-by-step procedures, we'll look at underlying questions that can shape and guide both your research and your paper.

Why Pursue Research?

The question seems obvious, but it is all too rarely asked. Research makes sense only if you have genuine questions that need answers—and those answers are not readily available or obvious. To ask those questions intelligently, and to find answers that matter, you must develop or uncover information that is not already at your disposal. You owe it to yourself and your readers to see what the best minds have had to say on the subject, so that you, in turn, can say something more, something new. The purpose of research is thus an ethical one: to acknowledge the work of those who have gone before you. Only by acknowledging that work can you build on it.

Genuine questions thus ask you to pursue intelligent answers by acknowledging and extending the work of others. Unfortunately, this is where misunderstandings can arise. Although research involves gathering information, the gathering process is not an end in itself. Information becomes relevant only insofar as it permits you to solve a problem. To make sense of your research paper and the research that leads up to it, you will do best to adopt a problem-solving perspective.

By thinking of research in terms of solving problems, you can set what might otherwise seem to be clerical tasks in a critical-thinking context. Your research will have precious little point if you gather and footnote information that confirms conclusions others have already reached. By simply "looking it up," you merely confirm the obvious by supplying footnotes. The motions you go through may resemble research but miss its inherent purpose. Genuine research hinges on your ability to build on work already done, to pose new or unsettled questions, and to arrive at and justify answers that would otherwise remain uncertain or unknown. Research, in short, hinges on your ability to recognize and solve new problems.

As you engage your research problem, the dynamic, evolving relationship among questions, answers, and reasons can help you make sense of the unknown territory you explore. You are already familiar with this relationship as a point of departure for general essays: as you question, gather, and sort, you arrive at an occasion, and reasons that justify a thesis. These elements can lend shape and purpose to your words. Let's consider how you can adapt this general method for shaping your writing to the special demands of research. Those special demands include the need to maintain a skeptical attitude, for research is an open-ended process in which questions, conclusions, and reasons constantly evolve. Research also demands that you relate your own work to those who have gone before as you develop primary source material or engage in library research.

Focusing Your Research Question

Because questions define the limits of what you know, they can help you focus your search to know more. Unlike questions, topics merely point to subject areas. Whether narrow or broad, these subject areas bear little relation to the problem that has you pursuing research. Your first task when starting a research paper is to shift from a topic orientation to a questioning stance—a stance in which you are constantly formulating and refocusing your research question. Questions are the engines that drive your research. Here's why.

• A research question motivates, focuses, and directs your work. It reminds you why your work matters and what purpose it can serve. Your research question also helps you define your audience, for a question is always answered *for* someone. Moreover, questions help demystify the research process by suggesting how and where you might direct your inquiry.

• Pointed questions help ensure that your project is workable given the time and space you have available. As you refine and focus your question, making it always more specific, you can avoid glib generalities of the sort you might find under a general topic heading in an encyclopedia.

• Unlike a topic, a question can help you see your way through the avalanche of information you are likely to encounter as you conduct your research. Questions help you identify the information you need and lend relevance to the material you gather. Moreover, only when you formulate a question can you put information to use.

• A question helps you to define and solve the unknowns in your project. The marvelous thing about a question is that it prompts you to look for an answer. Questions can elicit hunches that, even if vague or unformed, can lead to unforeseen conclusions.

• As you learn more, questions change. By adopting a questioning stance, you help guarantee that your research will evolve and grow, and not stop at a preliminary point where you may rehearse the obvious. Along with your core question, develop an array of related secondary questions to help you answer more specific issues. Your research question is itself a moving target that can keep your work on the move.

Finding and Evaluating Information

Unless you formulate a research question, heading off to the library to "do some research" can easily become a frustrating and fruitless stroll through the stacks. Why? Sheer information is not enough. Because any library will have far more information than you need or can use, you must be able to relate information to your own problem-solving concerns. If you don't, library work can become a distraction, not a helpful research tool. To set your question in relationship to the work of others, keep these points in mind.

• When you look for information, you will find that the library organizes its holdings by subject categories—in other words, topics. To tap the library's rich resources, you'll need to relate your research question to several of these categories. The danger here is that you might shift your attention to the subject headings themselves, in which case you'll quickly have far more information than you can handle. Remember, you are not looking for information on a topic, you are looking for answers to increasingly specific research questions.

• If you feel the need to do some general background reading to make sense of more technical information about your research question, keep in mind why you are reading. Don't content yourself with reading about your research question; read to find answers to the question or to ask your question more intelligently. If you don't, background reading can easily become a way to keep busy while keeping your research at arm's length.

• Your research question is more than a tool for gathering material. Also use it as a screen by which to sort and evaluate the relevance of the materials you find. Because you will come across more articles and books than you can possibly read in depth, look through them quickly with your research question in mind. Glance at the table of contents, skim the preface or introduction, and check the index for topics related to your concerns. Look for clues that tell you how or even whether you should read any one article or book.

As you find sources related to your research question, you must do more than read them for the information they contain; you'll also need to *evaluate* them in terms of the intellectual case their authors present, and in terms of the analysis or argument you yourself are developing.

• The importance of your own research question should remind you that other articles and books do not describe information neutrally or aimlessly. To collaborate with researchers who have gone before you, you must recognize that they themselves are asking specific questions and asserting and justifying answers. Don't read for content alone; you'll also need to recognize how other authors place information in the service of their own analytic or argumentative projects. Look at the introduction and conclusion of an article or book to help you recognize the shape of its ideas—its occasion, thesis, and main supporting points.

• Once you have understood a source in its own terms, you can then evaluate it in terms of your own purposes. How does its question at issue relate to your own? How does its thesis relate to the hypothesis you are beginning to form? How does the evidence marshalled in support of its point contribute to or question your own case? In short, how has the material affected your own understanding of the questions you are posing and the answers you are beginning to arrive at and defend? In turn, be sure to relate each article or book to your other sources. Does it reinforce or dispute other findings? How credible does your source appear to be? Remember that research requires active, purposeful reading. Look beyond discrete nuggets of information that you might passively note down to the relationships you might form among pieces of evidence. Before you record information, ask yourself why and how it might fit into your own project.

Although I have focused chiefly on library sources (or secondary research), essentially the same process goes on as you engage in primary research where you are collecting data yourself.

• Before you collect data, formulate your research question carefully. The method and design behind your experiment, interviews, or survey instrument will determine the data you collect. If you don't know what question prompts your work, the information you collect will either confuse or confound you.

• Keep careful notes. If secondary research requires that you find sources, primary research asks that you collect and record detailed observations or raw data. Don't put off writing down these observations in a notebook, for memory can easily trick you into recording what you would like to have seen or heard.

• Evaluate what you are doing. Every so often, take a step back from your work and ask yourself what it means. Does the data confirm your working hypothesis, or do you need to revise the questions you are asking or the tentative conclusions you are forming? What sort of information does your research design screen out? What remains ambiguous?

Writing the Research Paper

As you conduct your research, the specific nature of your question will change, as will your tentative hypothesis. At the early stages of your research, your inquiry will focus on your initial questions and on questions raised by the data or material you uncover. As you begin to write your paper, your focus changes—it now centers on testing and justifying the conclusions you have reached. Your goal should be to offer a tightly reasoned case that supports your conclusion on a question at issue.

Because of this shift in focus, the shape you lend to your case usually does not reflect the actual twists and turns in the process by which you arrived at your conclusions. Likewise, your paper will not include all of the information you have uncovered nor will it mention all of the insights you have won. The paper inverts the direction of inquiry—you are now reasoning from and supporting a conclusion rather than working your way toward one. Nevertheless, the questions you have used to draw relationships among ideas can prepare you to justify them.

• Your *research question* can serve as the basis for your paper's *occasion*. Just as your question focused and guided your inquiry, so too can your occasion launch your presentation of its fruits. You needn't voice all the preliminary research questions that led you to settle on your particular concern. In fact, you should avoid retelling the story of your research process. Focus instead on articulating the question at the heart of your project. That question, not the trail of your research, will engage your readers' interest and establish the relevance of your conclusion. How you frame your occasion will depend on the audience you address. If your audience is not specified, engage the question at issue much as you would for someone who entered the research process knowing only what you did yourself.

• The hunches and *tentative hypotheses* that helped direct the research process can serve as the basis for your *thesis*. As you draft and revise your paper, your obligation is to refine and appropriately qualify the conclusion you present. As with preliminary research questions, you needn't discuss those hypotheses that proved inadequate or were misguided. Your task is to articulate your best, reasoned opinion on a matter of dispute or concern. Drafting your research paper can help you arrive at conclusions and test whether you can justify them before intelligent readers.

• The *information* you gather during the research process will surely contribute to the *reasons* that project the organization of your paper. But to turn information into evidence, you must place information in the service of your analysis or argument. Having worked toward a conclusion, you must now call upon key pieces of information to serve as evidence in support of your point. You needn't—in fact, shouldn't—include all that you uncovered during your research. Your task is to justify your conclusion while answering whatever questions or objections skeptical readers may pose. To sharpen the analytic or argumentative edge your paper should carry, make sure that you organize it as carefully as a lawyer who is trying a case. If you simply reshuffle the deck of your note cards into loosely related topical headings, you may lend some surface organization to your paper but little if any logical coherence to your case.

By viewing the research process in light of the conceptual demands of analysis and argument, you can avoid the three pitfalls into which many novice writers fall.

• Their research papers often lack motivation, a reason to be written and read.

• The papers usually waffle on (or entirely avoid) a point or conclusion, opting instead to catalog existing views or moderate differing opinions.

• The papers often become little more than strings of sources overwhelming readers with an avalanche of information that might otherwise be used to build a tightly reasoned case.

By focusing on the shape and shaping of ideas, you can lend to your own work the continuity and coherence that others often lack. Don't let your research justify the old joke that you're simply moving bones from one grave to another. If you think critically from the start, you can find and justify the best possible answers to questions that matter. For you, as for your professors, this shared inquiry is what college is all about.

Laboratory Reports

Of the writing tasks you may encounter in college, none will appear more rigid and predetermined than the lab report you write for a science, social science, or engineering course. Formal lab reports typically have five standard sections: abstract, introduction, methods, results, and discussion. Forming your report merely seems to be a matter of duplicating an organizational format. Even your reports for instructional labs, though less formal, require you to follow a particular format, often specified by your instructor. So whether you are conducting ground-breaking research, replicating classic experiments, or acquainting yourself with basic scientific concepts, the report you write seems to offer little if any latitude.

More is at stake, however, than mimicking a prescribed structure. Unless you understand the problem-solving concerns that underlie such a structure and the reasons why a community of readers and writers adopt it as convention, you risk misusing or misapplying even the most straightforward formats. By looking for relationships among ideas, you can discover what motivates surface format. Those relationships can lend purpose and point to what might otherwise appear as the arbitrary prescriptions of your assignment.

Although you may think of the lab report as a way to communicate the fruits of your work, it also represents the scientific method at work. As with other instances of analysis and argument, the form you lend to your report can serve as a tool to discover and shape meaning. The report provides you with a means to think through and solve problems, not merely to describe what you did and what you found. Method motivates format. More than just a final product you hand in, the lab report provides a common set of guidelines to help you engage in scientific problem-solving. The report enables you to

- address a problem by articulating and testing a hypothesis;
- gather, present, and interpret evidence about your hypothesis that will confirm or refute it; and
- inform readers of your findings so that they can evaluate them.

The lab report has become a conventional form because members of the scientific community have developed shared expectations. They have reached consensus about useful strategies for engaging in and communicating the results of problem-solving activities. Let's consider, section by section, how the formal lab report reflects problem-solving strategies. For illustration, we'll call upon a lab report written by Andrea Feldman for an upper-division course in cognitive psychology. The title of her report is "Isolation Effect of Common versus Rare Words in a Free Recall Task."

The Abstract

As a succinct summary of the entire report, the abstract informs readers about the key aspects of your experiment or study: the problem addressed, the methods used, the results obtained, and the conclusions drawn. As you'll recall from the earlier section on summary, an abstract captures the essential features of your work in capsule form, often no longer than 150–250 words. Here's the abstract from Andrea's lab report.

Previous research indicates that subjects recall common words significantly better than rare words. Research on the isolation effect suggests, by contrast, that items departing from an organized structure have a greater recall than their familiar counterparts. In this study, the recall of two word lists with common versus rare words were compared, each list containing an isolated item. The two independent variables were the word lists and the isolated items. The dependent variables were the recall rates for words on each list. Results showed support for the recall of common over rare words; however, when isolated, rare words had greater recall than isolated common words. These findings indicate that interference from a distinctive item, rather than a departure from an organized structure, can cause the isolation effect.

Andrea's abstract does more than render main points. It also invites a community of readers—here her fellow students and psychologists—to participate in the scientific method. The experiments or field observations you conduct are not isolated undertakings; they take their place alongside other experiments and studies. The work of fellow members in your disciplinary community may corroborate or dispute your findings. Their work may have served as a foundation for your own efforts or may expand on the foundation that you yourself lay.

The abstract to your report makes this cross-fertilization possible. On the basis of your abstract, readers know about your work and decide whether or not to look at it. The abstract reflects and in part establishes the report's functional context. It serves as both your final summary and your readers' initial invitation. When seen in this light, the abstract should alert you that the full lab report, for all its rigid features, depends on the dynamic participation of readers in your disciplinary community.

Introduction

Why have you performed the experiment or study, and why should your readers take an interest in it? The introduction to your report answers both questions by establishing the occasion for your experiment. It helps you clarify your purpose or objective, and should in turn occasion your readers' interest.

In your report for a demonstration or teaching lab, the introduction may amount to only several sentences. Here's one from a chemical engineering lab.

It has been reported that excessive pressure drops are being obtained in a segment of plant piping. Such a drop could be caused by corrosion or scale (roughness) on the inside walls of the pipe. This project was undertaken to determine experimentally if wall roughness was a major factor in causing the pressure drop.

The introduction you write in your lab notebook for an exercise in introductory physics may be even more concise.

Purpose of experiment: 1) To determine that, for a body moving with constant acceleration, the distance that the body travels is proportional to the square of the time during which it is traveling; 2) To verify that gravity = 9.8 m/s^2; and 3) To measure my reaction time and that of my lab partner.

Yet even when the introduction seems short and perhaps informal, you would do well to make very explicit the exact purpose of your experiment. Only when you know its purpose can you conduct and evaluate your work.

Introductions to formal lab reports are often a bit more extensive. Even so, they share the essential features of occasions to essays in many humanistic disciplines. Like many of the occasions you have already considered, the introduction to your report should

• articulate the problem or question that you are addressing and the intent of the experiment;

• place your work in context by establishing a link between the text to follow and the intellectual and scientific discussion out of which it emerges;

• provide brief background information that can help readers appreciate the significance of your work, and its relationship to scientific theory or previous experiments; and

• set up the results and discussion sections by stating the hypothesis that was tested—a hypothesis that was confirmed, refuted, or modified as a result of the experiment.

The introduction to Andrea's lab report addresses these concerns and thereby establishes the occasion for her experiment. As you read her introduction, don't worry if you can't follow the details as a psychology major might; consider instead how she shapes the intellectual case for her work. (For your own lab reports, be sure to follow documentation styles accepted in your field and attach a page giving references in full.)

Tests of word frequency have indicated that subjects recall common words significantly better than rare words in free recall tasks. Hall (1954) had subjects look at common versus rare word lists and found 80% less memory of rare words. Yet when recognition, not recall, is studied, rare words fare far better. Shepard (1967) tested recognition of common versus rare words, and found better recognition of rare words. These findings indicate that recall is aided by familiarity, while recognition is aided by rarity. Both of these experimenters used word lists composed entirely of either familiar or rare words. This study considers the effect that one rare word might have when randomly placed in a list of common words. Its recall might be better than a similarly placed familiar word due to the Von Restorff or Isolation Effect (Cimbalo and Brink, 1982).

Numerous studies of the isolation effect indicate that unique physical properties of a single stimulus can influence recall. Lippman and Thompson (1981) studied the effect of different colors on recall of consonant-vowel-consonant (CVC) sequences and found a significant isolation effect. In their experiment, employing a between-subjects design, Lippman and Thompson found greater recall for a particular letter when a red rectangle surrounded it. A second finding indicated that frequency of particular CVCs influenced the magnitude of the effect. That is, repeated sequences which were highlighted in red had greater recall than similar sequences which were not repeated.

In a second study, Cimbalo and Brink (1982) compared the isolation effect on college students versus the elderly, using a between-subjects design, to test whether or not the ability to recognize and use structure and organization (their reason for the isolation effect) declines with age. The structure and organization hypothesis predicts that exceptions to previously encoded schemas will be more difficult for the elderly to recall. Other explanations for the isolation effect include interference, Gestalt processing, or orienting principles. In their experiment, Cimbalo and Brink used enlarged stimuli for the isolating items. They found that although the college students recalled the outstanding item well, the elderly did not. The data for the elderly showed no significant main effect for the enlarged stimuli. They concluded that the elderly population had ignored the isolated item because it forced them to adopt an unfamiliar organizational scheme.

Both experiments indicate that familiarity aids the isolation effect: in the first study, repetition of letters created familiarity, while the second study concluded that unfamiliar patterns interfered with recall in the elderly. In the research reported here, I tested the isolation effect by using common versus rare words as stimuli. My hypothesis was that the isolation effect occurs to a greater extent when the word does not fit the structure of the word list—in this instance, when that word is rare rather than common. This finding would lend support to the interference hypothesis for the isolation effect as opposed to the structure and organization hypothesis. The interference hypothesis predicts that the isolate will stand out and therefore be treated as noise. This noise could serve as a distinctive anchor and result in better recall for the isolated item. It would also suggest that the isolation effect can override familiarity in a free recall task.

I expect to find the usual primacy and recency effects of a free recall experiment—i.e., a serial position curve, with a peak for the isolation effect. I also expect an overall higher recall of common over rare words. I predict, however, a greater recall of rare words when those words are isolated. If the interference hypothesis is correct, then rare words would stand out as distinctive, whereas common words (among rare words) would not appear as unusual.

The challenges Andrea faced when writing the introduction to her report are similar to those that you and other writers face when establishing the occasion for almost any paper. In an effort to provide context, you may be tempted to include irrelevant background information—long histories on the general topic of your experiment or convoluted theoretical discussions. Unnecessary background can all but bury the point of your study and the hypothesis you wish to test. Note that Andrea only referred to studies that were directly germane to her hypothesis. As a useful rule of thumb, include only information that helps an intelligent reader in your general field (not a narrow expert or your own professor) understand *why* you have conducted the experiment.

Methods

Sometimes referred to as "Materials and Methods," this section of your report documents how you conducted the experiment or field study. It allows readers to evaluate your methodology and in turn assess the reliability and validity of your results. Because the method by which you obtain results determines what you find, this section is by no means trivial. The clarity and detail with which you discuss your methods lends credibility to the results you achieve.

Your task in writing the methods section is to provide readers with as much information as they need to replicate your experiment. Indeed, the interest in repeatable procedures and objective results accounts for many of the stylistic features in lab reports, among them the use of passive voice and the past tense. Although scientific communities are now beginning to debate the wisdom of these stylistic features, you should at the very least be aware why such features have long been a convention.

The specific nature of the information you provide will vary from experiment to experiment. In a physics lab report, for example, you may need to pay special attention to the materials and apparatus used and the procedures followed. In our psychology experiment, the report also focuses on the subjects involved in the study.

Subjects

Fourteen University of Colorado undergraduates in a senior-level cognitive psychology class participated in the experiment. The between-subjects design consisted of two groups of seven students each. Each group consisted of two males and five females. Subjects ranged in age from 19 to 45. The students were required to participate in the experiment as a class assignment. All were native speakers of English.

Materials and Apparatus

Prior to the experiment, I asked each subject to write his or her age, sex, nationality, and native language on the top of an answer sheet. I used a tape recorder to read the instructions and word lists to each group of seven subjects. In recording the lists, I used a metronome to time my reading, such that a new word was read uniformly every two seconds. Using a word frequency list (Pavio, Yuille, and Madigan, 1968), I created two word lists of 29 words each. The first consisted of 28 common words with a single rare word in the middle of the list (as number 14). The second list contained 28 rare words with a single common word in the same center position. The word lists are shown in Table 1. The words contained from one to three syllables and were controlled for alphabetical order as well as syllable length. In addition, I equated the concreteness values for both lists.

Table 1: Word Lists with Frequency Ratings

Item #	Group 1 (common words)	Group 2 (rare words)
1	hall (AA)	yacht (2)
2	air (AA)	abduction (0)
3	happiness (A)	offshoot (1)
4	blood (AA)	causality (0)
5	season (AA)	preview (1)
6	city (AA)	disconnection (0)
7	railroad (AA)	shriek (1)
8	direction (AA)	figment (0)

9	party (AA)	misconception (1)
10	ocean (AA)	gist (0)
11	advantage (A)	lice (1)
12	forest (AA)	inanity (0)
13	joy (AA)	unbeliever (1)
14 (isolated item)	ego (0)	idea (AA)
15	industry (AA)	kink (1)
16	baby (AA)	letterhead (1)
17	engine (A)	impotency (0)
18	knowledge (AA)	loquacity (0)
19	newspaper (AA)	mirage (1)
20	lake (AA)	hierarchy (1)
21	effort (AA)	noose (2)
22	master (AA)	blandness (0)
23	journal (AA)	pacifism (1)
24	development (A)	perjury (1)
25	chance (AA)	dalliance (0)
26	kiss (AA)	rating (1)
27	fact (AA)	semester (1)
28	material (AA)	footwear (0)
29	length (AA)	tidbit (1)

Ratings were on a scale from 0–100 according to text frequency, where 0 indicates the least frequent item. AA indicates the most frequent item (over 100 occurrences), and A indicates the next most frequent, with approximately 100 occurrences. Source: Pavio, et. al., 1968.

Design and Procedure

The experiment consisted of a between-subjects design in which the subjects were separated into two groups. Each group heard a list of 29 words, one of those words being an isolated item. For group one, the item was a rare word in a list of common words, while for the other group, the outstanding item was a common word among a group of rare words. In each list, the isolated item was number 14.

The instructions indicated an intentional learning task by stating explicitly that subjects would be asked to recall as many items as possible immediately after they heard the lists. The two independent variables were the items appearing on the lists (i.e., common versus rare words) and the dependent variables were the recall rates. The subjects were told that after they had heard the list of words, they would have seven minutes to recall all of the words they heard. Subjects wrote these words down on a piece of paper (answer sheet). In both groups, the subjects finished writing in five minutes.

The challenge you face when writing the methods section lies in determining the appropriate level of detail. Use your laboratory notebook to document your methods. Record all observations on the spot and keep copious notes. As you select material from your notes, bear in mind these general tips.

• Focus your treatment on all of the variables that might have influenced your results. Information about these variables (for example, duration of experiment, temperature, size and age of specimens, etc.) will be crucial to anyone who wishes to replicate your study.

• Do not provide extensive details about standard laboratory procedure (how you used a scale or sterilized test tubes), nor should you bother with specifics clearly irrelevant to the experiment (whether you used a plastic or metal spoon to sprinkle soil over the seeds you planted).

• As you describe your methods, be sure to indicate why you took certain steps or what role certain procedures played in the experiment's design. For example, you would want to specify whether certain steps served as controls or constants in the experiment, and which served as dependent variables.

Considered in its own terms, the methods section provides a straightforward narrative about your experimental procedure that, step by step, describes in detail the materials you used and the methods you employed. It indicates the *how* of your experiment. Yet in the context of the full report, the methods section hones the analytic edge that your report can carry. *How* has a bearing on *what* and *why*. The results you achieve and the significance you accord them depend in no small measure on the methods you employ.

Results

Rigorously descriptive in intent, the results section reports the major findings of your experiment or study without interpretative comment. Be sure to present your data objectively, for your results provide the evidence you need to support the analytic claims you advance in the discussion section that follows. The results provide the *what* that allows you in turn to address the question *so what?*

If you can report your results with one number—13 percent, let's say—this section may present little difficulty. But few experiments or studies are that straightforward. More often than not, you'll have various results to report—not one datum but a whole set of data. Mention all relevant results and report the data in sufficient detail to justify the conclusions of your report. You may need to report trends or include statistical information, draw comparisons between experimental and control groups or indicate patterns into which your results fall.

The results section for Andrea's psychology experiment uses a figure to communicate complex information at a glance. Written comments focus on the statistical significance of various factors in the experiment.

A between subjects t-test was used to test for differences in the number of common versus rare items recalled overall. As predicted, the number of items recalled for group one (common word list) was significantly greater than the number recalled in group two (rare word list). The mean recall scores for the common versus rare word lists were 11.43 (4.69) and 8.57 (2.89), respectively. The two groups were significantly different, $t(12) = 1.94$, $p < .05$.

Additionally, as Figure 1 indicates, subjects in group one showed a peak recall rate around item 14, while subjects in group two showed a trough for the same item. The rare item, "ego," in list one was recalled three times, as opposed to one recall of the common item, "idea," in list two. Note the arrow pointing to the difference in Figure 1.

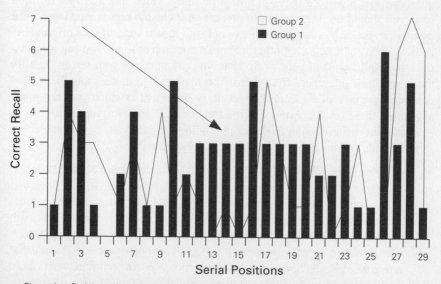

Figure 1.   Serial position curves of recall rates in two conditions: Group 1 (common words with one rare word) and Group 2 (rare words with one common word).

Given the complexities of your data, you may find it challenging to organize and clearly represent your results. Here are a few tips to help you marshall your data and orient your reader.

• Report your most significant or general results first, and then work your way toward more incidental or specific data.

• Group your results under one of several descriptive categories (growth rates, temperature changes, etc.).

• Use graphs and tables to capture complex information or to depict trends and comparisons. Let visual aids do as much of the detail work as you can; reserve written comments to draw your readers' attention to key patterns or trends, as reflected in tables or figures.

What are you to do if you have negative or unexpected results? Report them as you would any other finding. Don't discount data if they don't accord with your expectations; all of your data are useful. It's how you account for and interpret the data that makes virtually any experiment worthwhile. You accord data the respect they deserve by accurately reporting your findings.

Discussion

This final section of your report asks you to analyze your results in light of the questions that prompted the experiment or study. Much like a lawyer trying a case, you should use this section to present your closing arguments. Open your discussion section by stating whether or not your results support your original hypothesis. Having tested a hypothesis about a question at issue, you can now discuss the implications of your work. Here you can interpret your results, qualify them, and draw inferences from them. You may wish to discuss any theoretical consequences that follow from your results or the extent to which you can generalize from those results. Avoid making astounding claims for your study. As in Andrea's discussion section from her psychology experiment, be realistic about its magnitude and the implications you can draw from it.

> The present data lend clear support to earlier findings by Hall (1954) that common words tend to have greater recall than rare words. However, when occurring as an isolated item, a rare word (among common words) will have greater recall than a similarly isolated common word. This result is consistent with the interference theory for the isolation effect, which states that a distinctive item can serve as an anchor for recall. It is likely that a rare word would have such characteristics, while a common word would not. Moreover, these findings are inconsistent with the structure and orga-

nization hypothesis for the isolation effect, in that both lists contained items which violated their structure, but only the rare items in the list of common words had a peak of recall.

My choice of the isolated rare word for this experiment was the item "ego," chosen for its two syllable length, position in the alphabet (comparable to the isolated common word "idea"), and its abstract nature. The word, however, may have been particularly distinctive for this group of subjects, who were upper-division cognitive psychology students. While Pavio, et. al. assigned a frequency rating of zero to this word in the texts he examined, presumably this word might occur more frequently in the textbooks read by subjects in this experiment. Further studies would compare the performance of subjects when different two syllable rare words are chosen.

In addition to the peaks and troughs surrounding the isolated items, the reader may have noticed peaks around other items in the list. The usual primacy and recency effects occurred at the beginning and ends of both lists. However, some of the items in the center of the lists had significantly greater recall—namely items 10 and 16 ("ocean," "baby") in list one and item 17 ("impotency") in list two. The reasons for these peaks may be that the items in question hold some particular distinctiveness for this group of subjects. These results may therefore only be applicable to cognitive psychology students. Further testing should include larger numbers of subjects representing a variety of disciplinary fields, a control group in which only common or only rare words (with no isolates) are tested, and an additional group consisting of elderly people (in light of Cimbalo and Brink, 1982).

These results suggest that a distinctive isolated word catches the attention and is easier to recall than one that merely violates the organizational pattern but is a common word. Elderly people may have learned to ignore such interference, rather than show a weakening of organizational skills when they fail to recall isolated items. However, before any conclusions can be drawn, additional research is needed to compare recall rates for a variety of common versus rare words and for subjects at many age levels.

The specific issues you address in your discussion section follow, of course, from the results you obtained and the methods you used. Nevertheless, when discussing your results, consider answering these questions.

- Having obtained results, what can you infer from them?
- Do the results confirm or refute your initial hypothesis?

- What accounts for your results, and how conclusive are they?
- What other explanations might account for your results?
- What limitations or methodological problems might your results point to?
- How does your work fit into other work that has been done in the field?
- What further work would make your results more conclusive?
- What significance does your work hold for future studies?

By addressing these and other such questions, you are able to discuss the implications behind your findings—the *so what?* behind the immediate *what* in your data.

If you failed to confirm your hypothesis, do not consider the experiment a failure. Discuss why the experiment turned out as it did and consider how your hypothesis might be revised. Even if you feel you've botched the experiment entirely, your discussion section provides you with an opportunity to analyze what happened and why. The only experiment that truly fails is one in which you yourself fail to adopt an analytic frame of mind.

As the only part of the lab report that permits, indeed requires, explicit analysis, the discussion section can present you with all of the challenges you have come to expect with analytic writing. You must develop and articulate assertions that answer questions, and you must justify those assertions on the basis of the objective evidence provided in the results and methods sections. As in other types of analytic writing, you must take care to qualify your assertions appropriately, making sure that you do not claim too much or too little.

The pitfalls are likewise not all that different from the analytic writing you encounter in other disciplines. Here, too, it is easy to fall into description, which is what happens when the discussion merely repeats the results that have already been presented in the preceding section. At the other extreme lies the discussion that asserts what cannot be substantiated and leaps from evidence to claims that the data do not support.

Although the final section seems to be an isolated moment of analysis in what is otherwise an essentially descriptive project, the discussion section lends an analytic edge to the whole report. All of the preceding sections provide the basis on which the analysis proceeds; in the absence of that analysis, they would have little reason to exist. Yet the analysis you provide in this final section can be all the more rigorous and compelling precisely because you have established and made explicit the occasion, method, and evidence on which the analysis draws.

You might say that the lab report separates out modes of thinking and writing that usually intermingle in other writing tasks. Leaving the abstract aside for the moment, each of four questions is accorded its own section. *Why, how, what,* and *so what* become, respectively, the introduction, methods, results, and discussion. Only the discussion section engages analysis, yet the other sections provide the basis on which the analysis proceeds. If this arrangement seems a bit rigid and prescriptive, it is also conceptually and methodologically very powerful. By making explicit, each in its turn, the occasion, method, and results of your work, the report lays the groundwork for the probing analysis with which it ought to conclude.

    Although the sections of the lab report don't announce themselves in what are by now familiar terms—occasion, thesis, and reasons—they nevertheless reflect a similar preoccupation with shaping ideas. Why, how, what, and so what?—these are the conceptual tools that lie behind virtually any analysis. Whether in the lab report or the analytic essay, specific elements of form can help make explicit, both to yourself and to your readers, the relationships that underlie your thinking. Those relationships shape your ideas and lend form to your writing.

Business Memos

Although the memorandum—or memo, for short—serves as the communications workhorse in today's fast-paced corporate world, it is often far less effective than it might be. Who among us hasn't muttered "Not another memo" when we find our mailboxes cluttered with overlong tracts whose purpose, point, and plan remain unclear? Should you be asked to write a memo in your business class, you'll want to avoid the problems that frustrate managers and executives in corporate settings.

    Used well, the memo can make its mark; it can untangle knotty issues, argue policy, prompt action, and record decisions. But all too often a memo confuses the very problem it seeks to clarify. Long-winded, compulsive, and self-absorbed, the documents written by bureaucrats who fall victim to corporate memomania can frustrate, even alienate, the coworkers on whom business success depends. So widespread is its misuse—and overuse—that the memo deserves to be handled with care.

    The best way to get a handle on memos is to consider how format relates to form. The surface format that distinguishes the business memo can point you toward underlying principles of form that enable you to shape your ideas effectively.

A Functional Perspective on Format

Memo format is characterized chiefly by its heading—the "to, from, subject, date" listing that first meets the eye. Each organization may have its own distinctive house style for the heading; your business professor may ask you to use one of several common formats. Here's the heading from a typical memo that landed in my in-box. I've merely changed a name here and there to protect, as they say, the innocent.

> January 27, 1992
>
> TO: Deans, Directors, Department Chairs, Departmental
>   Secretaries, Faculty and Staff
> FROM: Correll N. Jameson, Provost
> SUBJECT: SB 91-140 — Collection Requirements

Enlightened? I wasn't. This heading, together with the information on the university letterhead, should orient me to the document and give me a reason to read it. Five long paragraphs later, I was still scratching my head. Only on a second reading did I uncover its point. As it turns out, the memo concerns a new law that changed the way the university collected debts owed to it. Sentence for sentence, the writing in the memo is competent. But a flood of information obscures its point. This happens with memos all the time; yet the time lost deciphering the memo convinced me that it was not doing its job.

Once you have completed the required heading, you may think that you are on your own, that it's free form from there on out. That free-form approach, however, did little to help me understand the memo on collection requirements. If you approach your memo in this same fashion, you lose sight of why the heading exists and how it can help shape your document. The result can be vagabond prose in a fast-paced, no-nonsense setting that has little patience for the long-winded ramble.

The memo heading is not a convenience for routing documents that has been devised by secretaries or the mail-room staff. It is a specific strategy for articulating the text's occasion. It's meant to guarantee a fast start and to point you and your reader in the right direction—namely, toward the point of the memo itself.

The heading, then, is more than a required four-line format at the top of page one. It is a format that can help you endow form throughout the document. Although the business memo may seem far removed from the analytic or argumentative essay, both require that you engage basic—and common—concerns.

- If the essay calls for an *occasion*, the memo likewise demands an *issue*, a rationale for being written and read.

- If the *thesis* lends point to an essay, the memo achieves focus through its *point* or *recommendation* and the action items that follow from it.

• If the reader of an analytic or argumentative essay appreciates *reasons* that forecast the shape of the discussion, busy executives likewise expect recommendations to be backed up with *cogent reasoning.*

So vital are these elements to effective communication that some corporations ask their employees to write memos that clearly specify issue, recommendation, and reasons.

The memo heading is designed as a prompt for clear, efficient communication. By recognizing its function, you can avoid the preliminary throat-clearing that often delays your most important ideas to page two—where readers will not care to look for them. Because a memo is essentially an internal document, a means of communicating within an organization, writers and readers can assume a good deal. They generally know the people who are writing and reading, the assumptions that govern how they interact, and the organizational context in which issues arise. With the memo on collection requirements, however, the writer might have assumed too much, especially given the memo's broad audience. Perhaps "Changes in the University's Collection of Debts" would have helped enlighten readers about its subject. Remember that the heading telegraphs essential context-setting information in just a few words, so choose them wisely. Indeed, before you write your first full sentence, try to set and clarify the occasion for what follows. With the heading already establishing audience and subject, you are then able to move directly to the particular issue that occasions your writing—and from there to the recommendation you offer, the reasons that support it, and whatever actions follow from it.

The Question of Audience

In specifying your audience, the memo heading can help you focus on your readers' needs and on your own rationale for writing to them. If recipients of your memo don't know why you have routed it their way, you haven't clarified the issue. Likewise, if readers don't know what to do with your memo once they've read it, you haven't made apparent what your point is or what actions follow from it. Of the millions of memos that clog corporate communications, only a small percentage do as well as they might in helping readers know why a memo landed in their in-basket and why they should do anything more with it than wad it up and round-file it.

But who exactly is your audience? When you write in an organization, you can never be entirely sure. The memo about collection requirements was a broad proclamation; it was sent to virtually everybody on campus. But many memos go to just several people—or so you think. The immediate or primary audience you address may not be the only audience that overhears your words. Memos may also reach a wide secondary audience less familiar with—but no less sensitive to— the personalities and issues you address. All memos amount to public proclamations. Unlike the confidential office chat, memos can't be whispered. On the page, indiscreet or hastily written words seem to shout. However carefully you select your immediate recipients, write your memos as if they could go public. Because memos are as much a political as a verbal act, they put a premium on savvy diplomacy. Before you fire off an angry memo, understand that people for whom it was never intended may read it.

Matters of audience also loom large because memos can assume a life of their own once you send them out. Written words endure. Although memos may disappear into filing cabinets for a while, they may reappear much later, as matters of record or as attachments to other reports meant for still other readers. To ensure that your words are not misunderstood—now or in the future—your memo should open with a brief but clear statement of the question at issue. What you take as self-evident in the heat of the moment may become perplexing (if not thoroughly foreign) to someone who reads your memo one week or some months later.

Your Point or Recommendation

If the needs and vagaries of audience define the organizational context in which you write memos, your recommendation can serve as a tool to motivate and shape organizational decision making. Although you probably don't think of a memo as having a thesis in the usual school-essay sense, it should nevertheless have a point. That point becomes dulled when information assumes value for itself, not for how it can clarify questions at issue or inform decision making. Unless you place information in the service of some kind of assertion, interpretation, or recommendation, you risk sacrificing the very get-to-the-point point of the memo. Without its recommendation, and the reasons and action items that accompany it, the memo loses its edge and becomes dull, ineffectual.

The memo on collection requirements, like most memos, bogs down under the weight of its own information.

On June 4, 1991 Senate Bill 91-140 was signed by Governor Romer. This bill addressed issues surrounding the collection of debts due the state. According to the State Controller's interpretation of that bill, effective this month, CU-Boulder must submit all BRS receivables and loan receivables that are past due to Central Collection Services (CCS). These past due charges can include tuition, parking and library fines, etc. To maintain the special relationship that an institution of higher education has with its students, faculty, staff, and alumni, the University and all of higher education sought an exemption from the law. Although the exemption was not granted, we will continue to seek one.

The Bursar's Office collects 99.6% of BRS billings within the fiscal year that they are billed. Internal collection efforts in succeeding fiscal years yield virtually all of the remaining outstanding .4% balances. Through our diligent efforts, the NDSL/Perkins default rate has been lowered over the years to a respectable 3.58%.

Had enough? I'd spare you more, but only now, well into the memo, do we get fragments of what could be the memo's point.

Unfortunately, the provisions of SB 91-140 will impact some alumni, students, staff and faculty. The Bursar's Office will no longer be able to choose the timing of nor the agencies to which it refers loan and past due BRS accounts. As of January 1, 1992, all accounts which are past due, regardless of dollar amount, must be placed with CCS. This means that all BRS accounts, including the ones which have been passively collected, must be turned over to CCS. Faculty and staff as well as alumni will be affected.

It is my intention to comply with SB 91-140 by sending the necessary accounts to CCS by January 31, 1992. The Bursar's Office has attempted to call all faculty and staff before these past due accounts are turned over for collection. The Bursar's Office will be sending a letter and a detailed bill to everyone whose account has been referred for collection. That letter will outline the procedure to follow for disputed charges.

I regret having to take this kind of action on these past due accounts, but the University must comply with the law. Should you have any questions you may call my office.

The penultimate paragraph, the real heart of the memo, should guide its revision. The author could open that revised memo by stating the occasion in no more than two sentences.

A new state law (SB 91-140) now requires the University to submit all of its past due accounts to a collection agency outside of the university. This change may affect many of you on our campus—faculty, staff, students, and alumni.

The point of the memo should come now, in its first paragraph.

> Although the University must comply with this new law, I am trying to mitigate its effects on members of the University community.

The remainder of the memo acquires its shape through the reasons that support this assertion. A very short memo need not forecast its organization, but in a memo of this length or longer, setting up the organization will make the document more readable.

> Although the University's initial request for an exemption was denied, we will continue to seek one. Moreover, I have instructed the Bursar's Office to call all faculty and staff affected by the change and to assist them in understanding the new procedures.

With the essential ideas made clear in the opening paragraph, the reader is now ready for the details. The second paragraph might provide some background information on the state law. The third paragraph could discuss efforts to gain an exemption, given the university's special status and its success in collecting debts. The fourth and final paragraph could then address efforts by the bursar's office to help people caught in the middle of this change.

Why bother making this revision when the original contained essentially the same information? For a memo to be read, its information requires a point. The saddest part about the original memo was that its bureaucratic tone and random organization hid the care and concern that surely motivated the author. Revision does more than sharpen the memo's point; it can give a human face to what otherwise might seem like uncaring communication.

Like the author of this memo and the readers who puzzled over it, corporate executives and managers are awash in information. They look to the memo to help them make, defend, communicate, and implement decisions. As such, the memo performs an inherently analytic and argumentative function. Memos certainly draw on information, but in so doing most memos are more than merely informative. They analyze, argue, cajole, and persuade. Virtually everything written under the exigencies of business decision making carries an edge. You can sharpen that edge by providing reasoned explanations for an assertion or recommendation that you make regarding a question at issue. If most memos are tossed out after readers put up with a paragraph or two, it is because their authors have not found or highlighted what is at stake when they write. Once you lose your analytic or argumentative edge, you've lost your audience. If your readers don't find something in your memo to be remembered, it will blend into the sea of paperwork that washes over each person's desk and into the wastebasket.

When Paper Replaces Performance

Before you can determine what you want your memo to say, you must consider what you want it to do. The memo's real work lies in prompting, informing, or directing action. Yet the memo itself will not get the job done. Oblivious to this point, compulsive memo writers will commit every meeting or water-cooler conversation to a memo. If it's not in a memo, it hasn't happened. In turn, they point to the memo as evidence that some real work has occurred. As a result, the business memo often substitutes for conducting business. Paper replaces performance.

When the memo begins to cover for work, rather than being a tool for getting it done, two excesses follow. One is that the memo becomes reduced to drivel. The second is that it becomes elevated to an exalted state of self-importance.

The former case arises when the compulsive memomaniac commits every trivial matter to a memo. The resulting barrage of paper can, in time, replace even personal contact—which all too many bureaucrats hope to avoid. If you consider the principles of form that underlie the memo, you'll recognize that audience and issue drive your writing from the start. If you don't have something to say, don't write. And if you do, consider whether you can't just walk across the hall and say it directly to your colleagues. You can help reduce the oppressive flood of memos in an organization if you simply question whether you have real occasion to write one.

As to the second excess, get-ahead types may be tempted to turn the common memo into their magnum opus. Every issue becomes for them an opportunity to write the great American memo. Convinced that a stellar memo will take them far, they go to great lengths to impress. The result is invariably a document so convoluted and self-satisfied that whatever point it tries to make is choked in verbal underbrush.

Meeting the Ideal of Brevity

To combat the excess of the magnum opus and to minimize the effects of the compulsive memomaniac, executives will often insist on brevity by implementing rules limiting memos to one page. Yet when memo writers dutifully comply, ideas can lose their shape and focus. Under the pressure to be brief, writers can baffle their readers by presenting the fragmented surface of an unarticulated argument or bald assertions without much support. Far from being a cure, the ideal of brevity can itself cause problems when it obscures the essential form of your analysis or argument. The university memo on collection requirements did in fact meet (but only barely) that one-page rule. But just because the memo fit onto one page did not make it easier to read or comprehend. The one-page rule merely spared us from reading more.

The only way to meet the ideal of brevity is to cultivate economy at its source. Economy follows once you define the shape of your ideas. Merely reducing your word count can never substitute for the cogent thinking that makes economy of expression possible. If you wish to be brief, cutting fat is not enough. You'll need to find and highlight the issue, recommendation, and reasons that lend muscle to your memo.

Writing within an organization can pressure the unwary writer to say what others would like to hear or to avoid saying what needs to be said. You needn't acquiesce with a polyester memo or fight back with a strident proclamation. By shaping your ideas to highlight reasoned analysis and debate, you can write memos that contribute to, rather than confound, corporate decision making.

Oral Presentations

When you speak before others, you shape ideas not just for the eye but for the ear. As such, oral presentations challenge you in ways that are at once familiar and unexpected. You must apply basic strategies for shaping an analysis or argument to the immediate exigencies of speaking before a live audience. Yet speaking need not be an afterthought; oral presentations can offer a fresh perspective on your own writing.

You'll face the live audience more often than you think. Upper-division courses and graduate seminars frequently require that you present papers or lead discussions. As a professional, you'll regularly be called upon to speak at staff meetings or even deliver papers at professional conferences. You may even stand before an audience more often than you sit behind a computer.

As a speaker, you'll find just how immediate and distinctive your rhetorical situation is as you look past your notes to the audience before you. You encounter real faces—earnest, curious, or perturbed—not the more abstract construct of your reader that you create for yourself as you write. Each person brings to the room particular interests and needs. As you try to gauge the overall mood of the group, you know full well that the particular and idiosyncratic always threaten to redefine whatever general picture of your audience you create for yourself.

The stakes are high because you have no opportunity for a repeat performance, another revision. If you are speaking extemporaneously, guided only by a few notes, you trade the safety of a prepared text for the flexibility, rapport, and creative tension that more spontaneous delivery affords. On the other hand, if you are speaking from a text, you opt for the security that written words can grant. Yet with that security comes inflexibility and a degree of indifference about whether your prepared words may elicit glassy-eyed stares from listeners whom you haven't reached. In either case, the risks you encounter take on a psychological, even physical reality: palms sweat, adrenaline pumps, nerves jangle.

As unsettling as any speaking experience may be, the live audience whom you address can serve as your most important ally. The effectiveness of your oral presentation hinges almost entirely on your ability to turn risk into a rhetorical resource. If the written word places audience at a temporal and physical distance, the spoken word gathers speaker and listener together in the same moment and virtually the same space. Although such immediacy poses its own risks, it presents you with opportunities that the written word finds hard to parallel.

To seize these opportunities, you must be willing to adapt your presentation to your audience and thereby connect—intellectually and emotionally—with the listeners who have gathered to hear you speak. Adaptation requires that you respond to clues about the needs and interests of your audience and recognize the issues you hold in common. Connection asks that you engage your audience as a person among people, that you meet them not just mind to mind, but heart to heart. Both strategies turn on one central notion; even though you may be the only one at the podium, you needn't go it alone. If tapped, the energy and interests of your audience can support and focus your own efforts and in turn reward your listeners for theirs.

Adapting to and connecting with your audience require, however, more than good intentions. In speaking as in writing, the shape and shaping of ideas can serve as a resource for finding your relationship to your audience—and, thereby, for discovering what you have to say and for saying it well. In turn, the shape you lend to ideas enables listeners to find the purpose, point, and plan behind your words and thereby participate in both its logic and emotional appeal. If you adapt key principles for shaping your writing to the demands of oral delivery, you'll avail yourself of a rhetorical resource that lessens the risks of speaking before others.

Hook Them

One advantage of speaking before others is that your *occasion* becomes immediate and concrete. When you speak before a live audience, your words are situated, contextualized. The people who gather to hear you talk deserve to be recognized because they are, in a very real sense, part of your presentation. To be sure, you may have a further, less immediate occasion to speak—a question or concern not limited to the group before whom you stand. But you should ground your talk in the immediacy of the moment. A joke or anecdote may at times hook your audience. But the safer strategy by far is to recognize—honestly and forthrightly—why you have come to speak and why they have come to listen. Only by recognizing and engaging your audience can you help them recognize what may be the more abstract or distant concerns that you wish to address.

Tell Them

If you speak, be sure you have something to say. What's more, be sure to tell them. Because your *thesis* is your core assertion, the very point you wish to get across to your listeners, you can't afford that they might not recognize it. Yet the risk that they might miss your point is higher than you might expect. Unlike readers of the written word, listeners have little active control over how they process information. They can't reread or skim ahead. They can't search for a thesis if they didn't catch one the first time through. Like the nervous speaker in front of them, they too only have one shot at the talk. As a result, you must make sure that your listeners recognize your point.

You needn't resort to obvious repetition, nor should you mechanically follow the advice that you "announce what you are going to tell them, then tell them, and then remind them what you've told them." But you do need to orient your listeners so that they pick up on your point. Brief but clear signals associated with your thesis should do the trick: "I wish to argue that . . ." or "Consider the following proposition: . . ." or "The point of my remarks today is simply this: . . ." A simple, forthright statement of your intention can do more for your case and your credibility than indirect comments or embarrassed hedges.

Point Them

Your listeners lack many of the devices that readers enjoy for discerning the shape of your presentation. In the absence of visual clues—paragraphing, breaks in the text to indicate a new section, or a page count that suggests length—your listeners must rely on whatever verbal signals and signposts you provide. Be sure you point the way for them. By projecting your organization at the very outset of your talk, you help your audience recognize both the *reasons* that support your assertion and the actual organization of your remarks. Then, as you move through your points, remind listeners where they are. Be explicit about how a prior point sets up the one now under discussion and how your current concern leads you to your next point. You may have to sacrifice complex details to help your listeners keep the overall shape of your remarks in mind. By signposting the shape and direction of your argument, you are drawing connections among your points and relating each back to the thesis that governs your talk.

A further tip: you may find it useful to tell your audience at the outset how long you're going to speak (if that has not been predetermined). "I'd like to spend the next ten minutes explaining to you exactly why I hold this position." To project time as well as organization works wonders in setting an audience at ease and winning their trust ("This person's in control of the material; he's not going to ramble on all night").

Hear Them

Although you may be speaking and your audience listening, an effective presentation makes these activities as mutual as possible. You, too, must listen. Perhaps your audience will speak by posing *questions and counterarguments* at the end of your remarks. But they will surely express themselves, if only in subtle ways, while you hold forth. Whether by furrowed brows or glazed eyes, they will communicate their questions, befuddlements, and objections. Your task is to respond to their signals, even as you expect them to pick up on your own. Better yet, anticipate their concerns from the outset. Because speaking before others situates your remarks, you have an obligation to respond to that situation by engaging your audience's questions and counterarguments. Never let the occasion that prompts your remarks slip out of mind. If you don't remind your audience why they should listen, they may not. In turn, if your audience doesn't have a sense that you are listening to them, you give them every reason not to lend you an ear—or an open mind.

Although the basic requirements of occasion, thesis, and reasons seem familiar enough, you may be surprised by the degree to which you must make them *explicit*. Three tools can help you highlight the shape you give to your remarks.

- a style crafted to the demands of ear not eye
- graphic aids that clarify your ideas
- a physical delivery that reinforces, in tone and manner, the intellectual content of your talk

Oral Style

A listenable style, like a readable style, responds to the needs of your audience. Because the ear cannot grasp as much or as quickly as the eye, you must adapt your syntax and diction to suit the occasion. If you are speaking extemporaneously, from just a few notes, you will quite naturally express your ideas in a conversational manner. But if you are reading a paper that has been crafted word by word, you are apt to remain in a written style that may prove impenetrable when delivered aloud.

To adapt your style from eye to ear, keep two distinctions in mind.

• Oral delivery requires a language that is simple to grasp. Keep your syntax clear by favoring an agent/action (or subject/verb) structure. Recast overlong sentences whose meaning cannot be grasped until the very last word. Avoid prepositional phrases and complicated "dictionary" words that make your ideas unnecessarily abstract.

• Pace your ideas more slowly than you would when writing. If you try to pack in concepts like so many sardines, your style will be so dense that listeners won't be able to follow you. Avoid what your particular audience would deem to be unusual or technical terms; if you need to resort to them, explain yourself fully. You may wish to illustrate your point with an analogy or metaphor.

You are better off speaking from notes unless the complexity of your subject and the expectations of your audience dictate that you read from a prepared text. If you must read, bear in mind that few written papers make for effective oral presentations; be prepared to translate your work to suit the ear, not the eye.

Test your style and pacing by speaking or reading aloud. If you have a hard time getting a sentence out, it will be next to impossible for your listeners to take in. Likewise, if you have trouble unfolding the logic of your case, it is unreasonable for you to expect your listeners to follow it.

Graphic Aids

Given our society's fascination with high-tech graphic displays, it's not surprising that many speakers seek to incorporate visual aids in their presentations. Tools that help you illustrate your point or make complex information easy to grasp can indeed make your talk more effective. But they can also distract your audience and even confuse the point you wish to make.

To use graphic aids well, you need to consider both your motives and your aims. All too often, speakers resort to visual props as a way to take attention off of themselves or to cover inadequacies in their talks. Likewise, they may use these tools to lend a bit of razzle dazzle to their remarks. Such motives are misguided. Graphics can make for a more effective talk, but only if they help you meet your two principle aims: your engagement with your audience and their engagement with your ideas.

For all the obvious benefits of graphic aids, they are not necessarily an advantage. Before you assume that graphic aids will elevate the mundane talk to gee-whiz status, bear in mind the following:

• Graphic aids can exact their own physical demands. If you plan to show 30 overheads in a ten-minute talk, your presentation can become a sideshow juggling act.

• Graphic aids can compete for attention. If your audience notices your graphics, not the points you illustrate by using them, you've lost their attention.

• Graphic aids can confuse rather than clarify. If your graphics are not easily comprehensible at a glance, your audience will be busy deciphering them instead of listening to your point.

• Graphics can undermine your own rapport with your audience. Handouts or complex blackboard diagrams can reduce, even eliminate eye contact. If your own attention goes to managing your stage show, you'll be far less able to relate to your listeners.

• Graphics can disrupt the continuity of your presentation and the coherence of your remarks. As you move from one overhead or display to the next, be sure that they relate to the immediate point you wish to make and contribute to the case you are developing. After all, illustrations should serve your ideas.

You should, by all means, consider using graphic aids when delivering your remarks. But if you use them, be sure to use them well.

Delivery

The manner in which you deliver your talk can contribute to the credibility and coherence of your argument or analysis. In this respect, delivery becomes a part of content, the impression you create an aspect of your case.

Given the importance of delivery, speakers often try to fashion for themselves a new personality—usually with little success. If you're shy, no amount of coaching will turn you charismatic; if you're a tenor, you'll never develop the classic radio voice of a bass-baritone. My best advice: don't even try. You're far better off being yourself. Self-confidence begins with a genuine willingness to be who you are. Because sincerity itself speaks volumes, don't try to be someone you aren't. Focus your attention instead on capitalizing on your strengths while minimizing what others may perceive as weaknesses. Here are some areas to note.

Poise   Although some speakers seem to have a natural stage presence, poise is something you can develop with practice. If you know your material well and rehearse your remarks, you'll acquire a natural poise that will outshine any shortcuts you might take to bolster your self-confidence.

Rapport and eye contact   Your engagement with your audience must be more than intellectual; it must be visceral and emotional as well. Eye contact is more than a matter of courtesy; it's your only way of reading audience reaction.

Body language   However awkward you may feel in your body, it's important to recognize that you speak through your gestures as well as through your words. You'll want to avoid unconscious habits: jangling keys or an incessant brush of the hand to your hair. But you shouldn't sacrifice natural gestures that can underscore the points you wish to make. Movement is one of the ways you can extend yourself to your audience.

Speed, pacing, and pitch   When adrenaline pumps, it's easy to talk too quickly. Slow down, especially at the outset of your talk, where your breakneck speed might easily blur information essential to your audience—your occasion, thesis, and reasons. (If you are reading, figure no less than two minutes per double-spaced page.) By varying your pitch and by altering your pace with a dramatic pause or a driving emphasis, you can reinforce key conceptual points. Voice and gesture have a language of their own. The challenge of an oral presentation lies in having your delivery match, if not reinforce, your ideas.

From Speaking to Writing

A final note: although oral presentations are important in their own right, they are doubly significant in that they bear relationship to your writing. Oral presentations needn't come after the fact, a mere add-on to the act of writing. They are often most useful when they precede or accompany writing, for they can remind you that the roots of writing begin with your engagement with others.

What, then, can speaking teach you about writing? It can remind you, in very immediate ways, of the rhetorical stance that you must also assume as you write on the page. Although less apparent than a live audience, your readers are still present. Moreover, when you deliver a talk, or even speak through your ideas informally, you are then better able to separate key points from confusing asides as you write. Direct contact with your audience evokes a certain honesty and efficiency that permit both speaker and listener to recognize a bluff or a weasel maneuver for what it is. As such, oral presentations can help you clarify and perhaps even rethink the shape you lend to ideas on the page. Finally, speaking develops your ability to write because it introduces you to rhetorical options and strategies you may not have considered while staring at the page. A live audience, for all the risks involved, remains a powerful rhetorical resource.

Whatever distance seems to separate the page from the podium, the best writers still speak to their readers—mind to mind, heart to heart.

Literary
Acknowledgments

Index